The Art and Science of Sociology

Key Issues in Modern Sociology

This series publishes scholarly texts by leading social theorists that give an accessible exposition of the major structural changes in modern societies. The volumes in the series address an academic audience through their relevance and scholarly quality, and connect sociological thought to public issues. The series covers both substantive and theoretical topics, as well as addressesthe works of major modern sociologists. The series emphasis is on modern developments in sociology with relevance to contemporary issues such as globalization, warfare, citizenship, human rights, environmental crises, demographic change, religion, postsecularism and civil conflict.

The Art and Science of Sociology

Essays in Honor of Edward A. Tiryakian

Edited by Roland Robertson and
John Simpson

ANTHEM PRESS

Anthem Press
An imprint of Wimbledon Publishing Company
www.anthempress.com

This edition first published in UK and USA 2016
by ANTHEM PRESS
75–76 Blackfriars Road, London SE1 8HA, UK
or PO Box 9779, London SW19 7ZG, UK
and
244 Madison Ave #116, New York, NY 10016, USA

British Library Cataloguing-in-Publication Data
A catalogue record for this book is available from the British Library.

Library of Congress Cataloging-in-Publication Data
Names: Robertson, Roland, editor. | Simpson, John Herman, 1936– editor. |
Tiryakian, Edward A., honoree.
Title: The art and science of sociology : essays in honor of Edward A.
Tiryakian / edited by Roland Robertson and John Simpson.
Description: London ; New York, NY : Anthem Press, [2016] |
Includes bibliographical references and index.
Identifiers: LCCN 2016003917 | ISBN 9781783085521 (hardback : alk. paper)
Subjects: LCSH: Sociology.
Classification: LCC HM585 .A78 2016 | DDC 301—dc23
LC record available at http://lccn.loc.gov/2016003917

ISBN-13: 978 1 78308 564 4 (Hbk)
ISBN-10: 1 78308 552 5 (Hbk)

This title is also available as an e-book.

CONTENTS

FIGURES AND TABLES

Figures

Tables

CONTRIBUTORS

Saïd Amir Arjomand (PhD, University of Chicago, 1980) is Distinguished Service Professor of Sociology and director of the Stony Brook Institute for Global Studies. He is the founder and president of the Association for the Study of Persianate Societies and editor of its interdisciplinary organ, *Journal of Persianate Studies*. He has published extensively in humanities and social science journals, and is the author of several books, including *The Shadow of God and the Hidden Imam: Religion, Political Organization and Societal Change in Shi'ite Iran from the Beginning to 1890* (1984; 2nd ed., 2010); *The Turban for the Crown: The Islamic Revolution in Iran* (1988); and, most recently, *Worlds of Difference* (with Elisa Reis, 2013) and *Social Theory and Regional Studies in the Global Age* (2014).

Hans Joas is the Ernst Troeltsch Professor for the Sociology of Religion in the Theological Faculty of Humboldt University, Berlin, and a professor of sociology at the University of Chicago, where he is also a member of the Committee on Social Thought. He holds honorary doctorates from the University of Tübingen (Germany) and Uppsala University (Sweden) and received the Niklas Luhmann Prize (Bielefelder Wissenschaftspreis) in 2010 and the Hans Kilian Prize in 2013. Among his recent books in English are *Faith as an Option: Possible Futures for Christianity* (2014), *The Sacredness of the Person: A New Genealogy of Human Rights* (2013) and *War in Social Thought: Hobbes to the Present* (with Wolfgang Knöbl, 2012).

Wolfgang Knöbl is currently professor of social science at the Institute of Sociology, Georg August University, Göttingen, Germany. In recent years he was fellow at the Freiburg Institute for Advanced Studies and the Max Weber Center for Advanced Cultural and Social Studies in Erfurt, Germany. His main research areas are political and historical sociology, social theory, and the history of sociology. Among his main publications are *Die Kontingenz der Moderne: Wege in Europa, Asien und Amerika* (2007); *Social Theory: Twenty Introductory Lectures* (with Hans Joas, 2009) and *War in Social Thought: Hobbes to the Present* (with Hans Joas, 2012).

Andrey Melnikov is associate professor in the Department of Sociology at East Ukrainian National University (Lugansk, Ukraine), where he has taught since 2006. In 2010 he received his PhD in sociology from Kharkiv National University (Kharkiv, Ukraine) with a dissertation on the sociological theory of Edward Tiryakian. He has published more than fifty articles and chapters in books in the fields of existential sociology, history and theory of sociology, social media, and the transformational processes in Ukrainian society. In 2009 he received The Best Young Ukrainian Sociologist Award from the Institute of Sociology of the Ukrainian National Academy of Sciences.

Alfonso Pérez-Agote is professor emeritus of sociology at Complutense University of Madrid. He is the coordinator of the research group, Groupe Européen de Recherche Interdisciplinaire sur le Changement Religieux. His main research topics are collective identities (cultural, religious, political), religious change and secularization and the contemporary crisis of democracy and the new forms of social mobilization. His books include *Les Nouveaux Repères de l'Identité Collective en Europe* (1999), *La Situación de la Religión en España a Principios del Siglo XXI* (2005), *The Social Roots of Basque Nationalism* (2006), *Religión y Política en la Sociedad Actual* (2008), *La Nueva PluralidadReligiosa* (2009), *Barrios Multiculturales* (2010), *Cambioreligioso en España: losAvatares de la Secularización* (2012), *Portraits du Catholicisme: Une ComparaisonEuropéenne* (2012) and *The Intimate: Polity and the Catholic Church* (2015).

George Ritzer, Distinguished University Professor at the University of Maryland, was named a Distinguished-Scholar Teacher there and received the Distinguished Contribution to Teaching Award from the American Sociological Association (ASA). He holds an honorary doctorate from La Trobe University, Melbourne, and the Robin William Lectureship from the Eastern Sociological Society. He has chaired four sections of the ASA: Theoretical Sociology, Organizations and Occupations, Global and Transnational Sociology and the History of Sociology. Among his books on theory are *Sociology: A Multiple Paradigm Science* (1975 [1980]) and *Metatheorizing in Sociology* (1991). In the application of social theory to the social world, his books include *The McDonaldization of Society* (8th ed., 2015), *Enchanting a Disenchanted World* (3rd ed., 2010) and *The Globalization of Nothing* (2nd ed., 2007). His books have been translated into over twenty languages, with over a dozen translations of *The McDonaldization of Society* alone. Most of his work over the last decade—and currently—deals with prosumption.

Roland Robertson is Distinguished Service Professor of Sociology Emeritus, University of Pittsburgh; professor emeritus of sociology and global society, University of Aberdeen, and Distinguished Guest Professor of Cultural Studies, Tsinghua University, Beijing. His authored or coauthored books include *The Sociological Interpretation of Religion* (1979), *Meaning and Change* (1978), *International Systems and the Modernization of Societies* (1968), *Globalization and Football* (2009) and *Globalization: Social Theory and Global Culture* (1992). His edited or coedited books include *Global Modernities* (1995), *Talcott Parson: Theorist of Modernity* (1991), *European Cosmopolitanism in Question* (2012), *Church–State Relations: Tensions and Transitions* (1987), *Religion and Global Order* (1991), *Globalization: Critical Concepts in Sociology* (2003), *Globalization and Sport* (2007), *Encyclopedia of Globalization* (2007), *Identity and Authority* (1980), *European Glocalization in Global Context* (2014) and *Global Culture: Consciousness and Connectivity* (2016). His work has been translated into more than twenty languages, and he has won numerous prizes and awards. He has held visiting positions in a large number of countries. His present work is centered upon globality and cosmology.

Alan Sica, professor of sociology and founding director of the Social Thought Program at Pennsylvania State University, was editor and publisher of *History of Sociology* (1984–87), and editor of *Sociological Theory* (1989–94) and *Contemporary Sociology* (2008–14). He has published five books about Max Weber in addition to editing *Social Thought: From the Enlightenment to the Present* (2004), *The Disobedient Generation* (with Stephen Turner, 2005), *Hermeneutics* (with Gary Shapiro, 1984) and other books. He also produced the "Max Weber" entry for Oxford Bibliographies Online.

John Simpson was educated at Whitman College, Seattle Pacific University, Princeton Theological Seminary and Stanford University. He is professor emeritus, Department of Sociology, University of Toronto. His papers (authored and coauthored) have appeared in the *British Journal of Sociology*, the *American Journal of Sociology*, the *Canadian Journal of Sociology* and elsewhere. In 2010 he collaborated with Richard Kehl, the Seattle artist and retired chair, Department of Painting, University of Washington, to produce a chapbook of poems and images titled *Older Lovers, Now and Then*.

Piotr Sztompka is a professor of theoretical sociology at the Jagiellonian University, Krakow, Poland. He is a member of the Polish Academy of Sciences, Academia Europaea (London) and the American Academy of Arts and Sciences (Cambridge, Massachusetts). Between 2002 and 2006 he served as an elected president of the International Sociological Association. In 1995 he received a major international award, the New Europe Prize. He has been a frequent visiting professor at universities in the United States, Mexico, Argentina, Australia and Europe and has been awarded fellowships at five Institutes for Advanced Study (Stanford, Berlin, Uppsala, Wassenaar and Budapest). His most important books in English include *System and Function* (1974), *Sociological Dilemmas* (1979), *Robert Merton: An Intellectual Profile* (1986), *Society in Action:*

The Theory of Social Becoming (1991), *The Sociology of Social Change* (1993), *Trust: A Sociological Theory* (1999), *Cultural Trauma and Collective Identity* (coauthored, 2005). The textbook *Sociology: Analysis of Society* (2012), which came out in Polish and Russian editions, has become a nationwide bestseller.

John Torpey is professor of sociology and history at the Graduate Center, City University of New York, and director of its Ralph Bunche Institute for International Studies. He is the author or editor of eight books, including *Old Europe, New Europe, Core Europe: Transatlantic Relations after the Iraq War* (edited with Daniel Levy and Max Pensky, 2005; Japanese and Chinese translations), *Making Whole What Has Been Smashed: On Reparations Politics* (2006, Japanese translation forthcoming), *The Post-Secular in Question* (coedited with Philip S. Gorski, David Kyuman Kim and Jonathan van Antwerpen, 2012) and, with Christian Joppke, *Legal Integration of Islam: A Transatlantic Comparison* (2013). His current work addresses the origins of world religions; changes in the nature of warfare in the contemporary world; and the nature of progress in human society since 1750.

Bryan S. Turner is the Presidential Professor of Sociology and director of the Mellon Committee for the Study of Religion, the Graduate Center, City University of New York, and professorial fellow at Australian Catholic University, Melbourne. He was the Alona Evans Distinguished Visiting Professor at Wellesley College, Massachusetts (2009–10). His most recent publications are *Religion and Modern Society* (2011) and *The Religious and the Political* (2013). With Oscar Salemink, he edited *The Routledge Handbook of Religions in Asia* (2014). He is founding editor with John O'Neill of the *Journal of Classical Sociology*, and with Irfan Ahmad of the *Journal of Religious and Political Practice*.

ACKNOWLEDGMENTS

The editors wish to acknowledge the assistance of Judith Velody, without whose help this book would have never come to life; and we are grateful for the help of Brian Stone of Anthem Press.

INTRODUCTION

Roland Robertson and John Simpson

Edward A. Tiryakian was born in Bronxville, New York, in 1929. However, at the age of six months his mother, who was of Armenian extraction, took him to France, and he was educated there from 1935 to 1939. On September 1, 1939, the day that World War II began, he and his mother boarded a ship in order to return to the United States. This was under strong advice from an American consul. His subsequent education led to his graduation from A. B. Davis High School, Mount Vernon, New York, where he was valedictorian, class of 1948. He then entered Princeton University and received a BA in sociology (summa cum laude) and was elected to Phi Beta Kappa honor society. After this he was accepted as a graduate student at Harvard, where he obtained an MA in sociology and, subsequently, a PhD (1954). His thesis was entitled, "The Evaluation of Occupations in an Underdeveloped Area: The Philippines." Upon entering Harvard he expressed an interest in working with Talcott Parsons, and the latter encouraged him to read Emile Durkheim in the original French. This interest in things French led him to a great knowledge of French (as well as German and Russian) philosophy.

Tiryakian developed an ever-expanding interest in "foreign" countries and their literatures, and it was in these terms that he was led to pursue dissertation research in the Philippines and to travel extensively in sub-Saharan Africa. This was a period of the burgeoning of interest in modernization, and it was in this particular context that he encountered the work of the French sociologist Georges Balandier, who was to become a close friend. The latter introduced him to a number of Francophone social scientists who belonged to a recently established organization, the International Association of French Speaking Sociologists (AISLF). This association had recently been launched by Georges Gurvitch and Henri Janne. Tiryakian was to become the only American to be elected to its executive committee and was elected to the presidency for the period 1988–92.

Tiryakian taught at Princeton University from 1956 to 1962 and at Harvard from 1962 to 1965. His first full-time academic appointment was at Duke University (1965), and there he rose to the rank of full professor in 1967, eventually retiring as professor emeritus in 2004.

During his years at Duke Tiryakian was pivotal in "internationalizing" the university curriculum, and he served as director of International Studies and as Distinguished Leader of the Fulbright New Century Scholars Program. He developed extensive international connections through lecturing and participating in conferences and congresses, including in Australia, Bulgaria, Canada, China, England, France, Germany, Hungary, Israel, Italy, Japan, Macedonia, Morocco, Lebanon, Mexico, the Philippines, Portugal, South Korea, Russia, Spain, Sweden, the United States and Wales.

He was a visiting teacher at Laval University, Québec; the UER de Sciences Sociales, Université René Descartes, Paris; the Institut d'Etudes Politiques, Paris; the Free University of Berlin; and an adjunct professor at Concordia University, Québec. He also served as associate director of Ecole Pratique des Hautes Etudes, 6e Section, Université de Paris.

Edward Tiryakian has served on many editorial boards, and as a grant referee, departmental visitor, consultant and advisor, and has attained a considerable number of leadership positions, including president of the American Society for the Study of Religion, and vice president and president of the Association Internationale des Sociologues de Langue Française. He was chair of the Theory Section and of the History of Sociology Section of the American Sociological Association (ASA). He was also the recipient of the Distinguished Scholarly Achievement of the ASA.

Other honors include appointment as a fellow of the Center for Advanced Study in the Behavioral Sciences, Palo Alto, California, and docteur *honoris causa*, Université René Descartes-Paris (Sorbonne).

It should be said that while at Harvard Parsons was Tiryakian's advisor, although Tiryakian has remarked that he was never a member of the "inner sanctum." Nevertheless, he certainly had the highest regard for Parsons as a great mind. One of the most unique and, to some, intriguing aspects of Tiryakian's career was his having been Pitirim Sorokin's teaching assistant while also having Parsons as an advisor. (Many will know that Parsons and Sorokin were, in a number of respects, at opposite ends of the sociological spectrum intellectually and temperamentally.) Tiryakian came to consider both men as mentors and role models. His "navigational skill" in this regard is exemplified in the Festschrift that he edited in honor of Sorokin—*Sociological Theory, Values, and Sociological Change*—first published in 1963, with a second edition published in 2013. One of the most unique features of this volume is the gracious contribution of Talcott Parsons.

Entitled *The Art and Science of Sociology*, the present Festschrift honors the long, provocative and fruitful career of Tiryakian. The chapters in this volume are all located within the trajectory of the scholarship of which the honoree has been a part. Tiryakian is not a one-tune composer, as the variety of the essays reflects. Unity exists at the level of context. Each individual piece illustrates something of an extension, summary or a point of interest of what he thought, spoke, or wrote.

Since Tiryakian entered American sociology much has changed, and the more significant of his own contributions have played a major part in that change. The divisions between and among peoples based on civilization, religion, gender, ethnicity, tradition and nationality have not by any means faded or been overcome, as some once thought (naively) that they would. In fact, such divisions and the conflicts associated with them have been central themes in Tiryakian's work right up to the present. It is the sociologist's task to shed light on how the human condition is constructed, deconstructed and reconstructed in all its aspects on humanity's "journey" through time and space, while at the same time being sensitive to disciplinary mutations. Tiryakian has certainly been very conscious of the latter. We reserve honor for sociologists who have contributed to that task in their scientific and artful expressions. Hence, this volume.

Chapter 1

THE DYNAMO AND THE DIPLOMAT: TIRYAKIAN'S ROLE IN PRESERVING SOROKIN'S REPUTATION

Alan Sica

The Protean Master and His Disciple

How was it that a scholar known and esteemed globally by readers from all walks of life, between the 1920s through his death in 1968, could have become by the early 1940s a source of embarrassment to his immediate colleagues at Harvard, unable or unwilling to form a "school" of acolytes and apparently destined to be forgotten posthumously? Moreover, how could it be that this man, demonstrably more creative, adventurous and productive than virtually anybody else in the guild of sociologists—which he himself had done so much to foster, first in Russia between 1919 and 1923, and then in the United States—had to wait until the eleventh hour of his professional life to be elected president of the American Sociological Association (ASA), an honor that many times had gone to far lesser scholars? One could believe that "cognitive dissonance" was invented as an analytic term just to illuminate this one man's life, so great was the gap between what he accomplished and how he was regarded by the most prominent practitioners of his craft during the last third of his life (see Nichols 1996 for concise details about this long-term battle). It is partly to address this puzzle that one man's scholarly labors and personal influence can be brought into play.

In a letter of February 27, 1963, Pitirim Sorokin (then 74 years old) wrote to Edward Ashod Tiryakian, 40 years his junior, to say he was "deeply touched by this superlative manifestation of your and [the] contributors' friendship to me." Sorokin was responding to the Festschrift in the former's honor, which Tiryakian had assembled over six long years of frustrating struggle. The "first copy today reached me. The volume [*Sociological Theory, Values, and Sociocultural*

Change: Essays in Honor of Pitirim A. Sorokin] is excellent in all respects. Your preface and [Arthur K.] Davis's article extol my achievements beyond their merits. I ascribe this high estimate to the *generosity of yours*" (emphasis added). After detailing "several unexpected pleasant surprises" that had recently come his way concerning translations of his work ("some 42" of them), and various awards he had received in his 74th year, Sorokin adds an uncharacteristic postscript: "I would like to order 20 or 30 copies of your volume to distribute it among some of my personal friends. I wonder can you help me in obtaining some discount on these volumes from the publisher?" (Tiryakian Papers, Box 6, File 2; *note*: all of Sorokin's quoted material appears precisely as he wrote it, including obvious errors).

Born in 1889 with about enough cultural capital to fill a thimble, yet supplemented by boundless energy and ambitious intelligence, this poor, motherless son of a Russian icon peddler from the Koni Land backwater asks in 1963 for help in securing cheaper copies of a book that celebrates his own scholarly achievements. It cost $5.95 in its clothbound edition, the first paperback version appearing several years later. Given that today the book's price would be over $45, Sorokin's request for aid is understandable. Yet, it also epitomizes the durable relationship between his ever-patient and helpful former teaching assistant and the great sociologist himself, whose hunger for professional esteem was understandably substantial, in part because it had eluded him between approximately 1941 and 1963.

Anthony Giddens has reflected on the career of Norbert Elias, based on their having taught together at Leicester University in the early 1960s, recalling that Elias comported himself then as if he were a world-class thinker and theorist, even though no one else would have at that time viewed him as such. Of course, Elias's scholarly self-estimate proved exactly right by the time he approached his 80th birthday and *The Civilizing Process* (1978) finally became known worldwide. With Sorokin the reverse occurred: he was precociously gifted and recognized as such, even by his dangerous political adversary, Vladimir Lenin who, within one year of the Bolshevik Revolution in Russia, had this to say: "*Pravda* today carries a remarkably interesting letter by Pitirim Sorokin [then 29 years old], to which the special attention of all Communists should be drawn. In this letter, which was originally published in *Izvestia of the North Dvina Executive Committee*, Pitirim Sorokin announces that he is leaving the right Socialist-Revolutionary party and relinquishing his seat in the Constituent Assembly. His motives are that he finds it difficult to provide effective political recipes, not only for others, but even for himself, and that therefore he 'is withdrawing completely from politics.'" This letter is worth mentioning, in the first place, because it is an extremely interesting "human document" (Lenin 1918/1974: 185).

As Sorokin explained in his autobiographies, despite holding a duly elected seat in the Constituent Assembly (having won over 90 percent of the vote in his province in the fall of 1917), he was summarily arrested by the "Cheka" on January 2, 1918, charged with the planned assassination of Lenin, and imprisoned to await execution. His experience as a political prisoner, packed as he was in a cell with dozens of others, some suffering from typhus, was terrifying and indeterminate, his cell mates being led away regularly at night for execution. Finally, on November 20, 1918, he published the letter to which Lenin referred, which helped win him a reprieve from the firing squad. He had earlier been told that his intellectual value to the new USSR might cause him to be spared, but his fate lay exclusively in Lenin's hands. The brutality of this experience shaped Sorokin's mature politics, as one might imagine it would, and the thrill of political labor enjoyed by the young man was redirected into apolitical scholarship—just as Lenin had hoped it would be. Sorokin already had won his undergraduate degree and a difficult master's in legal studies, requiring that he study 900 published items in only two years rather than the usual four. He was also almost ready to defend his doctoral dissertation, later published as *System of Sociology*. By regretfully setting aside a future in politics, Sorokin's contribution to scholarship in general, sociology in particular, was assured in a way that could not have been imagined when he served as Alexander Kerensky's secretary in 1917.

But, as he aged, the acclaim to which Sorokin was long accustomed significantly diminished, particularly among his sociological colleagues. And it was at this nadir in his professional reputation that he and Tiryakian were thrown together at Harvard, to the lasting benefit of both. Not unlike the case of Norbert Elias, who alone understood the importance of his early work, it was clear to Sorokin that his innovative ideas and writings in so many areas of sociology had developed earlier than anyone else's and were better than most who followed. He had begun producing seminal works very early, with his first book, at the age of 24, called *Crime and Punishment, Service and Reward* (published in 1913, in Russian; Elena Sorokin 1975: 9), appearing just prior to serving on the "executive committee of the All-Russian Peasant Soviet, 1917," and serving as "editor-in-chief of *Vollia Naroda*, newspaper at Petrograd, 1917" (as recorded in Sorokin's own short vita in the Tiryakian Papers). In 1922, after barely escaping political murder in the Soviet Union, he and Elena emigrated to Berlin, then Prague, and finally Minneapolis. In the United States, amid a pleasant familial setting, he wrote at a furious rate throughout the 1920s, producing *The Sociology of Revolution* (1925), *Social Mobility* (1927) and *Contemporary Sociological Theories* (1928), in addition to *Principles of Rural-Urban Sociology* with Carle Zimmerman (1929).

This torrent of fundamental works brought Sorokin to the attention of Abbott Lawrence Lowell, president of Harvard, and his colleagues, who had apparently been looking "for some twenty-five years" for a suitable scholar to start a sociology program—so claimed Sorokin in his second autobiography (Sorokin 1963: 238). Barry Johnston surprisingly noted that in fact Harvard had appointed E. E. Cummings's adored father, Edward Cummings, as "assistant professor of sociology" in 1893 but, based within the Economics Department, where in fact Sorokin also happily began his Harvard tenure in 1930 (Johnston 1995: 55–56, 290–92). Yet, despite the ballyhoo that accompanied announcement of Sorokin's mandate to found sociology proper at Harvard (as opposed to the outmoded "social ethics" program long on the books), Sorokin's lionization among sociologists ended when the fourth volume of his *Social and Cultural Dynamics* appeared in 1941. By then his methodology and scholarly posture did not match stylistic conventions of the time, and World War II distracted everyone from attention to his ponderous work of pessimistic social philosophy, the first three large volumes of which had appeared to widespread public notice four years earlier.

The about-face among American sociologists regarding Sorokin's work and reputation is well documented in a letter he wrote in August 1943 to Howard Paul Becker, coeditor of book reviews for *The American Sociological Review* (*ASR*), faithfully reproduced in a letter by Becker to Joseph Kirk Folsom, then editor in chief of *ASR*. Sorokin had registered his annoyance at a brief, unsigned review of his *Socio-Cultural Causality*, which had just appeared in the journal:

With a great deal of pleasure I read the anonymous contemp[t]uous note on my book for which note you, as editors, are responsible. The pleasurable reaction of mine is due to the following sociological uniformity: the more strongly my books have been damned by the reviewers of the *Review* (and previously by the [*American Journal of Sociology* (*AJS*)] the more important they have been shown to be. My *Mobility* was first damned contemptuously, but after the protest of Professor Cooley editors had to spank themselves and the book has been as vital as almost any book in recent sociology. The same is true of the *Contemporary Sociological Theories* (now translated into eight languages). Read Bain damned my *Crisis* to the bottom of hell (but he did not very strongly damn my *Calamnity* [*sic*] and it does not promise to be important as my other books). In spite of Bain the *Crisis* is now in the ninth printing and has a literature which in volume and complimentary tone (written by many first-class natural scientists, historians, economists, philosophers, and high dignitaries of statesmanship far exceeds the total and meager review- literature of the Bains, MacIvers, Lundbergs, and the whole gang of anonymous and non-anonymous "damners of Sorokin." So go on along the same line. I do not have any objections to and am sincerely glad of the damning by this whole group of ignoramuses, who, having no arguments, resort to the super-fascistic technique of dogmatic and smart damning. I regret only for the *Review* which in this way loses the last poor shreds of value and of a scientific spirit." (Sorokin 1968)

Referring to the likes of Read Bain, Robert MacIver, George Lundberg, Charles Horton Cooley et al., all of whom were widely esteemed by their colleagues, as "this whole group of ignoramuses" who "resort to the super-fascistic technique of dogmatic and smart damning"—whatever exactly that might mean—did not win friends among his professional peers. In spring 1941 this outburst recapitulated a ferocious exchange between Sorokin and his former friend, Read Bain, then editor of *ASR*, over rejection of Sorokin's "Declaration of Independence of the Social Sciences," a curt and denunciative jeremiad about the failures of social science, mostly inspired by familiar themes from his earlier work (see Johnston 1995: 140–43).

According to Becker, Sorokin had apparently given "his express permission" to reproduce this querulous letter, as written, in a subsequent issue of *ASR* as part of a proposed statement outlining the journal's book-reviewing policies so that no ambiguity would linger among its readers or reviewers. Becker pointed out to editor Folsom that the coeditors of the book-review section of *ASR* routinely gave guidelines to its reviewers, but never adjusted the content or tone of submitted reviews if the reviewers chose to personalize their attacks on a book's author or otherwise deviate from the journal's suggested reviewing norms. Thus, the *ASR* did not owe Sorokin an apology or a second review of his book, despite his facetious protestation that he "enjoyed" negative reviews by his fellow sociologists, their taste in books being so awful that they nearly guaranteed his success with other readers.

Repeated exchanges like this between Sorokin and some of his colleagues, most notably his nemesis at Harvard, Talcott Parsons, created a gulf between him and them—one that did not even begin to close until he was elected president of ASA in 1964, the year after the Tiryakian Festschrift was finally published. Some of his friends and former students believed that Sorokin, a sentimentalist at heart, was thin-skinned when it came to attacks upon his work, no matter how principled or reasonable those attacks might be. It was this hypersensitivity to critique that ignited his fury and gave rise to what seemed barely controlled rage as expressed in print. Thus, Sorokin at 74 was genuinely grateful to his former teaching assistant for persisting in his long-term effort to gather papers into a book that would honor him, most of them written by first-class sociologists. Sorokin would be dead within five years, but this momentary appreciation from a stellar clutch of writers pleased him very much, as it seemed to vindicate his own self-perception as one of the most important sociologists of his time. Tiryakian thus had a lot to do with this revised view of Sorokin in the early to mid-1960s, the same wave of momentary enthusiasm which caused the ASA, between 1969 and 1980, to name its top scholarly honor the "Sorokin Award," funded by Ruth and Eli Lilly (Johnston 1995: 268).

Diplomatic Generosity Meets Heroic Self-Importance

As he has told the story many times, in the fall semester of 1953 young Harvard graduate student Tiryakian was called to the office of Gordon Allport's secretary, Eleanor Sprague, who apologetically informed him that Allport had assigned Tiryakian to serve as Pitirim Sorokin's teaching assistant. Tiryakian was assured that, as a reward for this putatively punishing duty, he would be reassigned in the spring term to George Homans (Tiryakian 1996: 15; see also 1988: 8; 1989: 1; 1999: 5–7). Homans was a blue-blooded American aristocrat known for his stringent scholarly demands and interpersonal formality, but he was apparently regarded as easier to deal with than was Sorokin. Tiryakian was 24 years old, a second-year graduate student in the "Social Relations" department at Harvard, when he met Sorokin, then 64. For decades the latter had been a famous social philosopher and sociologist known for his encyclopedic learning and impatient dismissal of those he viewed as inferior in their thought and research. He embodied what later became known as "the public intellectual," based in part on his multilingual cosmopolitanism and his willingness to take chances in the realm of social thought, where few of his colleagues dared to tread. Partly because of his intimidating posture and tremendous output, he had become a pariah in the department run by his former underling, Talcott Parsons, whom he had hired years before and had evaluated with lukewarm approval for tenure.

Despite Sorokin's almost inhumanly large vita and his foundational role in establishing sociology at Harvard, compounded by his fundamental sociological writing in the 1920s and 1930s, by 1953 he was no longer allowed to teach graduate students in the very department he had created in 1931. Thus, had Tiryakian not been given the apparently burdensome task of helping Sorokin with a large undergraduate course in "the history of social thought," he would very likely never have gotten to know him, nor become his friend for those 15 years preceding Sorokin's death on February 10, 1968. This is because Sorokin was only permitted contact with graduate students during a brief "sherry hour" discussion with newcomers. Tiryakian recalled hearing Sorokin, in that setting, advising the fresh cohort of graduate students not to spend much time winning their doctorates, to race through the program, pursue a modest project for their dissertations, get the "union card" quickly, and only then settle down to produce "something serious and worthwhile" (Tiryakian 1999: 5–6).

This sentiment surprised Tiryakian, who had read enough of Sorokin's works to know that his preferred scholarly style pivoted on massive data collection, strenuous and broad-scale theorizing at the civilizational level and profound meditations on the human condition writ large. His favorite topics— famine, military destruction, revolution, class warfare, social change, shifting human values and so on—did not indicate any interest in the small-scale and instrumental research he was urging on the new Harvard graduate students. Hearing this august figure say that ambitious dissertations were a waste of time seemed to contradict everything Tiryakian and his mates knew about Sorokin, while also scotching Tiryakian's own silent ambitions for his grad-school writing plans. Like so many young scholars, he dreamed of "doing a doctoral dissertation that would be of the stature of *Social and Cultural Dynamics*, a precocious magnum opus that would justify my having been selected for graduate admission to the leading department in the country, *ad astra per espera* [*sic*]. I probably shared this secret ambition with the others in my cohort" (Tiryakian 1999: 5).

Yet his relationship with Sorokin blossomed enough so that even recently Tiryakian commented, "I consider Emile Durkheim and Max Weber as major totems; Talcott Parsons and Pitirim Sorokin as my major personal mentors" (Tiryakian 2009: ix). Against all odds, their relationship worked, each invigorating and sustaining the other between 1953 and 1968, and even thereafter, as Tiryakian continued steadfastly championing Sorokin's life and ideas long after most others had discarded him as an intellectual ancestor worth emulating. In fact, the last time that Sorokin was treated with the same respect as other founders of the sociological tradition was nearly 40 years ago when Lewis Coser committed a substantial part of his uniquely structured and much-beloved textbook, *Masters of Sociological Thought*, to the Russian polymath (Coser 1977: 465–508). Revealingly, though, the first edition of Coser's lauded text in 1971 did not include a chapter on Sorokin, which seemed to have been added almost as an afterthought—perhaps at the urging of Robert K. Merton, in whose series with Harcourt the book appeared. Merton, after all, was "the best student I ever had," according to Sorokin's own testimony, and it was by meeting Sorokin at a professional gathering in 1931 that Merton went to Harvard and became a sociologist (Merton 1996).

Barry Johnston's fine biography of Sorokin does not dwell on Tiryakian's role in his teacher's later life which, given the amount of other material to cover and the many scholars with whom Sorokin interacted, is not surprising. Johnston does wisely invoke Tiryakian's two articles about how intellectual traditions or schools are formed (Tiryakian 1979, 1986), agreeing that a "charismatic leader" is required. But the charisma in question has more to do with a body of work or ideas to which junior members of "the team" can cling, can "add their two cents," than it has to do with the leader himself. The diametrical opposition between Parsons's mild, straitlaced personality and Sorokin's fiery "primitive-warrior" style of interaction (Martindale 1972) demonstrates the case unambiguously, the ur-example that must have informed Tiryakian's theorizing. A Duke University graduate student, surely guided by Tiryakian, documented Sorokin's self-characterization as "a wild Jackass always kicking everything about" (Heeren 1975: 165). And Johnston hypothesizes, building on Alvin Gouldner's famous book (Gouldner 1970), that the cool "Olympus Complex" so much a part of Harvard's self-conception was jarred and disoriented by the Russian's blunt, argumentative, value-driven and ferocious moralism: "One wonders if perhaps Sorokin's style, use of language, and passion were not an embarrassment to the department and to Harvard itself, and as such, tended to keep him from being taken more seriously by students and colleagues" (Johnston 1995: 163). One learns an enormous amount about Sorokin in Johnston's book, but relatively little concerning Tiryakian, who is usually mentioned along with a group of other important Harvard students from the 1950s.

Happily, investigation of the evolving relationship between the master and the pupil can be done without much difficulty, after allowing for the intrinsic informational limitations peculiar to professional correspondence—even as it slowly transmogrifies into the personally revealing. The "Pitirim A. Sorokin Collection" is in the University of Saskatchewan Library (Saskatoon, Canada), 2,300 miles from Harvard. In it are 33 items created between May 1956 and February 1963, which bear on "Dr. E. A. Tiryakian" (Makahonuk 1979: 133–34). None of them has yet been digitized, but many of this group also exist in the "Edward A. Tiryakian Papers" in the Penn State library. In this latter set of documents are at least thirty-seven letters written by Sorokin to Tiryakian between May 21, 1956, and October 14, 1967, only four months before his death. In addition, the Penn State collection also holds six substantial letters from Elena Sorokin to Tiryakian (September 3, 1968 to April 11, 1974) and four detailed letters from Sergei Sorokin, Pitirim's younger son, mostly concerning Tiryakian's effort to keep Sorokin's name before the sociological public.

A few of the letters in Saskatoon that do not seem to reside at Penn State, and are otherwise unavailable, might provide insights into the epistolary relationship. For instance, "*Sociological Review*'s rejection of Tiryakian's article on role specialisation arising from birth order" and "Tiryakian's work on an article comparing the views of Heidegger and Durkheim on the relation of the individual and society" both originate during Tiryakian's beginnings as a scholar, when he was relying on Sorokin's sponsorship and advice in order to land a permanent academic home. Sorokin routinely sent news about academic openings to Tiryakian (e.g., at Syracuse University, Wayne University and others) while he was an assistant professor at Princeton from 1956 through 1962, after which he repatriated to Cambridge, Massachusetts, and taught at Harvard for several years. Tiryakian's permanent connection with Duke began in 1965, and it seems that Sorokin wrote in support of his job search at every instance—as did Parsons and others who had taught Tiryakian in graduate school.

Sorokin first wrote on May 21, 1956, in answer to a letter from Tiryakian, beginning formally with, "Dear Tiryakian." He congratulates him on finishing the doctorate so that "now you can start doing real scientific work," obviously a comment his student well remembered from their first acquaintance several years before. Sorokin also congratulates his student on publishing an article in the *Harvard Educational Review*, "the beginning of your scientific publications," and hopes for more in quality and quantity. After these brief comments, Sorokin establishes a stylistic pattern that is often repeated in his letters to Tiryakian, wherein he writes at length after the phrase, "As for myself." In this letter he iterates a list of his most recent publications, in this case, *Fads and Foibles in Modern Sociology and Related Sciences*, and the "somewhat popular" *American Sex Revolution*, in addition to "a number of articles on Religion, on Philosophy, on Ethics, on Creativity, and so on." He also notes the newest translations of his works, plus a Chinese primer about his ideas to be published in Hong Kong.

After what now has the tone of unseemly boasting to his young former student—and probably as well by the standards of conventional American academics of that era—he breaks into a quasi-lyrical report about a trip "with my family, of crossing and recrossing the continent by car, and to see Oregon, Washington, and all the scenic spots on the way, in between giving three graduate seminars at the University of Oregon during the summer session." He continues with mention of an important lecture series he will be giving at the University of Florida "in connection with the inauguration of its new President." The final flourish announces "standing invitations from Sorbonne, University of Brazil, National University of Mexico, not to mention a few American universities, but for the present I have declined them." He ends the letter with the only vital and relevant piece of information that Tiryakian needs to know: "Simultaneously with this letter I am sending to the Harvard Appointment Office my recommendation of yourself." That Sorokin intended to impress the young Tiryakian, searching for his first academic job, with his own professional importance on the international scene, in stark contradiction to his outcast status at Harvard, requires little psychoanalytic work to comprehend. That Tiryakian could kindly overlook the flagrant bravado of a man very likely past his prime illustrates precisely the fine balance he was able to establish between himself and the "mystical Russian," as Sorokin was mockingly named by some of his professional colleagues. A communicative pattern was thus set, which seemed to work well for both correspondents.

According to memoirs by his wife and one of his sons (Elena Sorokin 1975; Sergei Sorokin 1998), Sorokin did not spend every minute at his work desks at Harvard or the family home (at 8 Cliff Street in Winchester, Massachusetts). He worked steadily and with dedication, but he also found time to grow award-winning azaleas, enjoy the company of dinner guests and establish close friendships with Serge Koussevitzky (conductor of the Boston Symphony), Michael Rostovtzeff (the great ancient historian), Nikolai Kondratieff (the economic historian) and other notable emigrés. As far as possible he and his wife recreated in the United States a life that imitated what they would have had in Russia had the Bolsheviks not overturned their plans. This was constituted by a civilized level of hedonistic pleasures associated with fine dining in the home, the comradeship of extraordinary friends and guests, an active appreciation of nature and the wilderness and other standard accoutrements of an elite cultural lifestyle circa 1920. And yet, despite a genuine passion for music, culture, gardening and friendship, Sorokin's innermost being revolved around his writing, which he carried out, as he expressed it, in solitary fashion:

> I seem to belong to the lone-wolf variety of scholars who, if need be, can do their work alone without a staff of research assistants or funds. On a small scale and with some reservation I can repeat what Albert Einstein said of himself: "I am a horse for a single harness, not cut out for tandem or teamwork; for well I know that in order to attain any definite goal, it is imperative that one person do the thinking and the commanding." (Sorokin 1963: 274)

It was this persona that Sorokin impressed upon his young protégé, a single-minded dedication to scholarship that must have seemed, even to the most seriously oriented Harvard denizens, somewhat histrionic, even melodramatic, in its intensity. A few months after the first letter in the file, on August 28, 1956, Sorokin again wrote to Tiryakian, thanking him for his "friendly letter" and wishing him "everything good in your life and scientific activities." Sorokin reported obliquely about a surgical experience in June and convalescence "at my summer place in Quebec," the Sorokin family's dacha, as it were. The rest of the letter, irrelevant to Tiryakian's own life or ambitions, one would imagine, recounts the series of lectures Sorokin will be giving at "Cornell, St. Louis, Florida, and Brandeis," with more reporting about his recent publications. He then claims that some "big denominations" have offered him the directorship of "a very large research in the field of religious and moral phenomena," with a five-year grant to his "National Research Center for Creative Altruism." There is not any hint that Sorokin might offer Tiryakian a position or research support amid all this lucre. The letter reads more like that of a proud and matter-of-fact young man letting his loved ones know about his promising prospects.

After this, "My dear Tiryakian" is addressed on stationery from the University of Florida, dated February 8, 1957. He and his wife are being treated "as royally" [sic] by everyone from the president down, and he is dealing with "a veritable avalanche of letters, offers, invitations, etc., generated by my *Fads and Foibles* and my latest little volume: *American Sex Revolution*, not to mention two recent Symposia: published by Harper's: *This Is My Faith* and *This Is My Philosophy*" in which he shares space with "J. Maritain" (at the time a preeminent French philosopher, and seven years his senior). Sorokin cannot resist detailing his great accomplishments and the promise of even greater things to come. It should be noted that neither of the latter two books he mentions here were received at all favorably in sociologists' published reviews, the first seeming a betrayal of the discipline and widely enjoyed as such outside its ranks, and the second a sermon against sexuality of the tawdry kind, so he thought, that worshipped Marilyn Monroe. "As to the *Am. Sex Revolution*, besides an avalanche of letters, two television interviews, and several other television invitations, at least six offers from foreign publishers to grant them the foreign rights on that volume, and several offers for partial and serial reproduction of its parts from several foreign papers and magazines already came in."

Clearly, Sorokin is basking in public, global attention, even as his sociological peers denounce his work as "mystical," wrong-headedly moralistic and counter-productive. At the very time they are courting grants from agencies and foundations by virtue of highlighting their credentials as "real scientists," one of their most visible colleagues is rushing in the other direction entirely, all the while ridiculing their methods and substantive accomplishments in harsh terms. Either he did not care what other sociologists said about him, or he was extremely good at camouflaging his hurt feelings by reporting his victories at length to his young colleague:

It seems write-ups of this little book were published in thousands of papers throughout the world, (even in papers of such countries as Nigeria, Liberia, Tanganayka [sic], etc.), hundreds of editorials have been published, and are being published increasingly. Unexpectedly for myself, the book seems to be making plenty of "noise," also in the forms of hundreds of sermons and discussions preached about it, and so on.

The proud author also notes that "this little tempest produced by my semi-popular and certainly less important book in comparison with several [of] my other—and much more important—volumes which failed to make such a 'noise.'" Syntax aside, this loud proclamation of professional success as a writer and influential thinker lets his 27-year-old interlocutor know that being snubbed or treated negatively by US sociologists is of no consequence to him and, by broad implication, should mean equally little to the young man in his first year as assistant professor at Princeton.

Tiryakian wrote that Parsons was his "advisor from start to finish" during graduate school at Harvard, but that the "warm friendship" that developed between himself and Sorokin served as a "key stimulus for later theorizing" (Tiryakian 2011b: 2–3). He also became increasingly enthusiastic about Sorokin's later work on altruism and creativity, long after his student years:

> From Sorokin I gathered intellectual leaven with looking at the dynamics of large-scale historical processes in the comparative analysis of civilizations, including great cycles. And more recently, the latter-day research of Sorokin on altruism and altruistic behavior, which has been dormant from mainstream sociological notice, is an area that I find pregnant with research possibilities in an age of globalization.

Thus, beginning at Harvard and continuing for the 16 years prior to Sorokin's death, Tiryakian skillfully maintained cordial and professionally useful relations with Parsons, on the one hand, and, most unusually, with Sorokin on the other. Perhaps Parsons's superabundance of talented students and followers, plus a fairly typical Colorado-nurtured avoidance of public boasting, made it unnecessary for him to communicate in the prideful style Sorokin adopted when writing to Tiryakian. Even when communicating with Robert Merton (who, on at least two occasions, wrote long and self-revealing "testaments" to Sorokin, the first on October 10, 1945, the second on December 23, 1960, copies of which Merton sent to Tiryakian with explanatory notes), Sorokin would list his most recent publications and professional successes, but without nearly the detail he gave Tiryakian (see also Merton 1989).

As the years wore on and Tiryakian's career flourished while Sorokin's ill health from lifelong smoking diminished his energy, the letters from the ailing old man lost some of their self-promoting quality and shifted into a friendly, almost intimate mode common to old friends who care about each other at a personal, not just professional level. "Dear Tiryakian" became "Dear Edward" and finally "Dear Ed," and the signature "Sorokin" became "Pitirim." For a man as proud and upright as Sorokin, these small niceties meant something. On December 30, 1965, while recuperating from illness,

Sorokin wrote that "I continue to be lazy and wasting time in various easy pseudo-works," which was the sum total of a paragraph, and remarkably candid when put beside his usual epistolary rhetoric. Nevertheless, after an opening polite inquiry regarding Tiryakian's work and family, he would begin the core of his letters with "As for myself," followed by long paragraphs relating positive reception of his books and the inevitable translations that followed, about which he seemed especially pleased. Importantly, though, Sorokin could always be counted on to write a recommendation for his former teaching assistant, even if they were not, by today's hyperbolic standards, particularly detailed or fawning.

Also as the file of letters between the two men grew, Sorokin began to give "substantive" advice and opinions that were absent from the earlier missives; for example:

> Don't pay much attention to my remarks (or anti-messianic) in my previous letter. Your "explanation" of your references to Durkheim and Weber and some existentialists are quite comprehensible and correct. The purpose of my remarks has been that we, finally, have to go beyond Durkheim-Weber whose works, with a lag of a half-century, reached the sociologists of this country and are "chewed and overchewed" by them, without references to other sociologists and social thinkers—contemporaries of D. and Weber—who deserve as much attention as D. and W. (November 4, 1965)

This sentiment mimics the warning Sorokin forcefully gave Merton thirty years before, changing little in tone or substance, insisting that other thinkers aside from Marx-Durkheim-Weber deserved study and debate including, of course, his own work (Merton 1989). In another unusually long and dense letter (November 17, 1966), Sorokin thanks Tiryakian for sending his essay, "Sociohistorical Phenomena," and observes that "its thesis about history and sociology, about time past as present and the present as the future are certainly significant and interesting. As to your thesis about 'the irrational' I prefer to call it 'superrational' or 'invisible potential creative' force as the main invisible factor of human history. (See my essay …)."

Deep into a letter of January 22, 1967, which otherwise follows his usual format, Sorokin comments:

> All in all we all are in fairly good shape with possible exception of my health: recent check of my health found out, besides some unimprotant informities of an old age a suspicious spot in my lungth. They want to investigate further. But I declined it: if the spot is not malignant, the tests are useless / if it is malignant, it is doubtful doctores can eliminate it at my age. At the best perhaps they can

> prolong my life (in its tortuous shape) for a few months what is not very tempting.
> At my age or soon one has to be prepared to the final "exit" at any time. [*sic*]

As he loses his customary energy, his letters become increasingly reflective and meaning-driven, and much less about professional concerns, as one would expect. On February 10, 1967, Sorokin writes: "Dear Edward and Josefina: We both are deeply touched by your most friendly effort to help us to find a good place for recuperation and 'rejuvenation' of my 'brother-body.' Warmest thanks for your help." From the physicians he got an "ambivalent diagnosis" that, "regardless of its correctness or error, [indicated] that the moment of the final 'exit' from the kingdom of life is anyhow not far away, [so] my (and Lena's) mood and life-tonality became notably depressed. We hope this is temporary reaction and will pass eventually[; …] for the time being I have lost an interest in writing more papers, and in doing several things enjoyed before." This is not unlike Bach or Mozart or Schubert admitting to their friends that they had grown a little tired of writing music.

Perhaps this flurry of late-life letters inspired Tiryakian to continue writing positively, even quite recently, about his former teacher and longtime friend. For the first time, Sorokin mentions his family members, his worries about them, and writes letters that are recognizably "normal" when compared with others between scholarly friends. On March 8, 1967, for instance, he devotes a paragraph to concerns about his son, Peter, who may be drafted (as a medical doctor) despite all the protesting and petitioning letters of the Harvard Medical School and the National Department of Welfare (which had granted to him a five-year research fund), asserting Peter was an indispensable member of these institutions. "Of course, in his present capacity as an instructor in Anatomy (particularly lungs) and as a researcher he renders to this nation the greatest service he is capable of, but in this 'Sick Society' (and the Power Elite gone mad), everything is possible." In the penultimate letter in the file (September 7, 1967), Sorokin returns to this sore subject in his opening paragraph:

> I do not mind the protests against the most despicable, barbarous and at the same time, most damaging the U.S. Vietnam War; but, like you, such protests shall be done not as those of ASA but as either by individuals or by political bodies. Regretfully I must observe that all these protests do not have any effects upon our power-elite, beginning with the Executive branch and Pentagon (which seems to be ready to fight this war up to the last drop of blood of American youth and last depreciated dollar of American economy), and ending by big corporations and their executives (not to mention the majority of the Congress). This unfortunate war may turn out to be a landmark of the beginning of the decay of the great United States and of its democratic values. But this is just a "premonition."

How interesting that Sorokin, like so many older social scientists of that era, vastly underestimated the political power of the anti-war protest movement which, though slowly and over a decade, finally did indeed help end the war. On May 28, 1967 Sorokin calmly writes about tests over several days at Peter B. Brigham Hospital in Boston:

> The results are not cheerful. They found cancer in my lungs and tentatively give to me about one year of life. I am neither surprised nor greatly depressed by this result. At the age of 78 years one has to expect the final "exit" from life from this or that cause. I even prefer the short-time "exit" if it is comparatively painless and quick to a long, semi-senile, uncreative "existence" for several years. Such a "life-in-death" is not tempting to me.

And then, more personally, "If I would not have the pleasure of seeing you and Josefina, please, accept my thanks for your friendship and real services to me." By June he was selling his library and dealing with several universities that had offered to set up an archive of his materials, and to sponsor Sorokin Lectures "given every year about myself and my works by scholars/experts in Sorokin's 'yarns'" (June 3, 1967). The ailing elder seemed to "bounce back" in August and wrote a long letter detailing various events and publications associated with himself and his works. He thanks the Tiryakians for arranging lectures for him at the University of Puerto Rico, mentions more lecture plans in Colombia, and also a Sorokin Center being set up in the library of Leningrad University—almost unbearably ironic given how close he was to death under Lenin's rule. He asks "Edward" not to divulge percolating plans for an annual ASA Sorokin Award sponsored by a Lilly Foundation donation of $10,000.

On August 19, 1967, Tiryakian hears that Sorokin was told about a new paperback version of the Festschrift "in my honor," which had been published in 1963, and Sorokin makes a familiar request: "Can you tell Harper people to send a complimentary copy of it to me or, if you have a spear [*sic*] copy, to mail it to me. I am interested to have it. Today doctors took another X-rays of my respiratory system and it showed a notable accumulation of fluids." In a letter several weeks later, he reports that "Dr. Taylor (surgeon) drained almost a gallon of 'fluids' from my body and tentatively told me that 'one year is not unrealistic figure for duration of my life.'" He also thanks Tiryakian for sending the paperback he had requested and notes that the new president of Harper and Row might be more amenable to publishing his work than had been the case earlier based on a letter Sorokin received from him, but, alas, he has only a few essays as yet unpublished.

The final letter from Sorokin (October 14, 1967) regards a recommendation Tiryakian had requested in pursuit of an ACLS award; Sorokin writes,

"In all frankness, I am tired from this ill existence and would not mind to have my final 'exit' from the kingdom of life. Otherwise, the flattering reactions of various kinds continue to come to me daly [*sic*]." The dying man included a carbon copy of the brief recommendation which says in part: "At the present time he has a prestige of one of the leaders of sociology of the younger generation. Though his project is somewhat vague, nevertheless I would not hesitate to sponsor it and to recommend a positive answer to this application." This is not what by today's standards would be read as, to use the cliché, a "glowing recommendation" but, given Sorokin's blunt and crisp way of writing, it would not probably have been viewed askance.

In the years following Sorokin's death in February 1968, Tiryakian maintained warm and extensive epistolary relations with his widow and sons, published a string of essays about his old teacher and friend and also wrote new introductions to two books by or about Sorokin (one, called *Russia and the United States* [1944; reissued 2007], sold well in its fresh incarnation). There were other scholars who wrote knowingly about the fascinating and troubled professional life of the great Russian scholar (e.g., Barry Johnston, Lawrence Nichols, contributors to various Festschrifts, even Robert K. Merton), but none other had studied at Harvard in the 1950s while successfully balancing simultaneous friendships with Parsons and Sorokin. Tiryakian's natural gift for diplomacy and interpersonal kindness, for remarkable toleration and patience, mixed with intelligent appreciation for scholarly achievement, surely made this juggling act possible. One cannot know if the effort to maintain cordial, generous relations with Sorokin was worth it to Tiryakian, either professionally or personally. But what remains clear is that without his persistent and public attention to Sorokin's reputation, far fewer scholars would now know who the fiery Russian polymath was, nor why continuing to think about his life and prophetic sociology remains worthwhile. As Tiryakian might well point out himself, there was nobody like him during his lifetime, nor will there be anyone in the perceivable future whose world of thought and social analysis will match his in scope or daring. It was Edward Tiryakian's gift to his colleagues to have realized this already in 1953, long before others had any inkling of it, and to do what he could to protect and advance Sorokin's reputation no matter what others thought.

References

Coser, L. 1977. *Masters of Sociological Thought*, 2nd ed. New York: Harcourt Brace Jovanovich (Reissued by Waveland Press, 2003).

Gouldner, A. 1970. *The Coming Crisis of Western Sociology*. New York: Basic Books.

Heeren, J. 1975. "Functional and Critical Sociology: A Study of Two Groups of Contemporary Sociologists." PhD dissertation, Duke University.

Johnston, B. V. 1995. *Pitirim A. Sorokin: An Intellectual Biography.* Lawrence: University Press of Kansas.

Lenin, V. I. 1918. "The Valuable Admissions of Pitirim Sorokin." *Pravda*, November 21. (Reissued in Lenin's *Collected Works.* Moscow: Progress Publishers, 1974), vol. 28: 185–94. https://www.marxists.org/archive/lenin/works/1918/nov/20.htm.

Makahonuk, G. 1979. "A Guide to the P. A. Sorokin Manuscripts and Papers." The Pitirim A. Sorokin Collection, University of Saskatchewan Library.

Martindale, D. 1972. "Pitirim Sorokin: Soldier of Fortune." In *Sorokin and Sociology: Essays in Honour of Pitirim A. Sorokin*, edited by C. C. Hallen and R. Prasad. Agra, India: Satish Book Enterprise.

Merton, R. K. 1989. "The Sorokin-Merton Correspondence on 'Puritanism, Pietism and Science,' 1933–34." *Science in Context* 3, no. 1: 291–98.

——— 1996. "A Life of Learning." In *On Social Structure and Science*, edited by P. Sztompka, 339–59. Chicago: University of Chicago Press. Also available online: http://www.acls.org/Publications/OP/Haskins/1994_RobertKMerton.pdf

Nichols, L. T. 1996. "Sorokin and American Sociology: The Dynamics of a Moral Career in Science." In *Sorokin and Civilization: A Centennial Assessment*, edited by J. B. Ford, M. P. Richard and P. C. Talbutt, 45–64. New Brunswick, NJ: Transaction Publishers.

Sorokin, E. 1975. "My Life with Pitirim Sorokin." *International Journal of Contemporary Sociology*, January/April, nos. 1 and 2: 1–27.

Sorokin, P. A. 1963. *A Long Journey: The Autobiography of Pitirim A. Sorokin.* New Haven, CT: College and University Press.

——— 1968. *Pitirim A. Sorokin Collection.* Special Collections, University of Saskatchewan Library. Saskatoon, Saskatchewan, Canada.

Sorokin, S. 1998. "Life with Pitirim Sorokin: A Younger Son's Perspective." http://cliffstreet.org/index.php/sergei-sorokin-about-pitirim

Tiryakian, E. A., ed. 1963. *Sociological Theory, Values, and Sociocultural Change.* New York: The Free Press of Glencoe (Reissued with a new introduction by the editor in 2013 by Transaction Publishers, New Brunswick, NJ).

——— 1979. "The Significance of Schools in the Development of Sociology." In *Contemporary Issues in Theory and Research*, edited by W. E. Snizek, 211–33.Westport, CT: Greenwood Press.

——— 1986. "Hegemonic Schools and the Development of Sociology." In *Structures of Knowing: Current Studies in the Sociology of Schools*, edited by R. C. Monk, 417–41. Lanham, MD: University Press of America.

——— 1988. "Sociology's Dostoyevski: Pitirim A. Sorokin." *The World and I* 3, no. 9: 569–81.

——— 1989. "Sorokin Lives!" *Sociology Lives* 5, no. 4 (January 21), Harvard University, Sociology Department.

——— 1996. "Sorokin Remembered." In *Sorokin and Civilization: A Centennial Assessment*, edited by J. P. Ford, M. P. Richard and P. C. Talbutt, 15–19. New Brunswick, NJ: Transaction Publishers.

——— 1999. "Pitirim A. Sorokin, My Teacher: Prophet of Advanced Modernity." Paper presented at the International Symposium, "Pitirim Sorokin and Sociocultural Tendencies of Our Times." Moscow and St. Petersburg; February 4–6, 1999. Edward Tiryakian Papers, HCLA 6521, Box 06 GST/AF/6.09. Special Collections, Paterno Library, Pennsylvania State University, University Park.

——— 2009. *For Durkheim: Essays in Historical and Cultural Sociology.* Surrey: Ashgate.

————— 2011a. *Edward A. Tiryakian Papers, 1952–2011*. Collection Number 6521. 9.5 cubic feet. Historical Collections and Labor Archives, Special Collections Library, Paterno Library, Pennsylvania State University, University Park.

————— 2011b. Autobiographical manuscript, prepared for *Dictionary of Eminent Social Scientists: Autobiographies (DESSA)*. Mattei Dogan Foundation, Paris. Tiryakian Papers, Pennsylvania State University, University Park.

Chapter 2

EDWARD TIRYAKIAN AND MODERNIZATION THEORY: A VERY SPECIAL RELATIONSHIP

Wolfgang Knöbl

Anyone familiar with developments in the field of social theory during the last two or three decades should not have much difficulty in coming to terms with the contributions of Edward A. Tiryakian. In addition to the fact that his style of writing is as elegant as his arguments are precise, he obviously never leaves his readers in the dark with respect to which theoretical camp he belongs. Tiryakian was one of the first authors who theorized the geopolitical sea change after 1989, claiming that many of the assumptions upon which dependency theorists—such as the early Fernando Henrique Cardoso or world systems analysts such as Immanuel Wallerstein—had built their arguments, have turned out to be false so that there is time for rethinking macrosociology. Frequently quoting Talcott Parsons's work, Tiryakian seemed to have argued that, despite some major problems, the basic structure of classical modernization theory as developed in the 1950s and 1960s is not completely defunct and thus could be transformed in a fruitful way, leading to a new theoretical paradigm, which he suggested calling "'Modernisation II', or alternatively, 'Neo-Modernisation Analysis'" (Tiryakian 1991: 171–72).

In his attempt to restructure modernization theory Tiryakian was certainly not alone; he had quite a few companions all over the world, from Jeffrey Alexander and Paul Colomy in the United States to Piotr Sztompka in Poland or Wolfgang Zapf in Germany, all of whom tried to continue and to renew either the Parsonian legacy or the modernization approach and, by doing so, to come to a new and more fruitful understanding of social change (Alexander 1998; Sztompka 1993; Zapf 1991). And although it is not too difficult to find at least some differences between Tiryakian's endeavor on the one hand and the attempts of his colleagues just mentioned on the other, this should not prevent one from categorizing Tiryakian in terms of social theory: He is no Marxist, to be sure, no Postmodernist, no Critical Theorist and no follower of radical systems analysis à la Niklas Luhmann. Tiryakian is an admirer of Max Weber and, even more, of Emile Durkheim; he was a student of Talcott Parsons, which must have made him part of the "orthodox consensus" against which the leftist radicals within sociology protested in the late 1960s and early 1970s, and so it is no wonder that he situated himself within the camp of modernization theory even when he tried to renew this paradigm. In sum, Tiryakian is the product of mainstream American sociology as it came into being after 1945 under the leadership of Parsons, Robert K. Merton and Paul Lazarsfeld. Voilà, we have found the right sticker in order to characterize Tiryakian's work. That was not too difficult, was it?

The problem, however, is that this sticker will not stick. It will slip away at the very first moment one reads Tiryakian's texts more carefully and realizes that the differences between him and other neo-modernization theorists are often much bigger than one is prepared to believe at first sight, and when one looks for the reasons for these differences. And this is what I am going to do in this chapter: Convinced that Tiryakian is anything else but mainstream, I will try in the first section to give an account of his early work, which was particularly influenced by French existentialism and by French social scientists who, in the 1950s and 1960s, were not seduced by the fashion of Lévi-Straussian structuralism. This "French Connection," I would like to argue, has been at least as important for the development of Tiryakian's oeuvre as was the well-known fact that he was one of the rare sociologists who had worked both with Parsons *and* Pitirim Sorokin (I). The second section of this chapter shows how this rather heterodox intellectual socialization (at least from an American point of view) decisively formed Tiryakian's way of thinking about macro-processes of social change in particular, and about modernity in general. Pointing to the contradictory results of modernization, Tiryakian was from the very beginning more sensitive toward the tensions within modern societies than were most of his colleagues (II). In the brief third and last section I will demonstrate how Tiryakian's work is related to developments within macrosociology which, in the last two decades, have led to the debate on civilizational analysis and "multiple modernities" (III).

I

When in 1952 the young Edward Tiryakian decided to go to Harvard in order to do his PhD with Talcott Parsons in the famous Department of Social Relations for Interdisciplinary Social Science Studies, he entered an intellectual milieu that not only was shaped by scholars such as Clyde Kluckhohn, Samuel

Stouffer and, of course, Parsons himself, but also housed brilliant students such as Robert Bellah and Neil Smelser, who were just a little older than Tiryakian. Everything looked as if Tiryakian would easily follow the theoretical tracks laid out by Parsons and thus walk similar paths as the ones taken by members of the Parsons school. This, however, did not happen as smoothly as one could have expected; and certainly one of the major reasons was that in his second PhD year Tiryakian became a teaching assistant assigned to an undergraduate class organized by Pitirim Sorokin (Tiryakian 2011a).

It would certainly not be completely wrong to assume that Sorokin's world views and his theoretical ideas at least somehow inspired Tiryakian's intellectual development (Tiryakian 2013). Sorokin's model of social change certainly resembled anything but a linear story of progress, which explains Tiryakian's already-mentioned sensitivity toward the bleak sides of modernity. But even if one does not want to overemphasize Sorokin's *intellectual* influence and accepts Tiryakian's plausible claim that Parsons was undoubtedly the more systematic theorist, Sorokin was important for him in another respect as well: Sorokin had close contacts to French intellectual circles and was a friend of the then-famous sociologist Georges Gurvitch so that Tiryakian got the chance to get into a French–American network around the friendship between Sorokin and Gurvitch and to become acquainted with intellectual debates in the French humanities at that time. In fact, building bridges over the Atlantic was quite easy for Tiryakian, if only because of his language skills: Born in the United States, he had spent the first 10 years of his life in France until 1939, when his family decided to go back to in order to escape from the war in Europe. As Tiryakian himself claims, French was his first language, the "language of his heart" so that "he learned the history of the world through French eyes" (Tiryakian 2011a). Tiryakian's easy access to the cosmos of French intellectuals is only one thing, however; the more important question is to *which part* of this particular cosmos he felt attracted! An answer to this question is crucial in order to understand Tiryakian's own intellectual career.

Tiryakian, as already mentioned, wrote his PhD with Parsons, and his education was not exceptional at that time. Like other PhD students at Harvard, at the University of Chicago and some other places in the United States during the high time of modernization theory, he was ambitious enough to do field work in regions soon to be called the "Third World." He decided to go to the Philippines to study the occupational stratification system there. After finishing his work in Asia some interesting papers came out of this research (Tiryakian 1958, 1959, 1960); but it certainly would not be unfair to argue that the way Tiryakian presented his results was very much in the fashion of classical modernization theory, and that rather conventional Parsonian categories were used in order to theorize his empirical insights. More significant was the fact that Tiryakian was not only interested in the areas where he did his actual research but also in other parts of the world haunted by very different problems, insofar as he also focused on the religious roots of apartheid in South Africa at a very early phase of his career (Tiryakian 1957). But all that was not really surprising; on the contrary, such moves could be expected from a brilliant student who, in the middle of the 1950s, became assistant professor at Duke University.

What could not have been expected, however, was the fact that in 1962 Tiryakian published a book called *Sociologism and Existentialism*. True, the first part of the book was on Durkheim, not an exotic topic at all (Tiryakian 1962). The second part, however, focused on a variety of philosophers close to existentialism such as Karl Jaspers, Jean-Paul Sartre and even Martin Heidegger—a somewhat strange research topic, at least for an American sociologist at that time. What was so interesting in that book was Tiryakian's attempt to link two obviously rather different traditions of thought that were, according to him, able to enlighten each other with respect to their specific strengths and weaknesses. On the one hand, Tiryakian very much emphasized the sociological deficits of existentialism, its inability to give a plausible account of intersubjectivity. As he claimed with respect to Sartre, his "view on intersubjective relationships comes to be virtually identical with the Hobbesian notion of the war-of-all-against-all: every consciousness is in potential conflict with every other consciousness" (Tiryakian 1962: 133). For sociologists, so Tiryakian argued, it was not acceptable to speak—as most existentialists did—of society almost exclusively in terms of a cause for "inauthenticity" and "inauthentic being" (Tiryakian 1962: 137).

On the other hand, Tiryakian was well aware that Parsons's action frame of reference as developed in *The Structure of Social Action* and in Parsons's theoretical works around the "pattern variables" could not have been the last word on action theory:

> The theory of action could well profit from existentialism by seeing to what extent this [existentialism's emphasis of choice and decision; W.K.] and other existential notions may be incorporated in its frame of reference, for example, Heidegger's notion of *ambiguity* as a fundamental existential situation. (Tiryakian 1962: 166)

It seemed as if Tiryakian was trying to push Parsonian action theory in a direction not taken by Parsons himself—a direction that would lead into a field one could possibly denote as "philosophical anthropology" in the German meaning of that term. Only such an ambition explains why Tiryakian—basing some of his arguments on Durkheim's lectures on American pragmatism—emphasized the theoretical convergence of existentialism, pragmatism and the late sociological works of Durkheim (Tiryakian 1962: 157). And, by the way, it also explains why a couple of years later Tiryakian got into a rather fierce intellectual fight with Peter L. Berger, who accused him of carelessly using the term "phenomenology" (ASR 1966: 258–65).

The background of this exchange was a paper published by Tiryakian in 1965 with the title, "Existential Phenomenology and the Sociological Tradition" (Tiryakian 1965). In this text he had argued that there were and are important methodological and theoretical overlaps between major sociologists who were usually classified as belonging to different or even hostile theoretical camps. In particular Tiryakian had tried to show that there were at least some links between, for example, Max Weber, Georg Simmel, Emile Durkheim, Karl Mannheim and Max Scheler on the one hand and the phenomenological and existentialist tradition within philosophy on the other, and that even in the works of contemporary authors such as Parsons and Merton certain traces could be detected that all point to a major influence of existentialism and phenomenology on sociology. These links and influences were and are not accidental because, according to Tiryakian, basically all good sociologists somehow have to deal with existential questions and the problem of "Verstehen," which could be tackled by using both phenomenological or existentialist insights concerning perception, the body and other topics theorized by Husserl, Jaspers and their followers. In this context Tiryakian used the term "existentialist phenomenology" in order to make his argument. Berger, however, objected and rather harshly criticized Tiryakian's terminological move, accusing Tiryakian of grouping together too many different strands of thought and thereby blurring not only the methodological and theoretical differences between the sociologists discussed but also distorting the contours of phenomenology proper.

Berger's critique was not completely off the mark, but he obviously overlooked at least four important points: *First*, Tiryakian's use of the term "existential phenomenology" was not as strange as Berger had suggested, since figures such as Maurice Merleau-Ponty had indeed tried to combine existentialist and phenomenological insights so that the term was anything but Tiryakian's idiosyncratic invention. *Second*, Tiryakian did not discuss Simmel, Weber, Durkheim or Mannheim in order to give an appropriate account of their most important theoretical and empirical assumptions and, by doing so, glossing over their differences. In fact, Tiryakian's aim was not so much interpretative but constructive. His focus was on the then-dominant theories of action within sociology that he obviously regarded as deficient. And so he tried to mobilize basically the whole sociological tradition (from Simmel to Merton) and a variety of phenomenological and existentialist philosophers (from

Husserl to Jaspers) in order to encourage further work on a theory of action.[1] For him this seemed to be a particularly pressing problem since Parsons's theoretical development at that time was about to lead in the wrong direction: As Tiryakian argued in 1965, there are some major problems in Parsons's current theorizing insofar as the incorporation of Freudian ideas concerning the libidinal roots of behavior tends to push into the background the voluntaristic character of human action and thus gives Parsons's theory a rather strange utilitarian touch, which basically contradicts his most important insights in *The Structure of Social Action* (Tiryakian 1965: 684).

Third, Tiryakian obviously tried to emphasize the important achievements of existentialism, not for purely theoretical reasons; for him there was a task for sociologists in the world that included more than just being distant observers. Existentialism at least asked some important questions concerning the human condition and thus raised important questions relevant for the professional identity of sociology as a discipline. And although Tiryakian was not quite prepared to spell out what this really meant and, thus, was certainly more careful than Howard S. Becker who, two years later, pressed his colleagues to answer the question, "Whose side are we on?" (Becker 1966–67), it was evident that Tiryakian very much disliked the kind of "ironic skepticism" as suggested in Berger's widely read *Invitation to Sociology* (1963). This is why Tiryakian, in the aforementioned conflict between himself and Berger, ended his reply with the following words: "In a century of two world wars, genocide, colonial oppression, racial tension, Nazism, fascism, totalitarian atrocities, and with the ominous presence of thermonuclear war, of hellish demons appearing in the current monster craze, and other symptoms of global social and moral destructuration, it is time for a serious though compassionate sociological stance toward the social world instead of a nonchalant playing of our fiddles à la Nero. To give attention to a general theory of social existence is neither chimerical nor luxuriating, but rather a necessary creative alternative to nihilism, barbarism, or sterility" (Tiryakian 1966: 263–64).

Fourth, Tiryakian's interest in phenomenology and existentialism was not only motivated by the aim to better theorize social action and the human condition although that was important for him. As was mentioned before, he certainly sympathized with any intellectual endeavor close to philosophical anthropology, and he probably would not have objected at all to the kind of sociology of knowledge as developed by Berger and Thomas Luckmann (1966) in their famous and phenomenologically inspired *The Social Construction of Reality*, a book that mainly tried to understand how action is structured by implicit or explicit worldviews. Tiryakian, however, as a "'militant' for the phenomenological cause in sociology" (1973: 222) and thus in principle not too far away from Berger's theoretical position, read "his" existentialist and phenomenological texts differently, he at least was much more attentive with respect to one particular point: He claimed that it is one of the most important insights of existentialist and phenomenological thinkers to emphasize "transcendence"—and this in the various meanings of this term. As has been stressed by almost all authors within these two philosophical traditions (and here Tiryakian does not deny that there are major differences between, let us say: Heidegger's position and that of Jaspers), it is the very essence of the freedom of human beings to transcend and change their social world, even to transcend themselves via the relationship to a higher being (Tiryakian 1962: 156).

This emphasis on transcendence is interesting because—if it is not the strict axial-age-meaning of the term—it can easily be linked not only to Durkheim's sociology of religion but also, of course, to fundamental questions of social change. As Tiryakian a couple of years later explained (and this could be read as a more or less implicit critique of Parsons), it is the character of social reality to continuously transcend the current state of affairs; therefore an interactionist and Meadian understanding of the social fabric—an understanding inspired by phenomenological and existentialist insights and that acknowledges the non-identity between the person on the one hand and her/his roles on the other—is far superior to the majority of sociological role theories; therefore, it is (again a somewhat disguised critique of Parsons) insufficient to talk about values, norms and ideologies as if they were stored in some platonic heaven of ideas (Tiryakian 1968: 449–50) without taking into consideration the innovative potential and willingness of actors to transcend and change not only the institutionalized forms of these values and norms but also these values and norms in themselves. To sum up this point, Tiryakian was not so much interested in "the social construction of reality" (as was obviously Berger/Luckmann's main focus) but in the continuous production and restructuring of reality. And it is exactly this point that explains why Tiryakian was so much involved with some developments within contemporary French sociology—which we turn to now.

Some of Tiryakian's papers on existentialism and phenomenology were published in anthologies related to Georges Gurvitch, a French sociologist, today not very well known outside the French-speaking scientific community but who, in fact, together with Raymond Aron was certainly one of the most important sociologists in France during the post–World War II period. Gurvitch, as has already been indicated, was a friend of Pitirim Sorokin and whatever this friendship was based upon, these two important sociologists at least shared—in addition to their common Russian origins—a deep interest in philosophical questions and a sound skepticism toward linear and often naive theories of social change and toward an overly simplistic and one-dimensional picture of social reality. This explains why—as the historian of French structuralism, François Dosse, had pointed out—Gurvitch became the somewhat charismatic leader of a whole group of authors who desperately tried to stop the wave of structuralism that threatened to overwhelm the French social sciences in the late 1950s and early 1960s; among those authors were sociologists such as Pierre Ansart and Jean Duvignaud, philosophers/sociologists such as Henri Lefebvre and Lucien Goldmann and anthropologists such as Georges Balandier (Dosse 1999; Ansart 1990).

As becomes immediately obvious by reading the last part of one of Gurvitch's most well-known books, *Dialectique et Sociologie* (1962), he had a peculiar perspective on the main task of sociology: Because of his understanding of the particularities of the human condition, he argued that sociology must theorize above all the discontinuities and contingencies of social processes. Georges Balandier, one of Gurvitch's interpreters, explained Gurvitch's action theoretical starting point as follows: "Human liberty[,] which is experienced collectively as well as individually, is therefore doubly defined; it is voluntary, innovatory, creative action; it is 'forced to clear away, overthrow, and break down all obstacles and to modify, transcend, recreate all situations'" (Balandier 1975: 31–2; see Bosserman 1968). Balandier adds that it was indeed Gurvitch's aim to overcome the classical opposition between the possible and the contingent, something which can only be understood and achieved if one takes seriously Gurvitch's insight that action even transforms and transcends the actor and thus opens new horizons.

Taking all this into consideration, one also begins to grasp how Gurvitch's intellectual guidance might have influenced at least some important members of the French social scientific community at that time, which makes it plausible why, for example, Goldmann transformed Lévi-Straussian structuralism into a historically informed *genetic* one, or why Balandier tried to distance himself from both ahistorical and static functionalism *and* structuralism by propagating an *Anthropologie Dynamique* (Balandier 1967). And, of course, this also allows one to understand why Tiryakian was very much attracted to the ideas of the scholars just mentioned and to the surrounding intellectual debates, in which he began to take part,[2] and why a decade later he was quite irritated when Anthony Giddens, in his *New Rules of Sociological Method*, coined the term "structuration" without mentioning the French circles around Gurvitch, which had developed much earlier and had even used identical terms (Tiryakian 1978: 1024). Further, this also clarifies why Tiryakian more and more regarded *Les formes élémentaires de la vie religieuse* as Durkheim's most important work, believing that Durkheim's "collective effervescence" still is a term central to any theory of social change that takes the emergence and transformation of social symbols seriously (Tiryakian 1973: 212).

At the end of "Vers une sociologie de l'existence," a paper published in a 1968 volume organized by Georges Balandier in homage to Georges Gurvitch, Tiryakian gives some remarkable hints concerning his future work. There he claims that one of the most important tasks of an existential sociology is not only to analyze the structures of social existence but also to focus on symbols (Tiryakian 1968: 454) and their change, since it is the symbolic dimension of human action that is responsible for the production, reproduction and transformation of social reality. If this is so, then one of the most promising fields of future social research are phenomena such as the development of heresies, the ongoing sacralization and de-sacralization of the profane (Tiryakian 1968: 456), and (so one at least could assume) the rise and fall of eschatological visions, since Tiryakian regarded the end of the 1960s as a period of crisis in the Western world (Tiryakian 1968: 462). And, indeed, these and similar topics were very much at the heart of Tiryakian's interventions in the theoretical debates on modernity and modernization that began to dominate the discipline of sociology in the 1970s and 1980s.

II

In these debates one of Tiryakian's most remarkable texts of the early 1970s was his "Toward the Sociology of Esoteric Culture" (1972). As the title of this paper suggests, one reason for Tiryakian's intervention was the blossoming of esoteric cults during and immediately after the "hippie movement," which soon began to affect not only youth culture but also the broader strata of populations all over the Western world. Tiryakian did not stay at the surface of these phenomena, however, but immediately pointed to a theoretical problem insofar as these esoteric cults obviously "clash with the image of secularization" (Tiryakian 1972: 491) and thus must somehow affect theories of modernization, which quite often predicted an increasing and basically inexorable secularization and disenchantment of the world.[3] If this is so then one could have drawn at least three rather different conclusions: One could have abandoned secularization theory, with some unknown effects for the status of the modernization paradigm; one could have improved the theory of secularization by modifying the problematic assumption of secularization as a *linear* process and, instead, emphasize the importance of counter trends as long as they do not contradict the overall picture; last but not least, one could have denied that the emergence and spread of these esoteric cults were problems for secularization theory since these forms of belief were not religions proper, which means that they should not affect the story of secularization at all. Tiryakian, however, did not choose any of the three options but argued in a completely different way. He claimed that the idea of modernization is not secular but, on the contrary, nothing but an esoteric ideology. Thus, Tiryakian challenged sociological common sense that believed in the inescapability of disenchantment and modernization and argued that these processes are not rational per se but something based on ideological and esoteric grounds that look pretty much the same as that which the protagonists of the thesis of a "rational modernity" tend to deny.

As Tiryakian argues, modernization is an "ideology, which positively evaluates what is new as against what is old, which sees the unfolding present as a time of liberation and freedom from the yoke of the stagnating past, is an ideology of a new order of things to come and of a this-worldly salvation by human means—an ideology which at least one author [and here Tiryakian refers to Voegelin; W. K.] [...] has seen as a product of esoteric (gnostic in this instance) symbolism manifested in the development of the Puritan Revolution" (Tiryakian 1972: 502–3). In short, Tiryakian regarded modernization as product of the aforementioned continuous battle between the sacred and the profane, of the continuous sacralization and de-sacralization of social phenomena that contradict any linear picture of historical processes.

> We wish to argue that much of what is modern, even the ideology of modernization at its source, has originated in esoteric culture; paradoxically, the value orientation of Western exoteric society, embodied in rationalism, the scientific ethos, and industrialism, has forced esoteric culture into the role of a marginal or underground movement. That is, modern Western civilization (dating it back to the Renaissance and Reformation) has increasingly given to esoteric culture the mantle of a counterculture, while at the same time coopting many of its values and products. (ibid.)

If this is so, Tiryakian concludes, then modernization is certainly not something that can *only* be detected since the time of the European Renaissance; it must have started earlier; there must have been traces already in antiquity. But linking antiquity with the twentieth century is not—and this is very much emphasized by Tiryakian—an attempt to make a teleological argument. On the contrary, social change is a "stochastic process" (Tiryakian 1972: 509); its outcomes are hardly ever predictable because it was and is often the case that esoteric cultures indeed are the innovators in world history, even if they often try to get rid of their "esoteric" labels as soon as possible (Tiryakian 1972: 508).

These arguments as presented here make it rather difficult to characterize Tiryakian as someone belonging to American mainstream sociology in general and to classical modernization theory in particular. This is especially so since basically *all* of Tiryakian's major projects from the 1970s onward seem to escape this very characterization. *First,* Tiryakian is one of the earliest historically inspired sociologists who put into doubt the assumption of a rather smooth global process of modernization *by pointing to the enormous legacy of colonialism in different parts of the world.* Already in the middle of the 1960s, and influenced by Georges Balandier, Tiryakian emphasized that the life of the colonized in colonial societies continuously resembled "une 'situation limite' qui est limitation au même point que les autres situations limites discutées par Jaspers dans son *Existenzphilosophie*" (1968: 460–1)—with grave consequences for the post-independence history of these former colonies, which for this very reason probably will not be able to follow Western models as was assumed for a long time by the defenders of modernization theory. No surprise, therefore, that Tiryakian again and again (Tiryakian 1973: 216; Tiryakian 1974: 127) raised the question of colonialism, and that in the middle of the 1980s he even pleaded for the necessary integration of the study of colonial history into the curricula of sociology programs (Tiryakian 1986a).

Second, Tiryakian became one of the first sociologists who really took *nationalism* seriously by arguing against the widely shared assumption that nationalism is a thing of the past or at least some archaic remnant soon to disappear. In his empirical study, "The Politics of Devolution: Quebec, Wales, and Scotland" (Tiryakian 1981), he not only indicated his interest in nationalism in general, but also seriously asked whether nationalism might change, or even destroy, established political systems even in the Western world (See also Tiryakian and Nevitte 1983; Tiryakian 1989; Tiryakian 1995; Tiryakian 2011b). Nation-states have been changing all the time, and they still do, so that their current existence cannot be guaranteed forever, not in Canada, not in Great Britain—an insight which, of course, was caused by the wave of nationalisms in the 1960s and 1970s, but one that is still valid with respect to the referendum in Scotland in October 2014.

Third, Tiryakian was quite often far away from celebrating the United States; his home country was certainly not regarded by him as the sound and healthy embodiment of the principles of an "enlightened" modernity—as many modernization theorists have argued for a long time, and which many of them seemed to believe again in the aftermath of 1989–91 and the collapse of the Soviet Union. Tiryakian always emphasized the ambivalent and contradictory features of American culture, arguing that the Puritan value system established during colonial times has fostered a highly problematic picture of the world, one that "transforms systematically the world into a new, active moral community, while there has also been a parallel policy of ignoring or abusing the 'wretched of the earth,' those perceived as outside the pale of the extended Puritan community" (Tiryakian 1984: 126). All that, so Tiryakian's conclusion, makes a rational foreign policy nearly impossible, which also made him believe already in the middle of the 1980s that the United States quickly will lose its dominant position in a world in which East Asia soon will rise and become the new "epicenter of modernity" (Tiryakian 1984: 127).

Fourth, and connected to the point just mentioned, Tiryakian continued to be occupied with secularization theory, often focusing on the somewhat exceptional religious history of the United States. In an interesting twist with respect to Max Weber's classical interpretation of the Puritan revolution in the sixteenth and seventeenth centuries, Tiryakian claimed that the events involved have to be interpreted as, above all, processes of dedifferentiation. It was the separation (i.e., differentiation) between state and church—something that could rather easily be achieved since Puritanism within Britain's New England colonies in North America was the rare case of a majority phenomenon (Tiryakian 1982: 355)—which paradoxically also allowed the blurring (i.e., dedifferentiation) of the differences between secular and religious life (Tiryakian 1975: 17) and thus the beginning of dynamic processes in which (Puritan) religion—unrestricted by any state regulation—shaped civil society as decisively as nowhere else in the Western world (Tiryakian 1993: 47), that is, the thorough sacralization of the mundane, which makes it so difficult to apply secularization theory to the American case (Tiryakian 1982: 356). Therefore, and in contrast to Seymour Martin Lipset and other authors within the modernization paradigm, Tiryakian pointed to the potentially conflictive potential of religion in the United States, something one becomes aware of only if one is prepared to look particularly into the spiritual, de-institutionalized and not churched, aspects of religious life (Tiryakian 1975: 17).

Fifth, it was certainly not only Tiryakian's occupation with religious life in the United States that made him aware of the importance of processes of dedifferentiation, processes that—according to him—were rarely theorized within sociological theory, particularly not by those authors who above all had emphasized processes of functional differentiation such as Talcott Parsons or Niklas Luhmann (Tiryakian 1985a). As Tiryakian made clear, however, dedifferentiation happens basically all the time on many levels of social life. And although one must certainly not argue that dedifferentiation is more important than differentiation, it would also be false to claim that dedifferentiation necessarily is a pathological phenomenon that somehow has to be, or will be, overcome in the future (Tiryakian 1985a: 130).

Taking all these five points into consideration, it becomes clear that Tiryakian's thinking about modernization necessarily must have resulted in ideas that look anything but orthodox or mainstream. So when one carefully reads Tiryakian's already-mentioned plea for a new paradigm, to be called "Modernization II" or "Neo-Modernization Analysis," which was published in 1991, one immediately realizes that there is indeed much talk of "modernization." But, in fact, Tiryakian is very much aware of the problems of this term and does not use it with the optimism of the 1950s and 1960s. On the contrary, Tiryakian emphasizes conflicts, the problem of legitimacy in all modern societies, the possibility of exogenous factors[1] that might distort or redirect attempts to modernize particular countries, and the fact that the United States can no longer be the model of modernization, since one must always take into consideration the existence of different epicenters of modernity. The careful reader might wonder whether this is a systematic theory at all—and, indeed, one probably better understands Tiryakian's plea for "Neo-Modernisation Analysis" as a theoretically highly sophisticated tool kit that does not dare to make predictions, but at least allows one to understand the complexities of social change.[5] Tiryakian's continuous and systematic articulation of such a theoretical and, at the same time, modest position, however, did not prevent him from participating and decisively influencing new trends within social theory. On the contrary, Tiryakian could build upon insights already developed in the 1970s in order to enter the macro-sociological debate, which in the decades around the year 2000 increasingly began to focus on the concept of "civilization" and the idea of "modernities" (plural). This is the aspect of his work that will be analyzed in the last section of this chapter.

III

It is significant for Tiryakian's openness toward new theoretical currents that, already in the middle of the 1970s, he developed a strong interest in the concept of "civilization"—at a time when such a move was not *en vogue* at all.[6] He took part in debates (SA 1974) around the work of Benjamin Nelson, who—in a similar way as Shmuel N. Eisenstadt at that time—continued Max Weber's project of wide-ranging macro-comparisons but who, more than Weber ever did, theorized "civilizations" in order to understand the variety of intellectual and scientific developments in different periods and parts of the world (see Huff 1981). Although Tiryakian was attracted to Nelson's work and to Nelson's particular emphasis on the importance of *inter*-civilizational encounters,[7] he immediately realized what a few decades later would turn out to be the two decisive problems of civilizational analysis.

First, Tiryakian claimed that the talk of civilizational *encounters* is somewhat vague since there are simply too many ways by which civilizations and culture can "meet" each other—via exchange of goods as well as, for example, via violence and war. "Entanglement," as the phenomenon was later called in a rather fashionable way, is hardly a very precise concept! Tiryakian above all pleaded for the intense study of empires and colonialism as one of the most important aspects of inter-civilizational encounters. In this context he referred to the early work of Eisenstadt and his *The Political Systems of Empires* (Eisenstadt 1963), a remarkable reference, if only for the very reason that Eisenstadt's own type of civilizational analysis as developed from the late 1970s onwards (see, e.g., Eisenstadt 1977, 2000) rarely ever took such encounters into consideration and thus strangely neglected his own achievements as laid out in this early book (Knöbl 2001: 259).

Second, Tiryakian pleaded for the careful use of the concept of "civilization" because it is always accompanied by the danger of glossing over the many differences within a particular civilization. According to Tiryakian, civilizational analysis must pay at least as much attention to inter-civilizational encounters as to *intra*-civilizational ones. Therefore, and particularly with respect to cultural phenomena, he very much emphasized the continuous emergence of new heterodox intellectual currents such as Gnosis, mysticism, theosophy and pantheism in Western civilization, which certainly do not define the "West" but which, as undercurrents, are important enough to lead to rather conflictual and dynamic processes *within* this civilization (Tiryakian 1974: 127; 1996).

Tiryakian has up until now continued his interventions into the debate on civilizational analysis with important contributions, which also means that he quickly also became involved in the debate on "multiple modernities" (see, e.g., Tiryakian and Arjomand 2004; Tiryakian 2007, 2014). As has been pointed out in the last section, Tiryakian has developed a very sophisticated understanding of "modernization," one which already in the middle of the 1980s made him talk of "waves of modernity" and thus of "cyclical changes in the epicenters of modernity" (Tiryakian 1985b: 135). He was convinced that processes of modernization might not have started with the Renaissance and the Reformation but much earlier (Tiryakian 1985b: 137). It is no surprise, that in this context—and in accordance with his academic origins—he used the term "seedbed societies" (Ancient Israel and Greece) as developed in Talcott Parsons's writings from the 1960s (Parsons 1966: Ch. 6). But, and this should not surprise either, Tiryakian was also prepared to use the term somewhat differently: Whereas Parsons tried to sketch a whole variety of specific cultural and institutional elements of these two ancient societies which, according to him, turned out to be a legacy for times still to come, Tiryakian tended to be more careful. In accordance with his existentialist roots and links to French intellectual life, he only emphasized the new understanding of time that emerged in these two societies and framed this with the concept of "historicity," a concept that (a) was well-known within philosophical and circles of France in the 1960s and even became a central concept of Alain Touraine's sociology (which, by the way, in many respects was certainly not too far away from the project pursued by Georges Gurvitch) and that (b) is closely related to the term "transcendence" in the general meaning of the word: "In both societies we find for the first time a sense of a world historical process, of the transcendence of their situation, of historicity. These are aspects of a breakthrough that far wealthier, earlier, and later civilizations lacked" (Tiryakian 1985: 136).[8]

Thus, as can be seen in this quotation, although in the middle of the 1980s Tiryakian still believed in some Western origin of modernity, he quickly distanced himself from such a position since "historicity" and "transcendence" were "invented" and used within Western civilization.

This made him conclude—and here it is necessary to stress Tiryakian's proximity to the debate on the "Axial Age" (Bellah and Joas 2012)—that "modernity" and "modernization" also are not exclusively Western projects (Tiryakian 1992a: 308) so that it might be better (and this has already been referred to above) to speak of "modernities" or "waves of modernity." In addition, an emphasis on "historicity" and "transcendence" also means, of course, that there is no telos in history (Tiryakian 1992b: 82); that social change and modernization are continuously accompanied by processes of differentiation *and* dedifferentiation; that secularization, rationalization and disenchantment are anything but linear processes (Tiryakian 1992c: 83); that even the "place" of the sacred in society is never fixed—because of continuous trends of sacralization and de-sacralization (Tiryakian 1997)—and that eschatological visions are always possible, especially since the different waves of modernity can in themselves be regarded as articulations of such visions (Tiryakian 1986b).

Summarizing Tiryakian's theoretical moves and brilliant insights just mentioned makes one wonder how anyone could have acquired the strange idea that he might be a product of mainstream US sociology in general and a typical representative of modernization theory in particular. What a misinterpretation! Would it not be much better to classify him as member of that group of sociologists whom Hans Joas once aptly called "Konstitutionstheoretiker," or constitution theorists (Joas 1996: 230)—scholars such as Michael Mann, Anthony Giddens, Alain Touraine and Cornelius Castoriadis, who tried and tried to explain social macro-processes by referring to the creative potentials of individual and collective actors, who therefore always reckon with contingent outcomes and thus criticize the assumption of a telos of history? Without a doubt, that sticker is much better! But since one has to keep in mind that not only do human beings in general—but Edward A. Tiryakian in particular— have the capacity of creatively transcending their situations and developing new ideas, we might see more surprises in the future. So it can easily happen that even this sticker will slip away.

Notes

1 Tiryakian always continued with this kind of "ecumenical" work; see Tiryakian 1990: 19–25.
2 For a critique of Jean Duvignaud, see Tiryakian 1970.
3 One should add here that, in contrast to many modernization theorists, Parsons did not stick to the secularization paradigm (see Tiryakian 1999: 76).
4 In the 1990s—and while staying in Berlin—Tiryakian came into closer contact with the work of Hans Joas who, at that time, wrote quite extensively on war and social thought. Tiryakian, who was already occupied with this research topic, responded to Joas's analyses with his paper (Tiryakian 2000).
5 This honest and modest way of theorizing became even more evident when Tiryakian could look back to almost a decade of post-Soviet history in Eastern Europe, see Tiryakian 1998. Here, Tiryakian more than ever stresses the importance of the focus on collective actors (the necessary voluntaristic frame of reference of Neo-Modernization theory!) in analyses of social change indicating that theorists have to reckon with contingencies all over the place.
6 Note that Tiryakian's openness toward civilizational analysis might have been due to the early influence of Sorokin, who also used the concept of "civilization."
7 One of the reasons Tiryakian could so easily link his own ideas to the ones of Nelson was probably the fact that Nelson had a rather, as one might call it, phenomenological understanding of how to approach and analyze cultures and civilizations, something very close to Tiryakian's own position: "No matter how 'primitive' or 'complex' the nature of their societies, peoples cannot live together continuously, share common life ways, and speak common languages without creating expressive structures of meaning and symbolic designs—the cultural ontologies and mappings of their historically situated life-worlds—which constitute the immanent textures and media of their coexistence over time" (Nelson 1974: 131).
8 Here it would also be interesting to reflect in a systematic way on the possible influence of Voegelin on Tiryakian's thought (I owe this idea to Hans Joas).

References

Alexander, J. C. 1998. *Neofunctionalism and After*. Malden and Oxford: Blackwell.
Ansart, P. 1990. *Les sociologies contemporaines*, 3rd edition. Paris: Éditions du Seuil.
ASR—*American Sociological Review*. 1966. Vol. 31, no. 2: 258–65.
Balandier, G. 1975. *Gurvitch*. Oxford: Basil Blackwell.
——— 1967. *Anthropologie Politique*. Paris: Presses Universitaires de France.
Becker, H. S. 1966–67. "Whose Side Are We on?" *Social Problems* 14 (Winter): 239–47.
Bellah, R. and H. Joas. 2012. *The Axial Age and Its Consequences*. Cambridge, MA, and London: The Belknap Press of Harvard University Press.
Berger, P. L. 1963. *Invitation to Sociology. A Humanistic Perspective*. New York: Doubleday & Company.
Berger, P. L. and T. Luckmann. 1966. *The Social Construction of Reality*. New York: Doubleday.
Bosserman, P. 1968. *Dialectical Sociology: An analysis of the sociology of Georges Gurvitch*. Boston: Porter Sargent.
Dosse, F. 1999. *Geschichte des Strukturalismus. Band 1: Das Feld des Zeichens 1945–1966*. Frankfurt/Main: Fischer.

Eisenstadt, S. N. 1963. *The Political Systems of Empires.* New York: The Free Press.

——— 1977. "Sociological Theory and an Analysis of the Dynamics of Civilization and Revolutions." *Daedalus* 106, no. 1: 59–78.

——— 2000. *Die Vielfalt der Moderne.* Weilerswist: Velbrück.

Gurvitch, G. 1962. *Dialectique et Sociologie.* Paris: Flammarion.

Huff, T. E., ed. 1981. *On the Roads to Modernity. Conscience, Science, and Civilizations. Selected Writings by Benjamin Nelson.* Totowa, NJ: Rowman and Littlefield.

Joas, H. 1996. *The Creativity of Action.* Chicago: Chicago University Press.

Knöbl, W. 2001. *Spielräume der Modernisierung. Das Ende der Eindeutigkeit.* Weilerswist: Velbrück.

Nelson, B. 1974. "De Profundis…: Responses to Friends and Critics." *Sociological Analysis* 35, no. 2: 129–42.

Parsons, T. 1966. *Societies. Evolutionary and Comparative Perspectives.* Englewood Cliffs, NJ: Prentice-Hall.

SA—Sociological Analysis. 1974. "Symposium on Civilizational Complexes and Intercivilizational Encounters." Vol. 35, no. 2.

Sztompka, P. 1993. *The Sociology of Social Change.* Oxford and Cambridge, MA: Blackwell.

Tiryakian, E. A. and S. Arjomand, eds. 2004. *Rethinking Civilizational Analysis.* London: Thousand Oaks.

Tiryakian, E. A. and N. Nevitte. 1983. "A Typology of Nationalism." In *Introductory Readings in Government and Politics*, edited by M. O. Dickerson, T. Flanagan and N. Nevitte, 116–25. Toronto: Methuen.

Tiryakian, E. A. 2014. "Civilization in the Global Era: One, Many…or None?" In *Social Theory and Regional Studies in the Global Age*, edited by S. Arjomand, 91–112. Albany: SUNY Press.

——— 2013. "Introduction." In *Sociological Theory, Values, and Sociocultural Change: Essays in Honor of Pitirim A. Sorokin*, edited by E. A. Tiryakian, vii–xxvi. New Brunswick, NJ, and London: Transaction Publishers.

——— 2011a. "Remembering Talcott Parsons and Pitirim Sorokin: Interview of Edward Tiryakian." August 23, Las Vegas. http://cdclv.unlv.edu/archives/interactionism/goffman/tiryakian_11.html.

——— 2011b. "The Missing Religious Factor in *Imagined Communities.*" *American Behavioral Scientist* 55, no. 10: 1395–414.

——— 2007. "The Meshing of Civilisations: Soft Power and the Renewal of the Civilisation of Modernity." In *Modernity at the Beginning of the 21st Century*, edited by V. H. Schmidt, 89–113. Newcastle: Cambridge Scholars Publishing.

——— 2000. "Krieg: Die verborgene Seite der Moderne." In *Die Gegenwart des Krieges: Staatliche Gewalt in der Moderne*, edited by W. Knöbl and G. Schmidt, 194–213. Frankfurt/Main: Fischer TB.

——— 1999. "An Emergent French Connection: Revisiting Parsons's Durkheims." In *Agenda for Sociology: Classic Sources and Current Uses of Talcott Parsons's Work*, edited by B. Barber and U. Gerhard, 53–86. Baden-Baden: Nomos Verlagsgesellschaft.

——— 1998. "Neo-Modernisierung. Lehren für die und aus der postsozialistischen Transformation." In *Postsozialistische Krisen: Theoretische Ansätze und empirische Befunde*, edited by K. Müller, 31–52. Opladen: Leske & Budrich.

——— 1997. "The Wild Cards of Modernity." *Daedalus* 126, no. 2: 147–81.

——— 1996. "Three Metacultures of Modernity: Christian, Gnostic, Chthonic." *Theory, Culture and Society* 13, no. 1: 99–118.

———— 1995. "Nationalism and Modernity: A Methodological Appraisal." In *Perspectives on Nationalism and War*, edited by J. L. Comaroff and P. C. Stern, 205–35. Australia: Gordon and Breach Publishers.

———— 1993. "American Religious Exceptionalism: A Reconsideration." *Annals of the American Academy of Political and Social Sciences* 527, no. 1: 40–54.

———— 1992a. "From Modernization to Globalization." *Journal for the Scientific Study of Religion* 31, no. 3: 304–10.

———— 1992b. "Pathways to Metatheory: Rethinking the Presuppositions of Macrosociology." In *Metatheorizing*, edited by G. Ritzer, 69–87. Newbury Park, London, New Delhi: Sage.

———— 1992c. "Dialectics of Modernity: Reenchantment and Dedifferentiation as Counterprocesses." In *Social Change and Modernity*, edited by H. Haferkamp and N. J. Smelser, 78–94. Berkeley, Los Angeles, Oxford: University of California Press.

———— 1991. "Modernisation: Exhumetur in Pace (Rethinking Macrosociology in the 1990s)." *International Sociology* 6, no. 2: 165–80.

———— 1990. "Gurvitch et Parsons." *Sociologia Internationalis* 28, no. 1: 19–25.

———— 1989. "Nacionalismo, Modernidad y Sociología." In *Sociolgía del Nacionalismo*, edited by A. Perez-Agote, 143–61. Bilbao: Universidad del pais vasco.

———— 1986a. "Sociology's Great Leap Forward: The Challenge of Internationalisation." *International Sociology* 1, no. 2: 155–71.

———— 1986b. "Modernity as an Eschatological Setting: A New Vista for the Study of Religions." *History of Religions* 25, no. 4: 378–86.

———— 1985a. "On the Significance of De-differentiation." In *Macrosociological Theory: Perspectives on Sociological Theory*, Vol. 1, edited by S. N. Eisenstadt and H. J. Helle, 118–34. Beverly Hills: Sage.

———— 1985b. "The Changing Centers of Modernity." In *Comparative Social Dynamics*, edited by E. Cohen, M. Lissak and U. Almagor, 131–47. Boulder and London: Westview Press.

———— 1984. "The Global Crisis as an Interregnum of Modernity." *International Journal of Comparative Sociology* XXV, nos. 1–2: 123–30.

———— 1982. "Puritan America in the Modern World: Mission Impossible?" *Sociological Analysis* 43, no. 4: 351–67.

———— 1981. "The Politics of Devolution: Quebec, Wales, and Scotland." *Comparative Social Research* 4, no. 1: 33–64.

———— 1978. "Review of Giddens's 'New Rules of Sociological Method.'" *American Journal of Sociology* 83, no. 4: 1022–25.

———— 1975. "Neither Marx nor Durkheim…Perhaps Weber." *American Journal of Sociology* 81, no.1: 1–33.

———— 1974. "Reflections on the Sociology of Civilizations." *Sociological Analysis* 35, no. 2: 122–28.

———— 1973. "Sociology and Existential Phenomenology." In *Phenomenology and the Social Sciences*, Vol. 1, edited by M. Natanson, 187–222. Evanston: Northwestern University Press.

———— 1972. "Toward the Sociology of Esoteric Culture." *American Journal of Sociology* 78, no. 3: 491–512.

———— 1970. "Remarques sur une sociologie du changement qualitatif." In *Sociologie des Mutations*, edited by G. Balandier, 83–94. Paris: Éditions Anthropos.

———— 1968. "Vers une sociologie de l'existence." In *Perspectives de La Sociologie Contemporaine: Hommage à Georges Gurvitch*, edited by G. Balandier, R. Bastide, J. Berquem and P. George, 445–65. Paris: Presses Universitaires de France.

———— 1966. "Reply to Kolaja and Berger." *American Sociological Review* 31, no. 2: 263–64.

———— 1965. "Existential Phenomenology and the Sociological Tradition." *American Sociological Review* 30, no. 5: 674–88.

———— 1962. *Sociologism and Existentialism: Two perspectives on the individual and society.* Englewood Cliffs, NJ: Prentice-Hall.

———— 1960. "Quelques aspects négatifs de l'éducation de masse dans les pays sous-développés." *Tiers-Monde* 1, no. 1–2: 161–73.

———— 1959. "Occupational Satisfaction and Aspiration in an Underdeveloped Country: The Philippines." *Economic Development and Cultural Change* 7, July: 431–44.

———— 1958. "The Prestige Evaluation of Occupations in an Underdeveloped Country: The Philippines." *American Journal of Sociology* 63, no. 4: 390–99.

———— 1957. "Apartheid and Religion." *Theology Today* 14, no. 1: 385–400.

Zapf, W. 1991. "Modernisierung und Modernisierungstheorien." In *Die Modernisierung moderner Gesellschaften: Verhandlungen des 25. Deutschen Soziologentages in Frankfurt am Main 1990*, edited by W. Zapf, 23–39. Frankfurt/Main and New York: Campus.

Chapter 3

DEVELOPMENTAL PATH (*ENTWICKLUNGSFORM*): A NEGLECTED WEBERIAN CONCEPT AND ITS USEFULNESS IN THE CIVILIZATIONAL ANALYSIS OF ISLAM

Saïd Amir Arjomand

Edward Tiryakian offered a masterful formulation of a key neglected concept, dedifferentiation (Tiryakian 1985), and has proposed rethinking civilizational analysis (Tiryakian 2001). It therefore seems appropriate to dedicate the exploration of an idea for civilizational analysis that may prove seminal to him. In rethinking civilizational analysis, our paradigm for analyzing the relation between world religions and axial civilizations as adumbrated by Max Weber and S. N. Eisenstadt readily suggests itself as the best starting point, and yet it is too abstract and badly in need of being historicized. In proposing a concept to assist the task of historicization, I will briefly go back to a key referent of Tiryakian's concept of dedifferentiation, namely Herbert Spencer.

Much of my work in progress seeks to historicize Islam as a world religion and the Islamicate civilization that grew around it, from the Nile to the Oxus, by moving away from the monistic and ahistorical, one-ideal type, one-religion approach followed by many Weberians, and by applying instead Max Weber's own notion of developmental patterns to axial civilizations in their formative period(s) and beyond. As part of this work in progress, I here explore this historicizing approach in connection with a pluralistic conception of axial civilizations—in my case, the Islamicate civilization—as consisting of normatively autonomous (*eigengesetzlich*) domains, each with its own developmental pattern, which can interact or conflict with those in other domains.

In his seminal essay, "Progress: Its Law and Causes," written in 1857, the year before Darwin's *On the Origin of Species*, Herbert Spencer equated "social progress" with "social evolution," consisting in "changes of structure in the social organism" (Spencer 1972: 38–39). Spencer found evolution to be a universal process in nature and in human society: "in the development of Society, of Government, of Manufactures, of Commerce, of Language, Literature, Science, Art, this same evolution of the simple into the complex, through successive differentiations, holds throughout." In all these developments, "the transformation of the homogeneous into the heterogeneous is that in which Progress essentially consists." (Spencer 1972: 40). Furthermore, "The change from the homogeneous to the heterogeneous is displayed equally in the progress of civilization as a whole, and in the progress of every tribe or nation" (Spencer 1972: 41–42). By heterogeneity is meant the increasing differentiation of the forms of government, religion and manners or "ceremonial usages," both within each nation and between different nations (Spencer 1972: 44). Presumably, with this notion of heterogeneity both within and between different forms of social organizations in mind, Spencer added later that "Social progress in not linear but divergent and re-divergent" (Spencer 1972: 133), and redefined social evolution as increasing differentiation of structures and specialization of their functions, which need to be coordinated (Spencer 1972: 131–33).

These formulations have the merit of revealing Spencer's theory of social evolution as a special instance of the universal law of nature, a faithful translation of the idea of progress as the utopian regulative principle of the Enlightenment into the language of the scientism of the age of the counterrevolution in science (Gillispie 2007). Just as his contemporary, Karl Marx, relied on the scientism of the era to reduce evolution to that of the "mode of production," with government, religion and ethos relegated to the vaporous "superstructure," Spencer reduced evolution to that of "society," which in effect similarly disposed of government, religion and manners.

Although he insightfully analyzed the differentiation between the political, ecclesiastical and ceremonial institutions and within each of them in the early stages of evolution, as a British Dissenter faithful to the Enlightenment (Peel 1972), Spencer considered these institutions—and especially the state—as oppressive, restraining progressive individualism and providential freedom of the individual. Consequently, Spencer devalued his own pioneering contribution to comparative sociology and disabled himself for attaining what he considered "the highest achievement in Sociology," namely, "to grasp the vast heterogeneous aggregate" by considering "the inter-dependence of structures and functions [...] taken in their totality" (Spencer 1972: 132).

Spencer's heuristic conception of divergent and re-divergent evolution as a tool for understanding diversity of outcomes in evolutionary processes was vacated of all empirical reference by the abstraction "society." More recent reformulations of the idea of evolution by Parsons (1966) and Bellah (2011) have produced some new insights by moving toward historicization. Most notable among these are Parsons's idea of the emergence of evolutionary universals resulting from the generalization of the specific historical experiences of "seedbed societies." But these insights have not freed the idea of generic social evolution from its essentialist reference to society. In Bellah's latest formulation (2011), applied by Levine (2014) to demonstrate social pluralism in the single case of Ethiopia, the stages of social evolution are still five grades of *societies*: kinship, communal, archaic, axial and modern.

The incidental referents of society in the above-mentioned passages by Spencer himself are tribe, nation and civilization. When Eisenstadt (1966) used Parsons's evolutionary frame for the modernization theory, the nation-state became the sole empirical referent of society, albeit implicitly. He would only allow the possibility of eruptions "in the processes of modernization and the structure of modern society," leading "to breakdowns of modernization, to the development of regressive regimes, or deformed regimes with autocratic tendencies" (Eisenstadt 1966: 40). Even Charles Tilly (1970), a severe critic and advocate of historical sociology, while noting reversals within what was loosely thought of as society, remained trapped by the evolutionary schema he wishes to negate, coming up only with opposites such as devolution, dedifferentiation, shrinkage (instead of expansion) and the like. The plethora of failed nation-states in the global age, among other things, makes it impossible for us to make do with such tinkering devices as breakdowns of modernization, devolution and involution. We need new concepts to deal with the directionality of development in different societies, however more precisely defined, and that of different domains or spheres of life within each of them.

In the early 1970s, Eisenstadt himself realized the fault in the modernization theory could not be patched up, and he turned to the problem of "continuity and reconstruction of tradition," which in turn brought him to origins of major breakthroughs in human history during what Karl Jaspers called the Axial Age in 1980s, and finally led him, by the end of the century, to conceive of culturally specific and divergent paths of modernization as multiple modernities (Arjomand 2014: 32–33). Eisenstadt, however, described the consequence of the axial breakthrough that accounts for the dynamic potential of axial civilizations in broad and generic terms as the institution of a "chasm between the transcendental and the mundane." Two critical issues remained unresolved: (a) the historicization of the axial civilizations to show patterns of sociocultural change; and (b) analytical tools for tracing the culturally specific directionality of evolutionary processes and the consequent diversity of developmental paths. Only by resolving these issues would he move toward understanding the problem of diversity (divergent and re-divergent heterogeneity in Spencer's terms), which he considered the highest goal of sociology.

Unlike Spencer, Durkheim, Parsons and Bellah, Max Weber had little use for the abstraction "society" and instead analyzed "social action" in different spheres or domains of life that he considered normatively autonomous (*eigengesetzlich*). This gave him an enormous advantage for analyzing distinct developmental logics or patterns of rationalization within each that are captured by the term *Entwicklungsform*, literally developmental form/pattern, which I will translate as "developmental path." As each domain has its own normative order, it is in principle capable of engaging in encounters with other civilizations largely on its own terms, even in divergence from developmental paths in other spheres of social life.

In contrast to the impressive range of structural typologies—such as capitalism, patrimonialism, hierocracy and state—and historically significant ideal types—Protestant ethic, Confucian this-worldly rationalism, ethical and exemplary prophecy, theodicy of suffering and the like—Weber never formalized this concept, except for a single, grandest developmental path in human history, which he called rationalization. I believe I have demonstrated, however, that rationalization was somewhat incorrectly formalized by Weber in terms of instrumental and formal rationality, whereas the direction of the process set in motion by the world religions and the civilizations that grew around them was primarily that of value-rationalization. Religious rationalism that Weber (1915) saw as unfolding in different directions was neither primarily instrumental nor formal. What it involved, rather, was conceptual rationality or poetic construction of meaning. It was the process of value-rationalization that brought the heterogeneous, institutionally embodied developmental logics in different normatively autonomous spheres of life into a measure of meaningful consistency (*Zinnzusammenhang*). Such architectonic construction of meaning evolves gradually and often imperceptibly among cultural clusters through elective affinities that produce civilizational rationalities that we recognize as "civilizational style" (Arjomand 2004). Eisenstadt's basic premises of an axial civilization could only be regulative principles in the Kantian sense, and could never predetermine the direction of rationalization. The process of value-rationalization is historically contingent, and only its historical contingency can account for the diversity in the direction of change, be it in axial civilizations or in multiple modernities.

Although Weber's idea that civilizations or cultural worlds grow around the world religion is truly seminal, his application of the idea of rationalization to the development of the great world religions and civilizations, which is followed by some later Weberians such as Schluchter (1999), is too monistic and holistic to be historicized. It overlooks the directionality of specific historical trends *within* each and every civilization. Weber (1920) acknowledges this in the introduction to his collected essays on the sociology of religion, wherein he famously stated that a variety of rationalizations have taken place in different spheres of life, and what is rational from one point of view could be irrational from another. Let me suggest that, had he lived longer, he may have honed his idea of developmental paths for application to historical trends in normatively autonomous spheres of life, and to the interaction among them. In any event, we can do so as his heirs. We may differentiate different spheres of life analytically—say into the religious and the political—but need to specify rather than take for granted the relation between our categories and the more or less corresponding distinctions in the life world of the historical actors we are studying. I will illustrate my analytical framework with examples from the interlinked religious and political domains concerning the legitimacy of monarchy and the normative regulation of the political order. My aim will be to demonstrate how these two domains are brought into a measure of meaningful consistency (*Sinnzusammenhang*) in the context of the historical contingent developments in the Islamicate civilization.

We can begin to historicize the relation between Islam as a world religion and the Islamicate civilization that grew around it, and do so in two steps. First, by determining when in its formative history Islam acquired the characteristics typologically attributed to "world religions," and then tracing its interaction with the previous cultural worlds it inherited from the Nile to the Oxus—that is, with other civilizations it encountered and partially absorbed. This requires a basic distinction between the religious and the civilizational developmental patterns. The differentiation of religion (*din* = Arabic) from the world (*dunyā*) was presented as the religious developmental pattern belonging to the Medinan formative period under Muhammad and the first four caliphs. This differentiation was based on the Qur'an's distinction between the two and its increasing tendency to give faith (*imān*) a specific name in its later verses: Islam (Smith 1978). The Medinan period also generated Islamic sacred history in the form of the reports (singular, *khabar*) on the divine selection, teachings and wars (*maghāzi*) of Prophet Mohammad.

The developmental path of the differentiation of religion and politics as two interrelated orders or spheres of life was a later development in the second, imperial formative period. This Islamicate path of differentiation derived from the institutionalization of monarchy and the Islamic law in this second formative period. The two were reconciled in the Islamicate conception of the divinely ordained normative order consisting of the two powers—prophethood and kingship. According to this theory, God sent the prophets to lead humankind to salvation and appointed kings to maintain order as a prerequisite for their subjects to follow divine guidance through the teaching of the prophets. Prophecy as the basis of the Islamic ethico-legal order called the *Shari`a* was thus reconciled with kingship or monarchy as the political order.

This path of the normative differentiation of the two powers produced an analogous differentiation of sacred history in the works on the biography (*sira*) of Muhammad as the Seal of the Prophets sent by God for the guidance of humankind and the collection of his sayings (*hadith*), on the one hand, and the amalgamation of the *khabar* as the historical record of his activities and annalistic history (*ta'rikh*) into universal histories of empires. This double differentiation fitted well the empirical bifurcation of sovereignty into caliphate and sultanate from the second quarter of the tenth century onward and was elaborated by the practitioners of the new science of history. As stated by the great Ghaznavid historian and bureaucrat, Abu'l-Fazl Bayhaqi, a century later:

> Know that God Most High has given one power (*qowwat*) to the prophets and another power to the kings; and He has made it incumbent on the people of the earth to follow these two powers and thus to know God's straight path. (Cited in Arjomand 2010: 234)

This theory of the two powers was modified by the overthrow of the caliphate by the Mongols in 1258. The distinction between the political and the *shar'i* orders did not disappear with the caliphate but was accommodated within the framework of a distinctive type of regime that could be called "Islamic royalism," According to this conception, the ruler (*sultān*) maintained both the political and the *shar'i* order, and was therefore the "shadow of God on earth," the "refuge of the Caliphate" (*khilāfat-panāh*) and the "king of Islam" (Arjomand 2010).

We can now proceed to analyze the interaction between this developmental path in the political sphere of the Islamicate civilization with a new development in the religious sphere, namely the growth of popular Sufism from the twelfth century onward, and its paradoxical impact on the legitimacy of kingship in the political sphere. The two spheres of life in the Islamicate civilization remain analytically distinct, but their contingent historical intertwining opens a new developmental path in the Islamicate political order.

The reception of the idea of world renunciation in the Islamicate civilization was through the legend of the life of the Buddha (*Budhāsaf*) that was included in the broadly disseminated eighth/second century Arabic translations from the Pahlavi of the Indo-Persianate political parables, and independently through the Manichaean writings in New Persian somewhat later (Lang 1960). It is very significant that the story of the prince who renounced his royal estate in his search for enlightenment—according to this version, follow-ing the teaching of a world-renouncing ascetic, Belawhar—was incorporated into the Islamicate political ethic (rather than other branches of learning), giving the selection of the Buddhist parables for adoption a heavy political bias. Occasionally, as in the Twelver-Shi'ite-transmitted version, parables from other sources were added to illustrate the impermanence and nullity of worldly power (Mir-'Ābedini: 23–24).

Although Sufism was earlier attested for ascetic virtuosi throughout the Islamicate civilization, Sufism as a popular—first urban and then rural—movement spread in the eastern lands of the caliphate from the eleventh century onward and can properly be considered the core of Persianate Islam.[1]

As one would expect, world renunciation—detachment and withdrawal from the world—developed into a major value in Persianate Sufism. Let me take just two examples from the earliest to latest stages considered in the pres-ent chapter. The great Sufi master and Hanbalite Shaykh al-Islam of Herat, Kh^wāja 'Abdollāh Ansāri (d. 1088/481) was one of the early exponents of Sufism in elegant Persian prose. His magisterial *Chehel o daw fasl* (Forty-Two Essays) concluded with one interpreting a *hadith* attributed to the Prophet, "Be in the world as if you are a stranger (*gharib*) or a wayfarer, and consider yourself among the people of the tombs (*ahl al-qobur*)," where Ansari (1, 248) enjoined the Sufi wayfarer to be "among the people of the Hereafter so as to be a stranger in this world, as the people of Truth are strangers in both worlds." He further included the following among the hundred stages or battlefields (*meydān*) that culminate in the annihilation of the ego (99) and persistence in God (100):

> Stage 14: disengagement (*tajrid*) of the soul, the heart and the head;[2] Stage 82: solitary individualization (*enferād*) or the "stepping outside of the self and the two worlds." (Ansāri, 1:268, 320)

Mystical union with God required world renunciation in the form of disen-gagement and solitariness:

> Love based on unity (*tawhid*) aims only at the One Beloved. It demands disengagement (*tajrid*) from everything other than God, and solitariness (*tafrid*) with the Solitary. (Sam'ani in Chittick's tr., 2013: 244)

World rejection and the glorification of poverty (*faqr* in Arabic, *darvishi* in Per-sian) went hand in hand (Chittick 2013: 386, 412, 420). *Darvish* meant "poor' in Middle Persian. With the rendition of Sufi texts in Persian, it was used as a synonym for the Arabic *faqir* (poor man). Ansari (1, 65–66, 368–69) used *faqr* and *darvishi* interchangeably for poverty as a critical stage of spiritual progression on the Path.

To gain a comparative perspective, it is instructive to consider the impact on kingship of quintessential world renunciation in Theravada Buddhism, for which there is an outstanding study by Stanley Tambiah (1976). Tambiah shows that the salvation quest of the spiritual virtuosi—of the *bhikkhu* through world renunciation—is made possible within the larger society of humanity by a king from the warrior caste who performs the function of kingship "for the purpose," according to a tenth-century inscription, of "the alms-bowl and the robe of the Buddha" (Cited in Tambiah: 96). The *dharma* of kingship as the maintenance of society and polity in order to assure the prevalence, as prototypically in the first Buddhist empire of Ashoka, of "the ethos of Buddhism acting within the world of Impermanence, in pursuing Nirvana by creating the outward social conditions for such striving towards the overcoming of Attachment" (Tambiah: 62). Note the partial similarity of the Buddhist function of "Kingship" to the Muslim king's function of maintaining order to allow the pursuit of salvation according to divine guidance in the above-mentioned Islamicate theory of the two powers. As we shall see presently, however, there is an even more important parallel: the paradoxical effect of the Buddhist world renunciation consisting in the sacralization of the previously secular, Hindu conception of the *dharma* of the king as statecraft.

The thirteenth century shook the Persianate world and indeed the Islamicate civilization by disestablishing Islam for almost a century and seriously undermining the legalistic Islam of the ulema which, incidentally, promoted the Sufi shaykhs to the guardians of Persianate Islam. There can be no doubt that the fear of annihilation of Islam by the Mongols led the Muslim king to flee his native Khurasan after 1220 to take refuge with the Seljuqs of Rum (Anatolia). This threat to the survival of Islam was stimulus indeed to the spiritual mission of the Kubravi Sufi order to recruit the kings of Islam at the time when, as the Prophet, Muhammad, had predicted in a well-known *hadith*: "Islam began as a stranger, and again shall become a stranger as it began" (*Mersād*: 18; Algar tr.: 41). This, however, does not obviate the need for the solitary virtuosi, as each class of humanity had need for a spiritual guide (*shaykh*) in its education (*Mersād*: pt. 3, ch. 9):

> Give thy life, for union with Him is not given for trickery
> Drunkards are not given milk from the goblet of divine law.
> Where the detached solitaries (*mojarradān*) gather to drink
> Not a sip is given to the worshippers of the self. (*Mersād*: 222)

The function of the king, too, is defined within the framework of the education of mankind, where "the soil of the human frame was prepared in such a way that when the seed of spirituality was sown in it by the husbandry of the divine inhalation, and nurtured with the sunlight of God's grace and watered with His Law, there should grow from it the fruits of nearness and knowledge in [unimaginably] abundant measure" (*Mersād*: 111, Algar tr.: 132–33). Different classes of society perform their specialized functions to assure the cultivation of the seed of spirituality and knowledge, and each class needs the others to perform its functions. "Finally, a just and politic king (*pādshāh*) is needed to maintain equilibrium among the people and to repel evil and prevent the oppression of the weak from the strong, and to preserve and protect the subjects" (*Mersād*: 112).

Najm al-Din's mirror for the wayfaring of kings (*Mersād:* pt. 5; *Marmuzāt)* actually opens with Qur'an 38:26 on God's appointment of David as his deputy to rule among men with justice and with the *hadith* attributed to the Prophet: "The king is the shadow of God upon earth, in whom the oppressed take refuge." These together are taken to establish that "monarchy (*saltanat*) is the deputyship (*khelāfat*) and vice-regency of God Almighty."[3] The foremost divinely established principles of kingship are stated as follows:

> First, [God] said, "O, David, We made thee a deputy (*khalifa*)" (Q.38:26), indicating that the king must regard his kingship as God's gift and consider his kingdom the result of His beneficence: "Thou givest kingship to whom Thou wishes." (Q.3:26)[4] (Algar tr.: 397, slightly modified)

The next principle, however, introduces a Sufi note on the impermanence of temporal power:

> Second, there is a reminder to the king contained in the indication that God gave him kingship. [...] "Thou takest kingship from whom Thou wishes." (Q.3.26) He will therefore strive to attain true and abiding kingship by means of this *borrowed and transient kingship*, and not to deprive himself of fair reputation among men and reward in the hereafter. (Algar tr.: 397, *emphasis* added)

> The invidious contrast between the real kingship of God and illusory and impermanent earthly kingship is repeated in different forms at least a half a dozen more times. Nevertheless, the elevated station of kings in this world is immediately reaffirmed:

> Third, he will know that kingship is the deputy of God.

> Fourth, God said: "So rule among men with justice." (Q.38:26)[5] [...] (Algar tr.: 398)

This makes possible the paradoxical elevation of the rank of the mystically enlightened king to that of the divinely appointed Prophet/Kings of the Qur'an, most notably David.[6]

This sacralization of temporal ruler through world abnegation is expressed as follows:

> Kingship is the most complete instrument of wayfaring on the path of Truth/ God. The noblest benefit of kingship is its being the noblest instrument for conforming to the divine ethos[,] and the most perfect station of the wayfarers is to internalize the ethics of God [according to the maxim]: *takhallaqu bi-akhlāq allāh*. (*Marmuzāt*: 50)

Nevertheless, the sacralization of temporal rule did not spread instantly and, in fact, the greatest poets and mystics of the next generation, Mawlānā Jalāl al-Din Rumi (d. 1274?) and Shaykh Mosleh al-Din Sa`di (d. 1292) persisted in the Sufi devaluation of temporal power. The first chapter of Sa'di's *Golestān*, the most influential mirror for the prince in Persian literature, is on the tradition/ [normative] manner of kings (*sirat-e pādshāhān*), as the wielders of earthly power (see Arjomand 2004), and is followed by a second chapter on the religious elite or the wielders of spiritual power, who are significantly called "the dervishes" (*darvishān*). This ordering is quite remarkable because it shows that, after the Mongol invasion, the Sufi virtuosi as dervishes replaced the jurists (not to mention the proponents of philosophy as perennial wisdom) as the religious elite in Persianate societies. Furthermore, it is interesting to note that the most populist or democratic of *Golestān*'s parables is put in the mouth of a solitary world renouncer (*darvishi mojarrad*), who boldly asserts: "[K]now that the kings are for the guarding of the subjects (*ra'iyyat*), not the subject for obedience to kings:

> The king (*pādshah*) is the guardian of the poor (*darvish*)
> > Even though prosperity is through the royal charisma (*farr*) of his turn in power.
> The flock is not for the shepherd
> > But the shepherd for its service [...]
> The difference between kingship and servitude is removed
> > When the writ of [divine] judgment is issued.
> If the grave of the dead is opened,
> > It shows neither the rich nor the poor. (*Golestān*: 61)

Sa'di proceeds to admonish the prince just as pithily:

> Help [the needy], while you have your turn in power (*dawlat*)
> > As this turn in power and kingdom turns from hand to hand. (*Golestān*: 62)

There was a tremendous expansion of popular Sufism after the disintegration of the Ilkhanid empire in the second quarter of the fourteenth century and, with it, the religious and political prominence of the Sufi shaykhs. The highly changeable and decentralized successor Turko-Mongolian nomadic polities induced some of the leading Sufi shaykhs to draw on Shi`ite and esoteric and cabalistic wisdom and give popular Sufi movements a distinctly millennial inflection. We also have an intriguing, brief episode in the early fifteenth century, when one of the grandsons of Timur (Tamerlane), an initiate into the Horufi millennial movement who ruled Fars for much of the decade of warfare among his successors until 1414, claimed to be the "Mahdi of the End of Time," who unifies the apparent and real monarchy. In *Jāme'-e soltāni*, a work on astronomy informed by the new science of letters (*horuf*) for revealing divine secrets and astrology, a science he considered most useful for statecraft, Mirza Eskandar claims "the robe of apparent and spiritual caliphate" as the "shadow of God on earth." God has vouchsafed His favor on the prince, "both making his appearance the manifestation of the *minutiae* of expediencies of monarchy and kingship, and his reality the manifestation of *minutiae* of divine knowledge and sciences" (Yazdi 209; Binbaş 2014).

Sharaf al-Din Ali Yazdi (d. 1454/858), the long-time vizier of the Timurid principality of Fars under Mirza Eskandar's successor, Ehrāhim-Sultān b. Shāhrokh (r. 1414–34/817–37), is famous for his biography of Timur. Sharaf al-Din (Yazdi: 7–10) expounds the theory of the two divinely ordained powers—guidance of the prophets and punishment/policy (*siyāsat*) of the kings—while emphasizing the king's sword of punishment as the essential weapon for the maintenance of order in the world. In his history of the grandfather of his royal patron, Amir Timur (known for his modesty and refusal of the title of king), he is posthumously called the "Lord of the Auspicious Conjunction of the End of Time" (*saheb-qerān-e akhar al-zamān*), and is said to have "ascended, with God's help, the throne of caliphate and kingship" (Yazdi: 27–28). The theory of the two powers is reiterated with a Sufi twist,[7] according to which "world order (*nezām-e 'ālam*)" depends on "monarchy which consists in formal/apparent (*suri*) caliphate (Yazdi: 27)," but does so only in order to claim for the divinely ordained ruler both "the apparent and spiritual (*ma'navi*) caliphate and dual royal and religious princehood (*riyāsatayn-e molki o melli*)" (Yazdi: 29).

The final triumph of Sufism, and with it the culmination of the paradoxical sacralization of temporal rule through world renunciation, came with the empire established in 1501/907 by the youthful shaykh of the Safavid order, Shah Esmā'il. The Safavid Mahdist revolution (Arjomand 2005) introduced a radical change in the conception of kingship. This was facilitated by the fact that popular Sufism had become increasingly tinged with the Shi'ite expectation of the manifestation of the Mahdi since the mid-fifteenth century, and further infused a sacral element into the idea of kingship as temporal rule. Esmā'il's father (and grandfather), as the shaykhs of the Safavid Sufi order, had had sought the "unification of dervishhood and kingship" (*jam'-e darvishi o shāhi* (—that is, the material and the spiritual monarchy (Arjomand 2010: 264). The popular Sufi conception of unified material and spiritual monarchy was institutionalized under Shah Esmā'il. The Shi'ite conception of Ali as the *vali Allāh* was key in the fusion of the Sufi notion of *velāyat* (friendship of God) and the juristic meaning of the term as "authority"; and the Safavids conjoined both senses by calling themselves the "House of *Velāyat.*" In a decree issued in 1511/917, Shah Esmā'il claims divine sanction for his monarchy (*saltanat*) and caliphate by citing the Qur'an (Q.2.118 and Q.38.25) and referring to the Safavid House as the "dynasty of spiritual authority (*velāyat*) and Imamate," while assuming the title of shah at the outset, and thus combining it with the traditional legitimacy of kingship (Arjomand 2010: 264).

To conclude, the paradoxical sacralization of worldly kingship, under the eventual impact of the Sufi world renunciation that originally intended to prove the kingship's nullity, could not be deduced from the normative logic of either the Islamicate political order or of Sufism as it came to dominate the religious sphere. The normative logic of the Islamicate civilization was gradually modified with the decline of the caliphate and the rise of the sultanate in the twelfth century, and somewhat more drastically after the overthrow of the caliphate in the mid-thirteenth century. The Sultan became the head of the Islamic hierocracy without, however, eliminating the duality of the political and religious spheres. The developmental path in the religious sphere was marked by the rise of Sufism. The eventual sacralization of the ruler through divinely ordained spiritual authority was the paradoxical result of the two, interwoven, developmental paths in the religious and the political domains. Its development was far from linear and went through four centuries of unexpected vicissitudes that were historically contingent.

Nor did history stand still at the endpoint of our analysis. Sacral kingship proved impermanent because of the subsequent developmental path in the religious sphere as it changed sharply in the first half of the sixteenth century in Iran and the Ottoman Empire (and somewhat later in Mughal India). The development of the *madrasa*s (colleges of Islamic learning) by the Ottoman state created a strong Sunni hierocracy under the Sultan who was, as with all rulers, in accordance with the principles of Islamic royalism, the supreme temporal authority as well as the protector of the *shar i* religious order. In Iran, the rise of a Shi`ite hierocracy that became independent of the king after the fall the Safavids in the eighteenth century meant a further reduction of the status of the king to the one granted by the theory of the two powers. This meant that the Shah was the divinely ordained temporal sovereign while religious authority devolved exclusively on the Shi`ite hierocracy, which mercilessly suppressed Sufism.

Notes

1   *Kashf al-mahjub* (revealing of the veiled) by `Othman b. `Ali al-Hojviri of Ghazna (d. ca 1077) is an important treatise on the Sufi mystical path, in Persian, followed by the compendium *Hadiqat al-Haqiqa wa shari'at al-tariqa* (The Garden of Truth and the Law of the Path) by another Sufi and poet of Ghazna, Majdud b. Ādam, known as Hakim Sanā'i (d. 1131/525) But the greater trend-setter was Khʷāja `Abdollāh Ansāri (d. 1089), another early exponent of Sufism in elegant Persian prose. Rashid al-Din Maybodi (d. after 1126), Ahmad Ghazali (d. 1126) and `Abd al-Karim Sam`ani (d. 1167), were followers of Ansāri, the *pir-e tariqat* (master of the path), who wrote extensively in Persian in the twelfth century.
2   It is interesting to note, that Ansari (1:26) considers the famed Ebrahim son of Adham the greatest master of disengagement as he, like the Buddha, was a prince who renounced the world.
3   This *hadith* was already mentioned earlier, and is further cited and commented upon to prove that "kingship is the deputyship of Truth (*haqq*)" on p. 429.
4   These two are the most frequently cited Koranic verses for establishing the legitimation of kingship in the Sufi and non-Sufi texts alike. The so-called "authority Verse" (*ulu'l-amr*) Q.59.4, appears more rarely.
5   Later, an old maxim of Persian statecraft is added as the Prophet's endorsement of this principle: "Thus the Prophet, upon whom be peace, said: 'justice and kingship are twins'" (Algar tr.: 414).
6   Thus Rāzi in *Mersād al-'ebād*: "The supreme happiness and utmost turn in power (*dawlat*) consists in this, that a man of lofty aspiration be granted kingship of the realms of both religion and the world, for then, with the deputyship of "Ours is the first and the last" (Q.92:13), he will control the affairs of both realms. This rank was granted to David, upon whom be peace—(Q.38:26) (Algar, tr.: 397, slightly modified).
7   The statement immediately follows the above-cited verse of Najm al-Din Rāzi on the isomorphism of the human microcosm and the divine macrocosm.

References

Ansāri, Khʷāja 'Abdollāh. 1998–99 [1377]. "Sad maydan." In *Majmu'-ye rasā'el-e fārsi*, M. Sarvar Mawla'i, ed. Tehran: Tus.

Arjomand. S. A. 2004. "Rationalization, the Constitution of Meaning and Institutional Development." In *The Dialogical Turn. New roles for sociology in the post–disciplinary age*, edited by C. Camic and H. Joas. 247–75. Lanham, MD: Rowman and Littlefield.

——— 2005. "Rise of Shāh Esmā`il as a Mahdist Revolution," *Studies on Persianate Societies*, 3: 44–65.

——— 2010. "Legitimacy and Political Organisation: Caliphs, Kings and Regimes." In *The New Cambridge History of Islam*, vol. 4, edited by R. Irwin, 225–73. Cambridge: Cambridge University Press.

———— 2014. "Three Generations of Comparative Sociologies." In *Social Theory and Regional Studies in the Global Age,* edited by S. A. Arjomand, Ch. 1. Albany: SUNY Press.

Bellah, R. N. 2011. *Religion in human evolution.* Cambridge, MA: Harvard University Press.

Binbaş, I. 2014. "Timurid Experimentation with Eschatological Absolutism: Mirza Iskandar, Shah Ni`matullah Wali, and Sayyid Sharif Jurjani in 815/1412." In *Unity in Diversity: Mysticism, Messianism and the Construction of Religious Authority in Islam,* edited by O. Mir-Kasimov, 277–303. Leiden: Brill.

Chittick, W. C. 2013. *Divine Love. Islamic Literature and the Path to God.* New Haven: Yale University Press.

Eisenstadt, S. N., ed. 1986. *Origins and Diversity of Axial Age Civilizations.* Albany: SUNY Press.

———— 1966. *Modernization: Protest and Change,* Englewood Cliffs, NJ: Prentice-Hall.

Gillispie, C. C. 2007. *Essays and Reviews in History and History of Science.* Philadelphia: American Philosophical Society.

Lang, D. M. 1960. "Bilawhar wa Yudasaf." In *Encyclopaedia of Islam,* vol. 1, 1215–17. Leiden: Brill.

Levine, D. N. 2014. "Evolutionary Grades within Complex Societies: The Case of Ethiopia." In *Social Theory and Regional Studies in the Global Age,* edited by S. A. Arjomand, 221–66. Albany: SUNY Press.

Mir-'Ābedini, S. A. 1986 [1365]. *Introduction to Belawhar va Budhasaf.* Tehran, Amir Kabir.

Parsons, T. 1966. *Societies: Evolutionary and Comparative Perspectives.* Englewood Cliffs, NJ: Prentice-Hall.

Peel, J. D. Y., ed. 1972. *Introduction to Herbert Spencer on Social Evolution.* Chicago: University of Chicago Press.

Rāzi, Najm al-Din Abu Bakr b. Mohammad. 1973 [1352]. *Mersād al-'ebād,* M. A. Riyāhi, ed. Tehran Enteshārāt-e 'Elmi va Farhangi. (*The Path of God's Bondsmen from Origin to Return*), trans. by Hamid Algar. New York: Persian Heritage Series, 1982.

Rāzi, Najm al-Din Abu Bakr b. Mohammad. 1973. *Marmuzāt-e asadi dar mazmurāt-e Dāwudi,* M.R. Shafi'i-Kadkani, ed. Tehran: McGill University Institute of Islamic Studies.

Sa'di Shirāzi, Shaykh Moslem al-Din. 1966 (1345). *Golestān,* Sa'id Nafisi, ed. Tehran: Foroughi.

Schluchetr, W. 1999. "Hindrances to Modernity: Max Weber on Islam." In *Max Weber and Islam,* edited by T. E. Huff and W. Schluchter, 75–101. New Brunswick, NJ: Transaction.

Smith, W. C. 1978. *The Meaning and End of Religion.* New York: Harper and Row.

Tambiah, S. 1976. *World Conqueror and World Renouncer.* Cambridge: Cambridge University Press.

Tilly, C. 1970. "Clio and Minerva." In *Theoretical Sociology. Perspectives and Developments,* edited by J. C. McKinney and E. A. Tiryakian, 433–66. New York: Appleton-Century-Crofts.

Tiryakian, E. A., ed. 2001. "Civilizational Analysis: Renovating the Sociological Tradition," Special issue of *International Sociology* 16, no. 3 (Reprinted in S. A. Arjomand and E. A. Tiryakian, eds. 2004. *Rethinking Civilizational Analysis.* London: Sage).

———— 1985. "On the Significance of Dedifferentiation," In *Perspectives on Macro-Sociological Theory,* edited by S. N. Eisenstadt and H. J. Helle, 118–34. London and Beverly Hills: Sage.

Weber, M. 1948 [1915]. "The Social Psychology of World Religions." In *From Max Weber. Essays in Sociology*, edited by H. H. Gerth and C. W. Mills, 267–302. London: Routledge.

——— 1930 [1920]. *The Protestant Ethic and the Spirit of Capitalism*. London: Allen and Unwin.

Yazdi, Sharaf al-Din 'Ali. 2009 [1388]. *Monsha'āt*, Iraj Afshar, ed. Tehran: Farhang-e Irān-Zamin.

Chapter 4

THE EXISTENTIAL SOCIOLOGY OF EDWARD TIRYAKIAN: TOWARD AN INTEGRATED PARADIGM

Andrey Melnikov

Edward Tiryakian is a representative of the cohort of outstanding contemporary theorists. After six decades of intensive sociological studies and activities, he has produced a number of novel sociological concepts, approaches and theoretical trends. The basis of his theorizing is the original project of existential phenomenological sociology, and the study of religion, culture, nationalism, ethnic conflicts, disasters and social change.

Sociologists became interested in the works of Edward Tiryakian as long ago as the 1960s. In Soviet sociology, an influential paper was published by Leonid Ionin (1977), representing one of the best analyses of Tiryakian's ideas, although it was written under the critical censorship of "bourgeois sociology." Certain aspects of Tiryakian's theory were considered in the rare studies of the history of existential sociology (Alijevova 1984; Kisil 1985; Raida 1998), and its systematic studies have begun only recently (Gasparyan 1997; Melnikov 2010). Today, the name of Tiryakian is increasingly found on the pages of sociological literature, including textbooks and encyclopedias.

Edward Tiryakian became acquainted with the ideas of existentialism in the 1950s during his studies at Princeton and Harvard, although the ascendancy of structural-functionalism, led by Talcott Parsons, and his great appreciation of Pitirim Sorokin also had great influence. Tiryakian also met Jacques Maritain and John Wild as teachers and friends. As a teaching fellow in a course on "Ideas of Human Nature" by Clyde Kluckhohn and Henry Murray at Harvard, he was invited to give a lecture on existentialism, which in the 1950s became a rising alternative to analytical philosophy. While at Princeton, because of the young instructor, Harold Garfinkel, Tiryakian was introduced to phenomenological ideas as well.

In 1959, Tiryakian went to Paris, where he wrote his famous *Sociologism and Existentialism*, published in 1962 after discussions with Walter Kaufmann (Tiryakian 1962). The book presented a project for a new sociological discipline, called *existential sociology*. The logic of the book was a detailed comparative study and subsequent synthesis of the sociological views of Emile Durkheim and various existential thinkers, such as Soren Kierkegaard, Friedrich Nietzsche, Martin Heidegger, Karl Jaspers, Jean-Paul Sartre, Nicolas Berdyaev and Gabriel Marcel. Tiryakian showed the contradictory aspects of this synthesis—for example, in sociological categories of collective consciousness and public opinion, which categories are senseless for the existentialists because they mask abstractions only and have no ontological references. Similarly, the two approaches differ in their views on individualism and on levelling processes in society. Extreme individualism, in terms of the Durkheimian perspective, leads to inauthentic existence, destructive pessimism and nihilism. There is also a confrontation of sociologism and existentialism with respect to the interpretation of the problem of truth. Existential understanding of truth is reflected in a key thesis of Soren Kierkegaard: *subjectivity is truth* and, in affinity to pragmatism, truth is dynamic, multiple and useful. Whereas Durkheim admitted that truth depends on historical or cultural factors, he interpreted it in objective and supra-individual terms. Some similar aspects of these two perspectives are found in relation to the problem of transcendence. Along with the fact of being rooted in biological reality, both sociologism and existentialism recognize as a fundamental aspect of individual existence something that transcends that existence. For Durkheim, this transcendental factor is not something vague, encompassing, limitless, unknowable or divine, as the existentialists think, but is the social reality that is amenable to scientific study. These differences explain a problem of individual freedom.

Despite the confrontation, existentialism and sociologism share a general concern about the crisis of the individual and society and can be considered as complementary perspectives. Tiryakian argues that the main interest of Durkheim was an objective study of subjective, rather than objective, reality. According to this view, society is a psychic phenomenon consisting of beliefs, values and norms. It is existing reality that is conscious of itself and may be regarded as immanent transcendence or as an authentic dimension of society. The new sociological perspective needs to be developed for the analysis of society as subjective reality, and this perspective is existential sociology. The main objective of existential sociology is *societal existence*, or a study of macro-manifestations of various existential problems as described by existentialists, such as: authenticity, choice, responsibility, becoming, openness, care, anxiety, boundary situation, ambiguity, intersubjectivity. If existential sociology investigates the macro-level of these existential problems, the philosophy of social existentialism may overcome its isolation with respect to autonomous subjectivity through sociological concepts of solidarity, anomie, socialization, social status, social role, social distance, social movement, social mobility, social action and reference group. For example, the notions of authenticity and inauthenticity can be considered as analogues of societal conditions of solidarity and anomie. Since the contrast between authentic and inauthentic existence is acute in boundary situations, it may be assumed that societal solidarity and anomie are also manifested in boundary or catastrophic situations that destroy everyday patterns of social life.[1] Existentialism and sociologism can cooperate in a broader perspective of all-encompassing approaches and theories, such as the phenomenological method used by existential thinkers. The potential fields of study for these broader perspectives are perceptions of different social groups and their worlds, perceptive distances (the theory of reference groups), synthesis of the notion of existential choice and dichotomies of "pattern variables" (Parsons), sociology of the body, mass society, and so forth. The final thesis of Tiryakian's program book is, in effect, a paraphrasing of Mikel Dufrenne,[2] that objectivism and subjectivism, sociology and philosophy, sociologism and existentialism, are necessarily complementary approaches.

Sociologism and Existentialism became a widely known work. It was reprinted in the series *Perennial Works in Sociology* (1979) and translated into Spanish (1969), Japanese (1971) and Russian (2002, in abbreviated form). The American sociologist, Philip Olson, though critical of Tiryakian's interpretations of existential thought, noted that the importance of the book is the integration of the two traditions (Olson 1962). The main value of *Sociologism and Existentialism* is not the integration of the two traditions, but the result of this integration, which is the emergence of existential sociology as a new approach, provided with a general program for further development. The logic and main message of the book by Tiryakian reminds one of two other prominent sociological works: *The Sociological Imagination* (1959), by C. Wright Mills, with its appeal to the nexus between biography and history, and *The Social Construction of Reality* (1966), by Peter Berger and Thomas Luckmann, who described society as the interpenetration of society and humanity. Together, these studies represent relatively early steps in addressing the problem of the micro–macro link, which for many became the epitome of the fundamental question of sociology.

After *Sociologism and Existentialism*, Tiryakian developed his project of existential sociology with the ambitious goal of revising the theoretical sociological tradition in terms of its relation to a broad philosophical trend of existential phenomenology (Tiryakian 1965). This revision was intended to show that in sociological tradition there is a hidden consensus based on the fundamental methodology of *subjective realism* and its aim to elaborate a *general theory of social existence.*

Referring to the ideas of such phenomenologically oriented sociologists as Alfred Vierkandt, Max Scheler, Karl Mannheim, Georges Gurvitch and Harold Garfinkel, Tiryakian comes to the broad synthesis of existential phenomenology with the ideas of the sociological mainstream, including Max Weber, Georg Simmel, Emile Durkheim, William I. Thomas, Pitirim Sorokin and Talcott Parsons. For example, he argues that a theory of social action of Weber and his methodology of *Verstehen* correspond with the basic principle of subjectivity in existential thought originating from Soren Kierkegaard. Likewise, Durkheim's concept of anomie can be related to the existential critique of mass society. The Thomas theorem, and his endeavors to move a social science from abstract studies to field research, are also leitmotifs of existential phenomenology. Methodological integralism and the problem of social crisis in the sociology of Pitirim Sorokin demonstrate a strong tendency toward convergence with existential phenomenology.[3] Sorokin accepted the neo-Kantian distinction of sciences—a distinction fundamental to subjective realism—and stressed that sociocultural reality is a sphere of meanings that "transform the natural properties of objects" (Tiryakian 1965: 683). These diverse sociocultural meanings took root in macro-sociocultural systems. Eventually, the sociological theory of Talcott Parsons, seemingly incompatible with existential phenomenology, actually has certain connections through voluntaristic interpretation of social action, treatment of culture and an action frame of reference, which can be considered as a model of social existence. The important elements of this model are intersubjectivity, self-realization via social institutions, sentience and the "openness" of the actor.

Based on principles of relationism and transobjectivism, the methodology of subjective realism is oriented toward the need to avoid the extremes of materialism and idealism, and considers social reality as a phenomenal experience of actors. The relational principle is different from relativism and implies that truth for the social actor is always in his existential relation to his own situation.

The principle of transobjectivity directs the study beyond the object toward its more complete and comprehensive explanation as "total social fact" (Marcel Mauss). Generally, existential phenomenology in sociology tends to overcome institutional reality (the natural attitude), and focuses on the roots of social existence (the existential nature of social structures) and the dialectics obtaining between institutional and existential dimensions of society.

The ideas of subjective realism and general theory of social existence evoked both positive and critical reactions. Indian sociologist Rastogi argued that Tiryakian's standpoint is untenable because existential phenomenology cannot be a theoretical ground for sociology because of its subjective and, therefore, limited methodology. As a result, Tiryakian's project is undermining the achievements of positivistic, naturalistic and objectivistic methodology which, in the view of Rastogi, are indeed in the heart of sociological mainstream (Ragosti 1966). In their critical paper, Heap and Roth analyzed the phenomenological sociology of Tiryakian, Bruyn and Douglas and mentioned, that they "metaphorically" used the key concepts of phenomenology (intention, reduction, phenomenon and essence), so changing their original meaning (Heap and Roth 1973).

Comments on Tiryakian's existential phenomenology appeared in the pages of *American Sociological Review* (Kolaja 1966; Berger 1966; Tiryakian 1966). Kolaja made positive statements on Tiryakian's efforts, but argued that Husserl and Durkheim had developed opposite perspectives. Berger was more critical and maintained that existential phenomenology, in fact, does not exist as accepted entity and existentialism and phenomenology are significantly different approaches. He also emphasized the incorrectness of the reassessment of sociological tradition in terms of existential phenomenology. Tiryakian brought grounded counterarguments answering the critics and correctly pointed to, for example, certain bases for the synthesis of existentialism and phenomenology in the works of Maurice Merleau-Ponty, Maurice Natanson and others. He provided additional detailed explanations for the possibility of subjective realistic interpretation of the sociological tradition.

After the attempt to reinterpret sociological tradition in terms of existential phenomenology, Tiryakian continued to develop and strengthen this position. His new step became an address to that level of the general theory of social existence, which can be called a micro-existential sociology or theory of personality in existential sociology. On this level he presented a sketch of "the existential model of man" (Tiryakian 1968). The latter includes the existential self and the person, who, despite their connection, cannot be identified with each other. The person is the active subject placed in social space and time. It is the intersubjective self and the presence, or externalization, of the existential self in the social world. In turn, the existential self is the fundamental ontological structure and the source of possibilities that determine the person. If the person is the social mask of man or woman, then the existential self is his or her true face.

Along with the general division into the existential self and the person, the existential model of "man" consists of four basic elements—ontological and ontic levels of existence, openness and situation. Ontological and ontic dualism are related, respectively, to the authentic and inauthentic conditions of human existence and to the existential self and the person. The ontic expresses an external empirical world, a reality of finite and discrete things and objects; while the ontological refers to the transcendental basis from which the external empirical world arises. Authenticity of existence involves the awareness and realization of man's own ontological basis (existential self as true or real self) and the recognition of this basis in other persons. Inauthenticity, by contrast, is the perception of oneself and others as ontic objects. If the person becomes depersonalized and objectified, then he or she is estranged from the existential self and immersed in inauthentic existence. The fundamental characteristic of the existential self is its integral whole-ness, its totality that is expressed in the unity of the spiritual and physical in man. Since the existential self is never static and involves becoming and self-realization, another aspect of its integrity is temporal unity—the inher-ent manifestation of past (present-that-was) and future (present-to-come) in the lived present.

Important elements of the existential model of man are openness and situ-ation. Openness of the self to the world actualizes through the body, intersub-jectivity, social time (historicity) and a sacred realm of existence. Main modes of this actualization are language, nonverbal communication, internal reli-gious dialogue, responsibility and morality arising from the call of conscience. Openness to the world actualizes in social situations that transcend the physi-cal site by the meanings that are found in them. The situation addresses the existential self, demanding an authentic response. The deepest significance of the situation occurs in its *boundary* forms (Jaspers), when the institutional norms of the everyday world are collapsed, and the person is forced to open his or her existential self to respond to emerging challenges. In the social dimension, boundary situations tend to polarize the members of a social group, depend-ing on its behavior and existential values.

After outlining the existential theory of personality, Tiryakian directed his studies to another fundamental sociological problem and proposed a new exis-tential phenomenological theory of *structural sociology* (Tiryakian 1970). In this theory he comprehensively represented the theme of social change, which is a leitmotif in most of his numerous works. Previously, Tiryakian had con-ceptualized his interpretation of societal change, defining it as the process of radical change on the level of society as a whole. Societal change involves a qualitative leap and the total transformation of institutional structures under the significant growth rates of urbanization, sexual freedom and noninstitu-tional religion (Tiryakian 1967).

In Tiryakian's theory of structural sociology this conceptual scheme was further developed.

Tiryakian started with reflections on the problem of social order that needs to be connected with the problems of the crisis and societal transformations. He shows the connection of these static and dynamic aspects of social real-ity in his concept of institutional life, indicating the totality of existing social institutions. The phenomenon of institutional life illustrates that social reality is not confined solely to institutional, that is, rational, normative and orderly behavior, but is constituted by deeper social layers.

Using the term structural sociology, Tiryakian emphasized that social structures are existential foundations of social life that combine social order and social change into a single whole. Sociologists had developed a theory of structural functionalism but had not paid enough attention to the very concept of structure, which was traditionally understood as something static and timeless, but is in fact plural, dynamic and not reducible to static models or institutional order. The social structure is not a physical entity, but a moral or "normative phenomena of intersubjective consciousness which frame social actions in social space" (Tiryakian 1970: 115). In Durkheimian terms, this is the phenomenon of collective representations rooted in the collective consciousness. Therefore, social change is not so much a transformation of physical reality, but rather a transformation of consciousness through the processes of structuration,[1] destructuration and restructuration.

One of the main objectives of structural sociology is the revision of the problems of time and culture from the perspective of existential phenomenology and the methodology of subjective realism, with their basic principles: social reality includes a cultural dimension, irreducible to its physical or natural properties; object presupposes a subject—social objects do not exist without their relations (meanings) to social actors; meanings of social reality are not only an individual but also a collective phenomenon. Based on these principles, Tiryakian defined social reality as a "global phenomenon of intersubjective consciousness; that is, a social psychological reality" (Tiryakian 1970: 117). Phenomenon is what appeared to consciousness as perceived here and now for the subject, produced from the ground that structures its appearance. Referring to the studies of Merleau-Ponty, Tiryakian noted that perception consists of three main elements: sensory, cognitive (factual) and normative (moral). The meaning of every social phenomenon includes moral aspects that vary widely depending upon the subjects and their particular situations. No social phenomenon is ever static and always has a becoming aspect. Phenomena are becoming from the "existential ground of possibilities," which is latent, but the real social structure or culture. Becoming, or actualization of, social phenomena is a process of formalization of social existence, making it "visible." In turn, the formalization of social existence determines the processes of institutionalization. Social structures define the internal condition of interrelated elements, while the forms are external manifestations of these existential structures.

Social phenomena actualize from their existential ground in sociohistorical time or in the "ecstasy of time" (Heidegger), both different from absolute time. Both historians and sociologists make the same mistake when they take the part for the whole, or reduce ontological to ontic. Despite the fact that historians study the past, nothing ever happens in the past. For the subject, the historical meaning of the past is always associated with his present and future, so history as a temporal process cannot be objectified. Hence, until history is objectified, the ultimate meaning of historical events can be only transhistorical.

Sociohistorical time is not abstract and not homogenous. Social groups have different historical perspectives that are associated with the specifics of collective memory. So, the same period of absolute time may be qualitatively different for different social groups.

When historians objectify or reify history, they act as sociologists who try to objectify society. Society as a total and dynamic societal phenomenon contains a multiplicity of social structures that are capable of actualization on the institutional level. In the process of actualization, institutional and noninstitutional levels of society conflict, as they imply different perceptions of reality. From the institutional perspective, noninstitutional phenomena are irrational, and there is the problem as to how irrational or immoral from one perceptional perspective is rational or moral from another viewpoint. Under certain conditions, the latent social structures (analogous to the L subsystem in the AGIL paradigm of Talcott Parsons) break the institutional order and lead to large-scale transformation.

Tiryakian used metaphor, according to which society is mostly an inactive volcano. The solidified part of the volcano is a reified social structure or institutional order. Its hidden part is a magma of social existence, and sacred, consisting in a dialectical relation with the secular level that correlates with A and G subsystems in the scheme of Parsons. Institutionalized religion arises through the actualization of the sacred sphere, which is based on the antinomy of the divine and the demonic and transcends any sociohistorical reality. On the institutional level, the sacred is reflected in rational form, and the function of the institutional order is moralization, social structuration and the regulation of sacred forces. Structuration presupposes differentiation (Weber's routinization of charisma) and reversal of processes of structural deformation, dedifferentiation, destructuration and demoralization of institutional forms that lead to a state of anomie (Durkheim). Since social structures are covert, the mistake of sociologists is their main focus on the "visible" level of society, while its sacred part or source of "solidified lava" remains out of sight. There is another Tiryakian metaphor, of the spectator who merges into a movie (institutional order) and forgets about the screen, projector and director; that is, those structures that create the picture. Thus, sociological theory needs to be reoriented to the study of relations between institutional life and latent social structures. On the micro level the example of such studies is the perspective of ethnomethodology, and this approach should spread to macro-studies as well.

Along with the orientation of existential sociology to take into account the historical and temporal factors, it is also necessary to consider culture as the basis of society. Tiryakian criticized the traditional notion of culture as simplistic and defined it as a manifold, open and multileveled symbolic system of intersubjective consciousness that expresses value orientations. The cultural symbols are on an intermediate level between an institutional layer and the deepest realm of antithetical moral and religious forces. Consideration of non-institutional religion as the basis of culture is connected with the problem of societal change, since the latter is not so much a change in the institutional life, but transformation of the societal structures that define the accepted order. These societal structures constitute a moral and religious frame of reference for the social actor and are not an object, but are part of subjectivity. Societal changes arise outside the social order, and the foundation of social revolutions is a radical attempt to rotate the normative axis of institutional life, and not to transform only its political or economic sphere. Revolutionary change is a total social phenomenon that comes from deep religious or quasi-religious inspiration, different from the institutional perception of reality.

An important aspect of culture is the social anthropological interpretation of "primitive" systems of symbolic categorization of the world that defines social organization (left–right, up–down, dark–light, male–female, etc.). These symbolic categories can be considered as universal social representations of moral and religious forces that underlie social reality. For example, the left–right and up–down categories can be analyzed as basic structures of social mobility. Symbolic categories are not logical, but existential, because they manifest dynamic antithetical forces, each side of which is striving to become dominant. In this regard, a highly integrated society can be considered as a phenomenon of dynamic equilibrium of universal categories.

Tiryakian suggests that the range of variations of cultural systems and types of structuration are finite or relatively small. Since society is a total cultural phenomenon, some of its levels are irrational and cannot be institutionalized. Irrationality is manifested in the *cultural reality principle*, according to which planned institutional change is always influenced by unplanned factors, with enough power to change its course. Despite the fact that this principle makes the prognosis of societal changes almost unrealizable, the prognosis is possible on the basis of a probabilistic approach and a comparison of historical and structural states of societal change.

Concluding his conceptualization Tiryakian formulates a general definition of structural sociology as a theoretical macrodynamic approach to societal systems, focused on the cultural essence of a total society and on actualizations of its possibilities. Structural sociology constitutes a renovation of structural functionalism that needs to take into account the aspects of sociohistorical time and the noninstitutional level of society; considering the latter as an existential source of rationalized social order.

From the existential theory of structural sociology, Tiryakian returned to the theoretical synthesis of sociology and existential phenomenology (Tiryakian 1973). He placed a stronger stress on the phenomenological component and examined the main concepts of phenomenology, adapting them to the general sociological perspective. If consciousness of subject is a central category of phenomenology, then for existential phenomenological sociology, since any subject includes both "I-pole" and "we-pole," such a category is intersubjective consciousness. "We-pole" is the experience of shared reality, which through the socialization process inculcates to structure of perception the common meanings supported by traditions. As "we" experience *Mitsein*, or being with, intersubjective reality is multiple and includes class, racial, religious, ethnic and other forms.

Meanings of reality in consciousness are an integral part of perception and cannot be separated from the physical properties of perceived objects. Different subjects may have diverse meanings for the same object, but they assume that other subjects perceive this object analogously. The difference of meanings is available to the uninvolved observer only. Tiryakian called this the *Pirandello effect*.[5] Meanings may change under the influence of social time-space, status positions or linguistic terminology. For example, one historical event may have different meanings for different generations. Reification of the social object to a single set of meanings denies and reifies the subjectivity of the Other, who is able to have a different set of meanings for this object.

Based on the Adelbert Ames transactionist notion of the "assumptive world," Tiryakian proposed his concept of the *assumptive frame of reference* (AFR), according to which the experience of social objects is not direct, but is mediated by a multilayered system of meanings. AFR is the general subjective orientation to the world and it is not itself an object, but rather a latent structure of perception, through which situation is "defined" (in the term of William Thomas). Important elements of AFR are emotions, images, cognitive elements, moral values, expectations and trust. AFR is not static and may change toward positive, negative or indifferent perception of the social object. Another form of AFR change is destruction or loss of an object's meaning (*noema*). Destruction of the *noema* of a significant Other can occur under the influence of a third person (for example, a friend) and transform perception of the Other—what Tiryakian defined as *the Iago effect*, when the friend is perceived as an enemy, good turns into evil and so on. Change in the intensity of moral meaning leads to a modification of the scale or proportions of the object in perception and consciousness. An increase in intensity of meaning leads to the attainment of a sacral level when the meaning of the object is extraordinary (radiated) and unproblematic.

Tiryakian emphasized that it is very important for existential phenomeno-logical sociology to develop not only a micro, but also a macro perspective to the study of social change. From this perspective social change is a trans-formation in the structure of collective perception, consciousness and moral meanings. Intersubjectivity involves not only the subjective we-pole, but also a common lived experience by the historical peer group or generation that similarly perceives the same events and situations. The task for existential phe-nomenological sociology in the study of social change is the bracketing of the natural attitude of intersubjective consciousness and the uncovering of the conditions under which the totality of meanings of the object for all subjects is transformed or "exploded." This totality of meanings is a *noemata* that struc-tures collective perception.

The destruction of the natural attitude allows us to become aware of the social object in the broader perspective and to realize its alternative mean-ings. The overcoming of the natural attitude opens *a priori* structures of con-sciousness, which produce the meanings of reality. Tiryakian did not explain the differences between *a priori* structures and AFR (and social structures or culture), but pointed out that the sociological significance of these structures is their formation in processes of socialization and social interaction. *A priori* structures include sociolinguistic categories (collective social objects), cognitive categories (related physical objects), conventional procedures (used in typi-cal social situations), social theories (causal models of interpretation of social actions) and cosmological theories (explanations of "ultimate reality"). Sub-jects usually are not aware of *a priori* structures, and the natural attitude covers the very scheme of perception and its function of determining the meanings. The study of *a priori* structures and the "bracketing" approach focus on the primacy of experience in the situation of here-and-now or on "the things themselves." *A priori* structures, are *meaning-structures* through which the object appears for the subject.

In his idea for a new existential phenomenological perspective in sociol-ogy Tiryakian fastened on to the ideas of Emile Durkheim and Edmund Husserl through a "comparison of the spirit of positivism and spirit of phe-nomenology" (Tiryakian 1978b). The term "phenomenological" in sociology, explained Tiryakian, can be understood in several senses. The broader sense reflects the subjective and meaningful aspects of social reality. From this view-point phenomenological content can be found in the works of many classics that are not usually taken as representatives of phenomenological sociology. In a stricter sense the term refers to those sociologists whose approach is clearly associated with phenomenology, such as Alfred Schutz, Maurice Natanson, Harold Garfinkel, Peter Berger and Thomas Luckmann. It is appropriate to consider phenomenology not as separate direction of philosophy and sociology, but in its connections with existentialism. The synthesis of phenomenology and existentialism is presented in the works of Martin Heidegger, Karl Jaspers and especially Maurice Merleau-Ponty, whose contribution to the integration of sociology and existential phenomenology remains undervalued. General aspects for both existentialism and phenomenology are subjectivity and experience, but if phenomenology focuses on the meaning-structures of consciousness, existentialism orients itself more to sensory experience that is inseparable from meaning-structures.

Considering the nature of the confrontation between positivism and phenomenology Tiryakian notes that the main delusion of positivism is the assertion that the world exists independently of perception; and reality of a multiple consciousness is reduced to a single dimension. He refers to the history of the two paradigms and their "spirit," clearly expressed in the later works of Durkheim (*The Elementary Forms of the Religious Life*, 1912) and Husserl (*The Crisis of European Sciences and Transcendental Phenomenology*, 1936). Analyzing the contradictions and affinities of Durkheim and Husserl, Tiryakian concludes that despite obvious divergence these thinkers, in different ways, ultimately come at the end to the same crossroad, which is the transcendental consciousness (pure consciousness, consciousness of consciousness or structure of structures) and the awareness of civilizational crisis deriving from the loss of a transcendental foundation. Both Husserl and Durkheim sought fundamental principles of reality, and both did it in the direction from the exterior world to the inner world of transcendental consciousness. Relying on the legacy of Husserl and Durkheim, there is the opportunity to begin a new dialogue between philosophy and sociology in their joint concern about the crisis of modern society.

By the end of the 1970s Tiryakian had generally completed the original version of existential phenomenological sociology. During the ensuing decades he tried to apply this theoretical and methodological approach, often implicitly, in the study of a very wide range of social problems. Thus, for example, Tiryakian used existential phenomenology in his sociology of religion, trying to understand the role of religious factors in the process of societal change. Existential motifs present in his *sociology of esoteric culture* (Tiryakian 1972a), where the differentiation of exoteric and esoteric forms of culture is, in fact, a development of the existential theory of personality, with its elements of existential and social self, and their correspondence to noninstitutional and institutional levels of society respectively.

Since the mid-1970s Tiryakian's studies of social change were gradually transformed into a theory of modernization. In the context of this he proposed new concepts of "changing centers" and "metacultures" of modernity (Tiryakian 1985a, 1996), as well as methodological perspectives of "neo-modernization" (Tiryakian 1991, 1995a) and "civilizational" (Tiryakian 2004a, 2007a) analysis. In these studies, along with adherence to the noninstitutional religious aspects, existential phenomenological methodology manifested itself in its emphasis on nation and national identity factors of late modernization, particularly in their interpretation as a becoming and multiple phenomena of intersubjective consciousness (Tiryakian 2004b, 2006a, 2007b; Tiryakian and Nevitte 1983; Tiryakian and Rogowski 1985). In connection with ethnic factors Tiryakian considered the characteristic of the existential problem of alienation (Tiryakian 1972b, 1980), and one example of German society analyzed the phenomena of "negative identity" and "collective stigma" (Tiryakian 2006b). Among the most important aspects of the development and mobilization of collective identity that he marked were ethnic conflicts and wars (Tiryakian 1999, 2002), the existential meaning of which is revealed in the moral dimension and in the understanding, as collective boundary situations that destroy the natural attitude.

The existential phenomenological methodology of Tiryakian's modernization theory is to be seen in his synthesis of Weber's concepts of rationalization and disenchantment and with his own concepts of "dialectical counterprocesses of modernity," and re-enchantment, as well as dedifferentiation (Tiryakian 1985b, 1992). In this regard, the qualitative dialectical method of Tiryakian is close to the existential dialectics of Kierkegaard, Berdyaev and the dialectical sociology of Gurvich. Considering the multiplicity of meaning-structures in modern society, Tiryakian developed the concept of a "new world of new worlds" (Tiryakian 1994), as a qualitatively changed state of intersubjective consciousness arose after the collapse of the bipolar geopolitical system. The new world created both negative states of insecurity and fear (especially for ethnic minorities) and positive collective inspiration, in which the process of "collective effervescence" (Durkheim) fosters solidarity of societal community and macro-manifestation of charisma (Tiryakian 1995b).

The existential phenomenological approach of Tiryakian became one of the earliest attempts to construct interpretive, qualitatively oriented macro-theory in contemporary sociology. Despite considerable effort to adapt phenomenology to sociology, phenomenological sociology itself is obviously not one of his theoretical innovations. In this respect, the main achievements of Tiryakian are the *foundation of existential sociology* as an independent field of study, the integration of existentialism and phenomenology in sociology and the reorientation of existential phenomenological perspective to the macro-level of social reality.

The existential sociology of Tiryakian is a rather open project and less than a complete, or rigorous, theoretical system. Moreover, he did not fully implement this project in his studies of religion, culture, national identity and other fields, where existential phenomenological methodology is often used, if only implicitly. Perhaps, this is the influence of a central existential principle involving the avoidance of abstract conceptual precision, systematization and formalization. However, this does not mean the absence of any theoretical logic. Detailed analysis indicates the three fundamental theoretical and methodological principles of Tiryakian's existential phenomenological sociology. The first of these is *subjective realism (relationism)*, the position that social objects do not exist without their relation to social subjects and that social reality is always a perceived phenomenon of consciousness.

Second, *transactionism* is reflected in the concepts of culture, assumptive frame of reference and *a priori* of meaning-structures, according to which the perception of social objects is not direct, but mediated by a multilayered system of meanings, indicating the primacy of sociocultural reality over the physical world.

Third, *totalism (integralism)* is a methodological orientation to the disclosure of the existential totality of social phenomena in terms of how they are given in individual or collective experience. This orientation is built around the understanding of social existence as a process of becoming and self-overcoming, and also aims to integrate the rational, sensory-emotional and physical elements of experience.

Totalism includes the sub-principles of transobjectivity, transhistoricity and dialectics. Transobjectivity defines total social facts as the main object of sociological studies and is a shift beyond the boundaries of the object in order to achieve its more complete and comprehensive explanation in the context of a superior reality. Transhistoricity is the totalization of sociocultural time, underlying the impossibility of its being entirely objectified or reified. Dialectics reflects the contradictions between the ontic (institutional life, natural attitude, inauthenticity) and ontological levels of social existence (noninstitutional and sacred layers of intersubjective consciousness, authenticity). Concerning sociology itself, totalism is realized through a systematic synthesis of different, and often conflicted, theories, paradigms and disciplines.

Over the last fifty years many theories and paradigms have been accepted in sociology. Several examples are phenomenological sociology, symbolic interactionism, ethnomethodology, dramaturgy, action theory and grounded theory. Existential sociology became one of the rare cases of a peculiar ignorance in the history and theory of sociology. Another problem is the absence of integrative processes within existential sociology. After Tiryakian's works, several original versions of existential sociology appeared independently, with almost no links to his initial ideas.

In the 1970s the American sociologist Jack Douglas and his intellectual colleagues, known as the Californian school (Melnikov 2011), developed their novel project of existential sociology. The main ideas of their project were published in the trilogy, *Existential Sociology* (Douglas and Johnson 1977), *The Existential Self in Society* (Kotarba and Fontana 1984), *Postmodern Existential Sociology* (Kotarba and Johnson 2002) as well as in some other works[6] (Manning 1973; Kotarba 1979; Fontana 1980). Sociologists of the Californian school defined existential sociology as the study of human experience-in-the-world (or existence) in all its social forms. They stressed the relative freedom of individuals from sociocultural contexts and their ability to determine the meanings of social reality. There was also a strong focus on feelings and emotions, embodiment and the becoming of the self. Douglas and his students tried to avoid any paradigmatic labels or formalizations and used inductive methodology, beginning their studies from the standpoint of individual experience in natural settings of everyday social life.

Along with American developments, another original project of existential sociology was elaborated by the Belgian sociologist, Marcel Bolle De Bal. In 1985, in his presidential address at the congress of the International Association of French-Speaking Sociologists, Bolle De Bal presented this project as an alternative to abstract, quantitative, and "not enough human" approaches. It is noteworthy that, until the beginning of 2010, he apparently believed he had invented the term *existential sociology*, a term that had in fact been proposed decades earlier by Tiryakian and Douglas.

Bolle De Bal (2013) summarized his thirty years of studies in this field. His project was based on six main principles: consideration of existential sociology as a fundamental theory; "reliance" as a central concept; action-research as a fundamental mode of research; socioanalysis as a fundamental practice for sociologists; plurality of sociological models; clinical or applied sociology as a research, action and training field. As a fundamental theory the existential sociology of Bolle de Bal is characterized by stressing the importance of the person (the related individual versus the isolated individual) and of the actor (the active, engaged person). It is a humanistic sociology instead of a positivistic sociology. It is a more comprehensive (Weber) and phenomenological (Mauss) sociology that develops in close cooperation with psychology, philosophy, and literature, and pays specific attention to the dynamics of primary groups with their complex and often *paradoxical* dialectic between persons, communities and society. Furthermore, this existential perspective stresses the qualitative, dialectical (Gurvitch), dialogical (Morin) methods, and gives a prominent place to subjectivity, irrationality and affect. In fact, the existential sociology of Bolle De Bal was constructed around the central concept of *reliance*—a French neologism, that could be translated into English as "re-linking" or "re-binding." Bolle De Bal argued that social links in contemporary society are in a process of destruction and are producing a society of *déliance* (the phenomenon of the "lonely crowd" described by David Riesman). In reaction to this situation, individuals and social groups develop a need and deep aspiration for *reliance*—the re-linking of lost relations. For sociology itself, *reliance* is a re-linking of psychological, philosophical and sociological approaches; subjectivity and objectivity; essence and existence; theory and practice (through applied and clinical sociology); research and action (through the action-research method); and teaching and training through group dynamics.

Since the 1990s another European version of existential sociology has been developed by the Polish sociologist Piotr Sztompka, who has worked on several existentially oriented themes, such as social becoming, cultural trauma, visual sociology and everyday life. Like Bolle De Bal, Sztompka presented his *sociology of social existence* in the presidential address to the International Sociological Association, titled, "The Quality of Social Existence in a Globalising World" (Durban, South Africa 2006), in which he diagnosed a paradigmatic shift toward a sociology of everyday life. According to Sztompka, the sociology of social existence is a "third sociology" that continued the "second sociology of action" (Weber, Pareto and Znaniecki) and the "first sociology of systems" (Comte, Spencer and Marx). The main idea of this perspective is a change from understanding the object of sociology as society (macro) or social actor (micro) to social existence. Piotr Sztompka (2008) observed that the social experience of everyday life is both determined by social structures and influenced by freedom of the individual. As in previous cases, the existential sociology of Sztompka has no explicit links to other versions of existential sociology.

The deficiency of integrative processes in existential sociology has a negative effect for growth in, and institutionalization of, this field. One of the appropriate steps concerning this problem could be the development of *the history of existential sociology*. There is also a need for further elaboration and linkage of the main categories of existential sociology, such as social existence, situation, authenticity, choice and meaning. The most effective way to provide this categorical linkage is to focus on both social and sociological processes of *ontologization* and *authentification*, consisting in changes from the abstract toward the concrete or from speculative rational thinking to lived integral experience.

Existential sociology can be structured as macro-, micro- and numerous middle range theories and thematic subfields,[7] reflected and marked in different studies, such as the sociology of the absurd; the sociology of suffering; the sociology of disasters; the sociology of risk; the sociology of fear; the sociology of war; the sociology of everyday life; visual sociology; the sociology of the body; the sociology of emotions; the sociology of experience; the social ontology; and the existential theory of globalization. One should also mention publications in or by Wolff (2007), Craib (1976), Bogard (1977), Weinstein and Weinstein (1978), Hayim (1980), Armstrong (1981), Koev (1990), Semmes (2004), Farrall (2005), Tognonato (2006), Martuccelli (2011), Ginev (2014) and others. This comprehensive perspective presupposes not only a metatheoretical view, but also international cooperation for an integrated paradigm of existential sociology.

Notes

1 Tiryakian considered the societal boundary situation in his early paper (Tiryakian 1959), which is one of the first studies in the area of the sociology of disasters. Based on K. Jaspers's concept of "boundary situation," the sociology of disasters or, generally, the sociology of critical situations, is an important direction of existential sociology (See Melnikov 2013a).
2 Tiryakian refers to the paper of M. Dufrenne (1946), which chronologically is the earliest explicit work on existential sociology.
3 Biographer of P. Sorokin, Barry Johnston, developed Tiryakian's efforts and considered affinities between existential phenomenology and the sociology of Sorokin (Johnston 1999).
4 There is misunderstanding in the history of sociology that the author of the idea of "structuration" is Anthony Giddens, but not Edward Tiryakian (See Tiryakian 1978a).
5 Luigi Pirandello (1867–1936) was an Italian dramatist, Nobel Prize laureate in literature (1934) and forerunner of Theatre of Absurd. In his famous play *Six Characters in Search of an Author* (1921), using the "play within a play" technique, he depicted different interpretations of reality by different characters and the impossibility of finding its unified meaning.
6 The rare case of communication between Tiryakian and the Californian school is a review published by Tiryakian in *American Journal of Sociology* (Tiryakian 1985c). Sociologists of the Californian school briefly referred to Tiryakian, but without considerable integration or development of his ideas in their own studies.
7 If ontologization and authentification are considered as the main trends of existential sociology, it is possible to use the term "nanosociology" to point out changes in scale from micro to deeper and more detailed levels of social reality.

References

Alieva, D. 1984. "Existentialism in Modern American Sociology." *Czech Sociological Review* 20, no. 3: 276–90. (In Czech)

Armstrong, E. 1981. "On the Problem of Evidence in Existential Sociology." *Sociology and Social Research* 65, no. 4: 390–99.

Aspers, P. and S. Kohl. 2013. "Heidegger and Socio-ontology: A Sociological Reading." *Journal of Classical Sociology* 13, no. 4: 487–508.

Backhaus, G. and G. Psathas, eds. 2007. *The Sociology of Radical Commitment: Kurt H. Wolff's Existential Turn*. Lanham, MD: Lexington Books.

Berger, P. 1966. "On Existential Phenomenology and Sociology (II)." *American Sociological Review* 31, no. 2: 259–60.

Bogard, R. 1977. "Critique of Existential Sociology." *Social Research* 44, no. 3: 502–28.

Bolle De Bal, M. 2013. *Fragments pour une sociologie existentielle*, 3 tomes. Paris: L'Harmattan.

Bude, H. and J. Dürrschmidt. 2010. "What's Wrong with Globalization?: Contra "flow speak"—towards an Existential Turn in the Theory of Globalization." *European Journal of Social Theory* 13, no. 1: 481–500.

Craib, I. 1976. *Existentialism and Sociology: A Study of Jean-Paul Sartre*. New York: Cambridge University Press.

Douglas, J. and J. Johnson, eds. 1977. *Existential Sociology*. Cambridge: Cambridge University Press.

Dubet, F. 1994. *Sociologie de l'Expérience*. Paris: Seuil.

Dufrenne, M. 1946. "Existentialisme et sociologie." *Cahiers Internationaux de Sociologie* 1, no. 1: 161–71.

Farrall, S. 2005. "On the Existential Aspects of Desistance from Crime." *Symbolic Interaction* 28, no. 3: 367–86.

Fontana, A. 1980. "Toward a Complex Universe: Existential Sociology." In *Introduction to the Sociologies of Everyday Life*, edited by J. D. Douglas, P. A. Adler, P. Adler, A. Fontana, C. R. Freeman and J. A. Kotarba, 155–81. Boston: Allyn & Bacon.

Gasparyan, A. 1997. "'Existential Sociology' of Edward Tiryakian." Unpublished thesis. Moscow State University. (In Russian)

Ginev, D. 2014. "Social Practices from the Viewpoint of Trans-subjective Existentialism." *European Journal of Social Theory* 17, no. 1: 77–94.

Hayim, G. 1980. *The Existential Sociology of Jean Paul Sartre*. Amherst: The University of Massachusetts Press.

Heap, J. and P. Roth. 1973. "On Phenomenological Sociology." *American Sociological Review* 38, no. 3: 354–67.

Ionin, L. 1977. "Existential Sociology (conception of E. Tiryakian)." In *Criticism of Modern Bourgeois Theoretical Sociology*. oscow: "Science." (In Russian)

Johnston, B. 1999. "Existential Phenomenology and the Sociology of Pitirim A. Sorokin." *Journal of Sociology and Anthropology* 2, no. 2: 37–50. (In Russian)

Kisil, V. 1985. "Critical Analysis of the Social and Analytical Attitudes of the American Existential Sociology." In *Problems of Philosophy* 66, no. 1: 124–32.

Koev, K. 1990. "The Problem of the Ontology of the Life-World and the Existential Situation in Modern Social Science." *International Sociology* 5, no. 3: 279–86.

Kolaja, J. 1966. "On Existential Phenomenology and Sociology (I)." *American Sociological Review* 31, no. 2: 258–59.

Kotarba, J. 1979. "Existential Sociology." In *Theoretical Perspectives in Sociology*, 348–68. New York: St. Martin's Press.

Kotarba, J. and A. Fontana, eds. 1984. *The Existential Self in Society*. Chicago: University of Chicago Press.

Kotarba, J. and J. Johnson, eds. 2002. *Postmodern Existential Sociology*. Walnut Creek, CA: Alta Mira.

Lyman, S. and M. Scott. 1970. *A Sociology of the Absurd*. New York: Appleton-Century-Crofts.

Lyng, S. 2012. "Existential Transcendence in Late Modernity: Edgework and Hermeneutic Reflexivity." *Human Studies* 35, no. 3: 401–14.

Manning, P. 1973. "Existential Sociology." *Sociological Quarterly* 14, no. 1: 200–25.

Martuccelli, D. 2011. "Une sociologie de l'existence est-elle possible?." *Sociologies*, 18 October. http://sociologies.revues.org/3617

Melnikov, A. 2010. "Sociological Imagination of Edward Tiryakian: the Imaginative Logic of Constructing Sociological Theory." Unpublished thesis. Kharkov National University, Ukraine, 2010. (In Russian)

———— 2011. "The Californian School of Existential Sociology." *Sociological Studies* 11, no.1: 89–101. Lugansk, Ukraine: East-Ukrainian National University Press. (In Russian)

———— 2013a "'Boundary-Situations' (K. Jaspers) as a Category of Existential Sociology." *Religion and Socium* 1 (9): 67–71. (In Ukrainian)

———— 2013 "Perspective for the Study of Value-Normative Transformations of Ukrainian Society from the Position of Existential Sociology." *Sociology: Theory, Methods, Marketing* 2, no. 1: 52–72. (In Ukrainian and Russian)

Olson, P. 1962. "Review of *Sociologism and Existentialism* by Edward Tiryakian." *American Sociological Review* 27, no. 5: 699–700.

Raida, K. 1998. *Historical and Philosophical Studies of Post-Existential thinking.* Kyiv, Ukraine: Ukrainian Center of Spiritual Culture. (In Ukrainian)

Rastogi, P. 1966. "Existential Phenomenology and Sociology: A Critical Note." *Kansas Journal of Sociology* 2, no. 3: 107–12.

Semmes, C. 2004. "Existential Sociology or the Sociology of Group Survival, Elevation, and Liberation." *Journal of African American Studies* 7, no. 4: 3–18.

Sztompka, P. 2008. "The Focus on Everyday Life: A New Turn in Sociology." *European Review* 16, no. 1: 1–15.

Tiryakian, E. 1959. "Aftermath of a Thermonuclear Attack on the United States: Some Sociological Considerations." *Social Problems* 6, no. 4: 291–303.

———— 1962. *Sociologism and Existentialism: Two Perspectives on the Individual and Society.* Englewood Cliffs, NJ: Prentice–Hall.

———— 1965. "Existential Phenomenology and the Sociological Tradition." *American Sociological Review* 30, no. 5: 674–88.

———— 1966. "Reply to Kolaja and Berger." *American Sociological Review* 31, no. 2: 260–4.

———— 1967. "A Conceptual Scheme of Societal Change and Its Lead Indicators." In *Theory and Method in the Study of Total Societies*, 69–97. Garden City, NY: Doubleday Anchor.

———— 1968. "The Existential Self and the Person." In *The Self in Social Interaction* I, 75–86. New York: John Wiley and Sons.

———— 1970. "Structural Sociology." In *Theoretical Sociology: Perspectives and Developments*, 111–35. New York: Appleton–Century–Crofts.

———— 1972a. "Toward the Sociology of Esoteric Culture." *American Journal of Sociology.* 78, no. 3: 491–512.

———— 1972b. "Sociological Perspectives on the Stranger." *Soundings* 56, no. 1: 45–58.

———— 1973. "Sociology and Existential Phenomenology." In *Phenomenology and the Social Sciences* I, 187–222. Evanston: Northwestern University Press.

———— 1978a. "Review of *New Rules of Sociological Method*, by Anthony Giddens." *American Journal of Sociology* 83, no. 4: 1022–25.

———— 1978b. "Durkheim and Husserl: A Comparison of the Spirit of Positivism and the Spirit of Phenomenology." In *Phenomenology and the Social Sciences: A Dialogue*, 20–43. Hague: Martinus Nijhoff.

———— 1980. "Sociological Dimensions of Uprootedness." In *Uprooting and Development: Dilemmas of Coping with Modernization*, 131–52. New York: Plenum Publishing.

———— 1985a. "The Changing Centers of Modernity." In *Comparative Social Dynamics: Essays in Honor of Shmuel N. Eisenstadt*, 131–47. Boulder, CO: Westview Press.

———— 1985b. "On the Significance of Dedifferentiation." In *Perspectives on Macro–Sociological Theory*, 118–34. London and Beverly Hills: Sage.

———— 1985c. "Review of *The Existential Self in Society*, edited by J. Kotarba and A. Fontana." *American Journal of Sociology* 91, no. 3: 442–43.

———— 1991. "Modernisation: Exhumetur in Pace (Rethinking Macrosociology in the 1990s)." *International Sociology* 6, no. 2: 165–80.

————1992. "Dialectics of Modernity: Reenchantment and Dedifferentiation as Counterprocesses." In *Social Change and Modernity*, 78–94. Berkeley and Los Angeles: University of California Press.

———— 1994. "The New Worlds and Sociology." *International Sociology* 9, no. 2: 131–48.

———— 1995a. "Modernization in a Millenarian Decade: Lessons for and from Eastern Europe." In *Social Change and Modernization. Lessons from Eastern Europe*, 249–64. Berlin and New York: Walter de Gruyter.

———— 1995b. "Collective Effervescence, Social Change and Charisma: Durkheim, Weber and 1989." *International Sociology* 10, no. 3: 269–81.

———— 1996. "Three Metacultures of Modernity: Christian, Gnostic, Chthonic." *Theory, Culture and Society* 13, no. 1: 99–118.

———— 1999. "War: the Covered Side of Modernity." *International Sociology* 14, no. 4: 473–89.

———— 2002. "Third Party Involvement in Ethnic Conflict: The Case of the Kosovo War." In *The New Balkans: Disintegration and Reconstruction*, 207–28. Boulder, CO: East European Monographs.

———— 2004a. "Civilizational Analysis: Renovating the Sociological Tradition." In *Rethinking Civilizational Analysis*, 30–47. London: Sage.

———— 2004b. "'Old Europe/New Europe': Ambiguities of Identity." In *Migration in the New Europe: East-West Revisited*, 215–31. New York: Palgrave Macmillan.

———— 2006a. "For the Nation…but Which One?" In *Worlds in Sociology*, 431–42. Sofia: St. Kliment Ohridski University Press.

———— 2006b. "Coping with Collective Stigma: the Case of Germany." In *Identity, Morality and Threat: Studies in Violent Conflict*, 329–65. Lanham, MD: Lexington.

———— 2007a. "The Meshing of Civilizations: Soft Power and the Renewal of the Civilization of Modernity." In *Modernity at the Beginning of the 21st Century*, 89–113. Newcastle: Cambridge Scholars Publishers.

———— 2007b. "When Is the Nation no Longer?" *Nationalism in a Global Era*, 55–74. New York: Routledge.

Tiryakian, E. and N. Nevitte. 1983. "A Typology of Nationalism." In *Introductory Readings in Government and Politics*, 116–25. Toronto: Methuen.

Tiryakian, E. and R. Rogowski, eds. 1985. *New Nationalisms of the Developed West*. London: George Allen & Unwin.

Tognonato, C. 2006. *Il corpo del sociale: appunti per una sociologia esistenziale*. Napoli: Liguori.

Weinstein, D. and M. Weinstein. 1978. "An Existential Approach to Society: Active Transcendence." *Human Studies* 1, no. 1: 38–47.

Chapter 5

COMPARATIVE REFLECTIONS ON SOCIOLOGY AND CONSERVATISM: THE CONTRIBUTIONS OF EDWARD A. TIRYAKIAN

Bryan S. Turner

Introduction: Classical Sociology

A product of Harvard's famous Department of Social Relations created by Pitirim Sorokin, Professor Tiryakian's academic work has ranged over many issues, but the intellectual focus of his sociology has primarily been Emile Durkheim and the legacy of the Durkheimian School (Tiryakian 2009). Tiryakian's work has engaged with various controversies, both political and academic. Situated in the borderland between American and European social theory, Tiryakian often found himself drawn into the professional and ideological conflicts that erupted in the 1960s and onward between various generations of scholars. Many of these confrontations in the academic world of sociology were influenced by student radicalism in 1969, the Vietnam War and the civil rights movement. He has recently complained that scholars have forgotten the profound disruptions around 1969 on both sides of the Atlantic (Tiryakian 2013: xxiv). More specifically, the ideological conflicts hinged on the charge that sociology—especially in the elite university departments—was inherently conservative, both culturally and politically. For Tiryakian, part of the attraction of Pitirim Sorokin was that he was also famously a critic of mid-century American sociology in his *Fads and Foibles in Contemporary Sociology and Related Social Sciences* (Sorokin 1956). Consequently Tiryakian's interpretation of Durkheim has been distinctive in rejecting the conventional view that Durkheimian "functionalism" was ultimately a conservative reaction to social change. Sorokin's marginal and often maverick position in American sociology and his view of large-scale civilizational change influenced Tiryakian's deep engagement with Durkheim's key notion of anomie.

Another distinctive feature of this engagement with Durkheim concerns the problematic relationship between philosophy and sociology, on the one hand, and between normative and empirical analysis on the other. In *Sociologism and Existentialism* Tiryakian (1962) lamented the separation between philosophy and sociology that was bound up in the opposition between the Old World and the New World. This separation was mutually problematic. By ignoring sociology, philosophy—while seeking universal truths—remained bound implicitly to specific cultural contexts. By ignoring philosophy, sociology worked at the microscopic level and failed to address problems of a global significance. The general result was that sociology has failed to develop a global perspective and "research projects accumulate, but are not cumulative. Sociological theory of a general and systematic nature is seen as something esoteric and recondite, not as a practical necessity to the development of sociology" (Tiryakian 1962: 4). We can understand Tiryakian's oeuvre as directed at bridge-building between philosophy and sociology with the aim of defending general and systematic sociological theory as a practical necessity.

In his preface to *Sociological Theory, Values, and Sociocultural Change. Essays in Honor of Pitirim A. Sorokin*, Tiryakian (1963: xi) observed that for the nineteenth-century founders of sociology, and for Sorokin in particular, "the central problem is the crisis of modern society, how this is related to a moral crisis, and how to go about reconstructing modern society so as to overcome its tendencies of anomie." In that short statement, Tiryakian captured much of the social and political agenda of conservative thought and its paradoxical relationship to sociology. In crude terms, we might say that broadly speaking there were two ideological responses to that crisis. For socialism, the crisis of capitalism was a function of the economic contradictions of the system that were manifest in class struggle, the destructive business cycle and human alienation. The socialist solution required the state (via the party apparatus) to intervene to stabilize the market and to create new institutions to manage the problems of civil society. For conservatism, the problem was a crisis of morality that was manifest in Durkheim's notion of anomie. The crisis of modernity had to be overcome by the revitalization and adaptation of traditions to contemporary needs rather than by wholesale destruction of tradition.

In the introduction to the Transaction edition of the Sorokin collection, Tiryakian (2013) reflected on the revival of interest in Sorokin and his sociology. One explanation was that Sorokin's crisis-oriented sociology matched the events and mood of the closing decades of the twentieth century, especially following the collapse of the Soviet empire in 1989–92. Thus, Sorokin's macro-sociology was more in tune with "the mood of the times, for a new generation had shifted to favour conflict, alienation, subjectivity, counter-cultural norms, and even social and revolutionary change" (Tiryakian 2013: xv) than either the microsociology of empirical research favoured by professional American sociology or Parsons's approach in *The Social System* (1951). In Russia the intellectual vacuum was suddenly filled by Sorokin's perspective on crisis and decay in cultural wholes, and by Nikolai Kondratieff's theory of waves of economic boom and decay. It is possible to interpret Sorokin's approach to civilizations in terms of waves of civilizational change parallel to long-term economic change. Sorokin's theories of civilizational change were identified with new developments by S. N. Eisenstadt (1986) in his edited collection, *The Origins and Diversity of Axial Age Civilizations*, and by Samuel Huntington (1996) the "clash of civilizations." Robert Bellah, also a product of the Harvard department and a former student of Talcott Parsons, published *Religion in Human Evolution* in 2011. There were many influences on his interpretation of evolutionary change in religious cultures, but one principal influence was Durkheim's *The Elementary Forms of Religious Life* (Turner 2014).

Given Tiryakian's lasting appreciation of Sorokin's approach to long-term social and cultural change, it is not surprising that the theme of anomie has played such a large part in Tiryakian's sociological imagination. Furthermore, we can interpret socialism and conservatism, not as polar opposites, but as parallel responses to industrialization and as themes that have occupied Tiryakian's sociology throughout his career. The overlap between socialist and conservative responses is indicated by two dominant ideas—anomie and alienation—that were given an objective definition as social science concepts, but both have a heavy normative underpinning. However, while socialism aimed to be an international movement, conservatism has been associated more closely with the defense of community and nation against the threat of an all-powerful state. Conservatism is generally neither cosmopolitan nor internationalist. As Russell Kirk (2001: 485) famously observed, "Hostile toward every institution which acts as a check upon its power, the nation-state has engaged, ever since the decline of the medieval order, in stripping away one by one the functions and prerogatives of true community—aristocracy, church, guild, family and local association." Conservatism aims to protect and restore such intermediary associations, whereas "actually existing socialism" has typically treated such associations as barriers to equality and as the bulwark of authoritarian traditions. Conservatism also supports national traditions and is politically often associated with nationalism against socialist commitments to internationalism. It distrusts cosmopolitan intellectuals. The contrast between socialism and conservatism, in turn, points to the importance of drawing an adequate set of distinctions between nations and societies, and between national society and nation-states. Without a careful analysis of these concepts, there is much confusion in the literature about the relationship between nationalism and modernity (Tiryakian and Rogowski 1985).

Given Professor Tiryakian's long-standing interest in Emile Durkheim and French sociology, such an inquiry into sociology's relationship to conservatism is appropriate to a publication in his honor. In this essay, I will focus on the United States, which emerged, alongside republican France, as a revolutionary society, and England which, after the civil war of the seventeenth century, escaped a revolutionary period during its emergence as a modern industrial society. Its society has consequently often been interpreted as one in which gradualism and compromise were two dominant responses to social change.

Sociological Traditions

Sociology is often thought of as a secular science with explicit connections to socialism. Karl Marx is without question a founding father of sociology. However, the relationship between Marxism and sociology has been, according to Tom Bottomore (1979: 118), "a close, uneasy, contentious relationship." For Tiryakian (17: 190), the sociological tradition stretching from Saint-Simon to Durkheim shared a "common denominator," which was a "repugnance of political upheavals" and, hence, unlike Marxism, sociology was "a healing and stabilizing science." The connection between sociology and socialism had its origin in the work of Auguste Comte and Saint-Simon. Their analysis of the evolutionary stages of society, their positivist epistemology and their belief that the crises of industrial society required leadership from secular science meant that they sought to establish an enlightenment basis for both socialism and sociology. There were, however, important differences between the two men. Saint-Simon had turned to religion in 1825, with his vision of the "Nouveau Christianisme" as a religion of humanity. Comte broke with Saint-Simon over the issue and was contemptuous of the conservatism of Joseph de Maistre, who was promoting the idea of a supernatural Christianity (Gane 2006). One defining issue in the debate about sociology's ideological origins in its relation to socialism and conservatism is the attitude of sociologists to religion. It hardly needs saying that the study of religion played a central role in the work of Max Weber, Emile Durkheim and Georg Simmel. In this cohort of "founding fathers," Durkheim's relationship to conservatism and socialism was, as we shall see, ambiguous.

Within the history of twentieth-century social thought, conservatism has of course been much debated by sociologists. Perhaps one of the most famous contributions came from Karl Mannheim in *Ideology and Utopia* (1936) and in his *Conservatism: A Contribution to the Sociology of Knowledge* (1986). For Mannheim, conservatism emerges from a psychological attitude towards traditionalism for those social groups that experienced both the rise of the modern state and the rationalization of society as harmful and threatening. Thus, rising and falling social strata were important in the reception of either ideology or utopia. In particular, conservative thought stands out against the legacy of enlightenment rationalism. Conservative thought rejected the individualism of bourgeois society and promoted the idea of society as an organic whole that is compromised by the liberal emphasis on individual freedoms. In his sociology of knowledge, Mannheim (1986: 176) saw "bourgeois sociology" as the heir of the Enlightenment in its propensity to relativize thought, thereby treating socialism as a utopian dream rather than as a science of society. In this theoretical framework, Weber appeared as a manifestation of "late bourgeois thinking" by recognizing the steady rationalization of society, but also lamenting the consequences of the disenchantment of the garden of meaningful existence. One response to the cold secularism of an emerging bourgeois civilization celebrated "life" over the rationalized world—a response that was articulated in Georg Simmel's *The View of Life* (Simmel 2010).

This tendency to treat socialism as utopian thought partly explains why Bottomore described the relationship between socialism and sociology as "uneasy," in which both claimed a scientific status. In twentieth-century sociology, Robert Nisbet (1967), in his influential *The Sociological Tradition*, challenged the conventional interpretation that sociology is an academic companion of socialism, arguing that the "unit ideas" of sociology were drawn primarily from the conservative reaction to the French Revolution, from the urbanization of European societies and from the rise of a militant working class. He saw the decline of community as the key issue in the "Reactionary Enlightenment" in Haller, Bonald, de Maistre and others. The French Revolution had simply replaced the religious millenarianism of Christianity with a political and secular ideology of progress.

Within this analysis of the origins of "classical sociology," Durkheim's response to modernity and secularism in France placed him in an uncertain position. He has been all too-often regarded as straightforwardly conservative (Coser 1960; Nisbet 1965). Yet, as Tiryakian (1979: 190) notes, Durkheim was a civil servant of the republican regime and did not move in conservative circles. More importantly, the "Dreyfus Affair" of 1894–1906 had divided France into two hostile camps. The anti-Dreyfusards were pro-army, Catholic and tainted with anti-Semitism; the pro-Dreyfusards were anticlerical, republican and politically left. Durkheim, himself a secularized Jew from a familial line of rabbis, was drawn into the pro-Dreyfusard camp for the obvious reason that the First Republic had liberated the Jews from the restrictions of the *ancient regime*. Consequently, he became a target of Catholic conservative criticism, especially because the Church was apprehensive over his influence within the

French educational system. However, his view of the crisis was "conservative" insofar as he saw the "affair" in moral rather than political terms (Lukes 1979). This stance was consistent with Durkheim's basic concern for the mores of society, which was illustrated in his belief that contracts were not effective without a foundation in trust—itself arising from moral presuppositions. For the same reason, Durkheim was ambiguous about the role of the state. For him, the role of the state was moral insofar as it exercised a regulatory function over society. However, while supporting the role of the state in counteracting the anomie of modern societies, he followed Alexis de Tocqueville in believing that civil society was critical for individual liberties in acting as the mediating institutions between the individual and society.

This focus on conservatism in the evolution of sociology is justified on the grounds that classical sociology saw religion, especially in its decline, as a critical component of the moral crisis that Tiryakian identified in his preface to the collection of essays on Sorokin. We can summarize Tiryakian's view of Durkheim and his school with respect to conservatism with this observation: "The Durkheimians were not nostalgically seeking a prerepublican regime[;] ... politically speaking they were not conservative but rather progressive" (Tiryakian 2009: 164).

In his essay on Durkheim in the Bottomore and Nisbet edition on the history of sociology, Tiryakian (1979: 188) divided Durkheim's contribution to sociology under three headings. The first was to create a scientific discipline, and the second to provide for the unity of the social sciences. The third was "to provide the empirical, rational, and systematic basis for modern society's civil religion." This third observation brings me back to the theme of this essay, namely the relationships between conservatism, religion and sociology. This focus is closely associated with the legacy of Parsons, who followed Sorokin as chairman of the Department of Social Relations at Harvard University, and who placed religion at the core of any analysis of the anomic tendencies of modern societies, and in his essay in the Sorokin collection he observed that in the field of comparative civilizational studies "the problem of the role of religion and its relation to social values stands in a particularly central position" (Parsons 1963: 34). To conclude this introductory section, what Sorokin, Parsons and Tiryakian have in common is that to some extent they stand outside "the highly empirical atmosphere of American sociology" (Parsons 1963: 34), while also raising large questions about significant social and political issues. In recognizing the contributions of Professor Tiryakian to sociology, I attempt to raise some large questions about how and why has religion, especially in relation to politics, played such different roles in America and England? Having opened this discussion with a brief commentary on the historical relationship between conservatism, socialism and sociology, I now move towards a more contemporary analysis of conservatism, focusing on England and America as my case studies with a view to understanding sociology as a "healing and stabilizing science."[1]

Twentieth-Century Conservatism

Edward Tiryakian did much to promote comparative sociology. I shall try to follow his example in offering a comparison of modern conservative thought in America and England. Perhaps a more relevant comparison would have been America and France in the light of Tiryakian's career. I have two intellectual excuses for selecting America and England. The first is that the "special relationship" suggests some similarities between the two countries. The second excuse is that, in an interview with Dmitri Shalin in 2011, Tiryakian confessed that "My heart speaks in French. My head in English." In this commentary I focus on Tiryakian's head.

When considering the impact of religion on conservative politics in America, we should think about comparisons that may be useful. In historical and political terms, it is obvious that Britain and America have important historical, political and cultural connections. The early foundations of New England were forged by English Puritan settlers who sought religious freedom in a territory that was to be free from political control. After independence, France and the United States, as republics, had more in common—at least in political terms—and through much of the nineteenth century the relationship between Britain and America was one of competition rather than cooperation. In the twentieth century there were two important turning points. The first was the role of Winston Churchill in attempting successfully to bring the Americans into World War II. Volume 3 of his history of the war is called *The Grand Alliance* (1950), which referred both to the grand alliance of the Duke of Marlborough that defeated the Franco-Bavarian army in 1704, and the alliance between Britain and the United States that with the Soviets had defeated Hitler's forces. The second turning point was the convergence of ideas (the "special relationship"), especially over foreign policy, between Ronald Reagan and Margaret Thatcher. Thatcher's early visits to the United States in 1967 on a "leadership program" and in 1969 on a speaking tour, were enough to convince her that US-style free markets, free society and private health care were to become the model for a revitalized Britain. The United States offered her a platform for demonstrating that she could exercise leadership in both foreign and domestic policy. The Reagan–Thatcher relationship was about forging a common foreign policy in which Thatcher saw Britain as American's principal ally. The second wing of this relationship was economic and, hence, "Reaganomics" and "Thatcherism" are often treated as equivalent economic doctrines. While there is much confusion between the notions of "neocon-servatism" and "neoliberalism," Thatcher and Reagan are closely associated with the subsequent global triumph of free-market principles. Despite the fact that Thatcherism and Reaganomics are often seen as parallel policies arising from their mutual respect, Thatcher thought Reagan lacked any intellectual capacity, but she was quick to exploit the opportunity to influence American politics, especially in the area of foreign policy (Campbell 2011: 260).

The idea of a special relationship survived the end of that political part-nership and became the foundation of the foreign policy consensus between George W. Bush and Tony Blair, the Labour prime minister. While Reagan and Thatcher were "natural" allies, the relationship between a Catholic left-of-center British prime minister and an evangelical right-wing president was not immediately obvious; they clearly agreed over the invasion of Iraq on the suspicion of the development of "weapons of mass destruction." The subsequent disillusionment with foreign wars in partnership with the United States has eroded the notion of any special relationship, and David Cameron's attempts to massage the relationship has been seen, on both sides of the Atlan-tic, to be artificial.

Thatcher and Reagan had similar ideas about economics and international affairs. However, while Thatcherism represented a significant departure from English conservatism, Reagan's politics were a reaffirmation of the Republi-can agenda. Thatcher and Reagan were successful in projecting a promise of renewal and revival for their respective societies. Thatcherism aimed to put "Great" back into "Great Britain" and to restore Britain's internal influence. In his 1984 presidential campaign, Reagan adopted the slogan, "It's morn-ing again in America," both to suggest renewal and to describe the fact that more Americans were going back to work every morning. While Thatcher's style was more abrasive, and her policies consistently controversial, in many respects she was the most successful (peacetime) British prime minister of the twentieth century, being elected on three occasions between 1979 and 1990. The prime ministers from both major parties who followed her have gener-ally been unsuccessful. While the Thatcher–Reagan relationship was mutu-ally beneficial, the cooperation between Tony Blair and George W. Bush was undermined, at least in Britain, by unpopular wars in Iraq and Afghanistan.

Having recognized the historical and political connections between the two societies, we can explore whether there are any deeper cultural foundations to the special relationship. In particular, in this commentary it is important to examine the place of religion in the two societies and especially the relationship between religion and conservatism on both sides of the Atlantic. I conclude that, given the very different characteristics of religion in the two societies in terms of both history and constitutional arrangements, the character of political and religious conservatism was also different. The conclusion is that the special relationship was an invention of Thatcher, but it had relatively little depth. While subsequent British leaders have periodically appealed to the idea, it has struggled to survive the Iraq debacle.

Varieties of Conservatism

The principal argument of this chapter is simple. While religion plays an important role in politics in the United States, it has been largely absent in Britain and, specifically, in England. Religion is strangely present in American politics and strangely absent from English political life. Furthermore, while the secularization thesis has become unpopular in the sociology of religion, organized religion in Britain has declined throughout the twentieth century. Bryan Wilson's diagnosis of secular society has been much criticized, and has been somewhat replaced by Grace Davie's notion of "believing without belonging" (Davie 1994). While this phrase is an accurate summary of the situation in Britain, the reverse—'belonging without believing' is equally true. The controversy in 2014 over Prime Minister David Cameron's lecture recommending a return to a more evangelical Christianity is indicative both of decline and difference in the United Kingdom's relationship with the United States. His claim that Britain is a Christian country was widely condemned as simply false and also inconsistent with the actual needs of a multifaith society. Public criticisms of Cameron's appeal to the idea of Britain as a Christian country pinpoints important differences between the two societies.

One further preliminary observation is in order. Despite the development of modernization theory and the secularization thesis—the two were inevitably combined—scholars such as S. M. Lipset (1996) recognized the importance of "American exceptionalism." On a variety of measures, the United States, it was argued, had unique characteristics. One obvious example was the absence of a successful socialist party—which had been famously discussed as early as 1906 in an essay in Germany by Werner Sombart: Why is there no Socialism in the United States? (Sombart 1976). While political sociologists concentrated on the notion that America, unlike Britain, had not had a history of working-class politics, the notion of exceptionalism has also been used to emphasize the fact that America has not gone through a process of secularization and, indeed, religion was and is a force in American public life, including its political life.

After the seminal work of Mannheim on "conservative thought," sociology has contributed relatively little to the academic analysis of conservatism. Much of the analysis has come from political, not social, theory. One example is Corey Robin (2011), who treats "the reactionary mind" as a continuous tradition, from Edmund Burke to Sarah Palin. Robin argues that what conservatives have in common is a sense that they are fugitives in a world that has turned against their values and way of life. Conservative defense of tradition, hierarchy, organic social wholes and religion is an expression of conservative nervousness about the direction of social change. Thus "in response to challenges from below, conservatism has none of the calm or composure that attends an enduring inheritance of power.... Conservatism is about power besieged and power protected" (Robin 2011: 28). There is much to support Robin's interpretation, for example from the collection of essays on *The Radical Right* (Bell 1962) that first appeared in 1955 and was revised in 1962. The authors were primarily concerned with the growth of anti-Communist ideology and anti-intellectual sentiment that was defined by the umbrella term. "McCarthyism." in 1950 by reference to Senator Joseph McCarthy (1909–57) who traded on anxieties about Russian intelligence infiltration of major American institutions, including Hollywood. This anti-Communist movement was, according to Lipset (1962), made up of three distinct but interrelated waves: Coughlinites, McCarthyites and Birchers. These organizations were not entirely congruent in ideology and background, but Lipset thought their resentment against society, especially the role of banks, was driven by status anxieties. While research on "status incongruities" had generally been "unfruitful" in explaining right-wing movements, Lipset (1962: 403) quoted research data indicating that "the general assumptions about the relationship of status strains of an open society and the type of political protest represented by McCarthy may have some validity."

Recent research on the Tea Party suggests that there is a good deal of continuity with previous conservative protest movements. Theda Skocpol and Vanessa Williamson (2013: 81) conclude with the observation that, "To say that Tea Partiers are part of a long-standing conservative tradition is to agree with many of our interviewees, who celebrate previous generations of conservatives as their political forebears." As in the past, they regard Woodrow Wilson's Progressivism, Franklin D. Roosevelt's New Deal. LBJ's Great Society and Barack Obama's attempts at medical insurance reform as part of the modern problem. They conclude that the Tea Party is "an embattled community of conservatives" (Skocpol and Williamson 2013: 137). In short, much of this research suggests that conservatives are cut from the same cloth; they are social groups that, for a variety of reasons, feel excluded, misunderstood and embattled as they see their world disappearing in the face of social change.

But are all conservatives the same? A more precise definition, but one consistent with Robin's position, can be found in Brian Barry's *Political Argument* (1965: 54), where he defines conservatism as "any view to the effect that all attempts to transform societies in accordance with principles (whether they be want-regarding or ideal-regarding principles) are pernicious: dangerous and self-defeating at once." He goes on to argue that conservatism can be either anti-political conservatism (for example the thought of Friedrich Hayek) or anti-rationalist conservatism (Edmund Burke and Michael Oakshott). In short, conservatives have many reasons to fear social change, and they explain (or justify) these fears by arguing that neither direct political intervention nor rationalist planning can solve our problems—in part because we can never predict or anticipate the unintended consequences of such actions. It is better to rely on tradition, religion and intuitive judgment.

These interpretations of conservatism clearly are persuasive and have scholarly merit, but they overlook important differences within conservatism. In this chapter, I want to treat Thatcherism as a major break with the English conservatism of the past. There is an important question about just how conservative Thatcher was. On the one hand she clearly feared revolts and social disruption by the working class, as illustrated by the Miners' Strike and the response to the Poll Tax. Her economic and social policies promoted inequality; intellectually she favored individualism, as in the infamous claim that "there is no such thing as society." On the other hand one might say that she did not fear social change enough. Her economic policies changed Britain irrevocably, with disruptive and divisive consequences that have not diminished over time. Thatcher's conservative values were a radical attack on the aristocratic wing of the Conservative Party, and older Tories "were shocked by her unsentimental scorn for tradition or past practice" (Judt 2005: 541). Harold Macmillan accused her of selling the "family silver," and Edward Heath thought her encouragement of rampant profiteering had exposed the "unacceptable face of capitalism." Thatcher was a truly radical conservative, and she "did serious harm to the fabric of public life. Citizens were transmuted into shareholders, or 'stakeholders', their relationship to one another and to the collectivity was measured in assets and claims rather than in services or obligations" (Judt 2005: 543).

Her aim was not to conserve Britain but to change it radically, for example, by privatization to destroy the "Nanny-state." In the light of these considerations, I am persuaded that conservatism comes in many shapes and sizes, and that it obviously changes over time. Thatcherism was not about conserving, but transforming and, hence, it is widely recognized that she departed from the "One Nation" conservatism of Disraeli and launched a "Two Nation" version that was less caring and more abrasive. Because Thatcher's support came, not from any traditional Tory background, but from a disgruntled working class, many of her policies—such as the privatization of council houses—were very popular. Allowing tenants of council houses to opt out of local-authority control was one component of what she called "Popular capitalism," but the result in the 1980s was a significant increase in the number of homeless people who were forced to live on the streets.

Thatcher's style of politics was better described as "authoritarian populism" rather than traditional conservatism. The phrase was coined by Stuart Hall in an article in 1978 in *Marxism Today* and reprinted in *The Hard Road to Renewal* (1988). Hall's article gave rise to a dispute about just how popular Thatcherism was and whether she had popular support for her attempts to cut back on welfare expenditure (Jessop et al. 1988). The gist of this argument concerns the tension in her policies between libertarianism and her expansion of the state (through the police where necessary) to enforce her policies (on the trade unions and opposition to the Poll Tax). If there was any consensus, it was that Thatcher's economic policy, especially support for free markets, was not matched by support for individual liberties. Thatcherism was thus summarized in the title of a book by Andrew Gamble (1988), *The Free Economy and the Strong State*.

American conservatism also changed dramatically in the second half of the twentieth century, from a time when conservatives saw themselves as an embattled minority, to the 1970s, when they became the silent majority (Nash 2006). Libertarians, who favored self-assertion and resistance to the state, and traditionalists, who promoted self-restraint, discipline and probity, often clashed. However, these conservative factions often disagreed over principles while often agreeing over practice. There was a general consensus around support for the private market and private enterprise, opposition to Communism and socialism, and agreement over the need for a strong national defense. Conservatives were also generally opposed to liberalism, which they saw as the ideology of bureaucratic welfare states and a corrupting force in the moral foundations of America. In sociology, figures like Robert Nisbet belonged to the new conservatives who rejected rampant individualism and secular rationalism in favor of more collectivist principles such as the importance of community. Nisbet (197) thus found himself aligned with writers such as Edward Banfield (1970) in *The Unheavenly City*, which challenged the liberal activist agenda and talk of urban crisis. Banfield, who was an adviser to Richard Nixon, Gerald Ford and Ronald Reagan, was a friend and colleague of Leo Strauss and Milton Friedman at the University of Chicago. Nisbet became associated with this emerging movement of dissenting university professors, such as Irving Kristol, Nathan Glazer and Daniel Patrick Moynihan. Many of these writers had been Left radicals in their youth, but came to occupy a position that was a fusion of various conservative traditions. As the new conservatives gained in numbers, they also gained in confidence. During the 1970s American liberalism appeared to be in retreat.

Leo Strauss (1899–1973) is perhaps the most controversial figure in American conservatism, and his ideas are often interpreted as the basis of modern neoconservatism. It is claimed that many in the administration of George W. Bush were Straussians (Drury 1997; Norton 2004). Academic interpretations of Strauss have argued that philosophy by definition is hostile to custom and tradition, because the "conservatism of the philosopher is thus always a conservatism of convention and convenience" (Tanguay 2007: 87). In style, background and temperament, Strauss and Nisbet were very different conservatives. If they shared any common ground, it was with regard to the influence of Thomas Hobbes with respect to his theory of the state. For Nisbet, the growth of the centralized, bureaucratic and centralized state was the critical turning point in the history of the West. In Nisbet's theory of community, the erosion of the family, the guild, the local church and the neighborhood were crucial intermediary institutions between the individual and the state.

Alan Wolfe (2009: 260) sees conservatism, especially popular conservatism, as the main enemy of liberalism, warning us that putting populism and conservatism together produces a "very dangerous brew." The conservatism that could at one stage offer some "restraining role, elevating ordinary people to reach for something higher in life," has long disappeared, and "instead class resentments are mobilized to reinforce class inequalities" (Wolfe 2009: 261). This interpretation of conservatism may well fit the Tea Party version of conservative politics following the election of Barack Obama. Clearly this form of conservative populism is far removed from the high Anglican conservative critique of modernity that one finds in T. S. Eliot's *The Waste Land*.

Religion and English Conservatism

All British prime ministers have asserted their belief in God, despite the fact that they have not been noted for their personal spirituality. Because the Church of England is an "established" Church, once politicians are in power they have generally avoided religious issues in order to avoid political controversy. Thatcher was a Methodist by upbringing, and her religious views certainly influenced her private life, but not so obviously in her political role. Winston Churchill was agnostic and 'found no intellectual reward in theological exercises' (Manchester and Reid 2012: 18). Harold Macmillan was a One Nation Tory and a pragmatist. Edward Heath was, in the late 1940s, the news editor for the *Church Times* and was assumed to have strong Anglican beliefs. Finally, Tony Blair converted to Roman Catholicism after he had been forced out of office. On balance we could say that British politicians often have religious beliefs that influence their moral standards but, generally speaking, religion has been kept out of British politics.

However, Roger Scruton, one of England's leading contemporary philosophers, wants to take religion seriously as a component of conservatism. In his
career, Scruton has defended the English conservative tradition against the
Thatcherite revolution over a number of years and from various locations. He
was a professor at Birkbeck College (1971–92) and subsequently held positions
at Boston University, the American Enterprise Institute and the University of
St Andrews. In 1982 he helped found *The Salisbury Review*, a conservative political journal he edited for 18 years. He had originally embraced conservatism
in opposition to the student protests of May 1968 and, at the time, described
the French students as "an unruly mob of self-indulgent middle-class hoo-
ligans." His reaction is in line with the secondary literature that interprets
conservatism as a reaction against social unrest.

Scruton has produced a variety of publications in an attempt to define the
conservative tradition in opposition to Thatcherism. In essence, his defense of
traditional conservative views involves a one-nation approach, whereby society is understood as an organic entity in which unequal social groups are,
nevertheless, woven into the social whole. At the same time, in *The Meaning
of Conservatism* (1980) he defended the importance of duty and authority over
individualism. In the tradition of Edmund Burke, he has been skeptical about
the large claims made by human rights advocates (Scruton 2012). His more
recent publications are characterized by a nostalgia for church and country-
side. We might add here that traditional conservative prime ministers such as
Churchill and Sir Alec Douglas Hume (1903–95) identified with country life
("The shire") and activities such as fishing and hunting. Hume was the Mar-
quess of Salisbury and a member of the House of Lords. Serving as prime
minister for under a year (1963–64), he was a traditional landowner, who
engaged in traditional sports such as grouse shooting on his estates and was
regarded as the last of the great landowners to wield extensive political power.
By contrast, Thatcherism essentially involved a suburban lower middle-class
vision of England. In line with this memory of England as "a green and pleasant land," Scruton also celebrates the English landscape and its communities:
"And this is the way the English loved their country. England, for them, was a
place of clubs and teams and societies: it was a land saturated with the sense
of membership" (Scruton 2001: 72).

Scruton's conservatism has become an increasingly nostalgic and romantic,
appealing to a village, community-based, Anglican culture that has been seriously eroded by secularization, the rise of multiculturalism, and social diversity. Scruton is a fox-hunting philosopher and lives on a farm with his wife in
Wiltshire. In more recent publications, such as *Our Church. A Personal History of
the Church of England* (Scruton 2013), he has treated Anglicanism as the cultural
and religious foundation of English conservatism. The Anglican Church is

seen to be an example of English political wisdom—latitudinarian, broad, caring and inclusive.

Scruton's position is, in fact, closely related to the eccentric and anachronistic thinking of Maurice Cowling (1980): *Religion and Public Doctrine in Modern England*. Cowling and Scruton were both connected with Peterhouse College Cambridge—probably the most conservative and elitist college at Cambridge—and the Peterhouse Right. Peterhouse College was closely connected with the development of *The Salisbury Review*. Cowling, however, recognized that England was no longer Christian. "In the modern world a mainly Christian culture has been replaced by a mainly post-Christian one (xii). [...] In England there is a sea of voices with a plurality of doctrines which are joined together by the liberal doctrine that plurality is desirable" (xiii). The version of conservatism held by both Cowling and Scruton makes no sense in the absence of a viable national religious tradition. Hence, their view of England is inevitably retrospective and untenable. It is a conservatism of a land that has already disappeared with the loss of empire, industrial decline, urbanization, multiculturalism and the general impact of globalization. In short, it is a backward-looking conservative cultural politics of a rural and relatively homogeneous society.

Scruton, recognizing the decline of the Church of England and the erosion of a civilization he admires and defends, must present cultural conservatism in terms of a lament. Thus, in the "Epilogue" of *Our Church*, he offers a list of developments that have transformed England in ways he disapproves of, such as the European Union, the European Court of Human Rights, Celtic legislative independence, and discrimination against the Christian view of marriage in order to avoid any affront to the homosexual minority. In conclusion, he notes: "English society is no longer explicitly Christian, and our Parliament is no longer sovereign. The unique position of the Church of England depended on the belief that England was an autonomous, largely Christian nation, regulating its affairs through the Parliament of Westminster" (Scruton 2013: 188).

Conclusion: Two Divided Nations

I began this contribution to the celebration of Edward Tiryakian's sociology with a quotation from his own tribute to Pitirim A. Sorokin, in which Tiryakian saw the crisis of modernity as the core interest of the discipline of sociology. The title of that collection of essays from the 1960s was *Sociological Theory, Values and Sociocultural Change*. In this brief conclusion, I bring this discussion to an end with the crisis of modernity as it is currently experienced in England and America. The conclusion also, therefore, acknowledges how sociology might contribute to the analysis of both social change and values. Durkheim's vision of the moral crisis of modernity, the erosion of religion, and the growth of anomie is fully borne out in the cultural and political crisis that has shaped modern conservatism. While American and English conservatism are different and distinctive, they share a common sense of loss in which their world is under threat. In America, the crisis was articulated by Nisbet as a loss of community. In England, it is articulated by Scruton as the erosion of a way of life based on rural pursuits, Anglicanism and its ancient churches, and the growth of society dominated by market objectives and corporate values.

If we can date Durkheim's concern for the social and political unity of France from the Dreyfus Affair that deeply divided France, we might conclude that America and England are now deeply divided societies suffering from imperial decline, racial conflict, fear of outsiders that finds its expression in Islamophobia, the failure of political leadership in the face of rising Chinese global influence and Russian authoritarianism, urban terrorism, controversies over sexuality (especially same-sex marriage), and a rising number of young people with no religious affiliation (Hout and Fischer 2002). These anxieties about anomie are seen to be behind the rise of the Tea Party in American politics and the drift of English politics toward the radical right in the shape of the English Defence League and UKIP. In these uncertain times, it is hardly surprising that conservative thought in calling for a re-valuation of values and a restoration of religion is, in fact, creating new values. Whether these values are relevant to the "sociocultural change" envisaged in the Sorokin collection with which I started this essay remains to be seen.

Note

1 In this chapter my usage of "Britain" and "England" and "the United States" and "America" is somewhat inconsistent. My intention is to compare America and England, because my examples are specifically about England. Furthermore the political traditions of Scotland and Northern Ireland would require separate treatment. The referendum on Scottish independence in September 2014 offered ample evidence of the religious and cultural differences between England and Scotland. However, on various occasions—for example during World War II—it only makes sense to refer to Britain. This clarification is important historically, but also in contemporary political terms.

References

Banfield, E. 1970. *The Unheavenly City. The Nature and Future of our Urban Crisis.* Boston: Little Brown and Co.
Barry, B. 1965. *Political Argument,* London: Routledge & Kegan Paul.
Bell, D., ed. 1962 [1955]. *The Radical Right. The New American Right Expanded and Updated.* Garden City New York: Doubleday & Co.
Bellah, R. 1967. "Civil Religion in America." *Daedalus* 96, Winter: 1–27.

———— 1978. "Religion and Legitimation in the American Republic." *Society* (May/June): 16–23.

Bottomore, T. 1978. "Marxism and Sociology." In *A History of Sociological Analysis*, edited by T. Bottomore and R. A. Nisbet, 118–48. London: Heinemann.

Campbell, J. 2009. *The Iron Lady. Margaret Thatcher from the Grocer's Daughter to Prime Minister.* London: Penguin.

Chapp, C. B. 2012. *Religious Rhetoric and American Politics. The Endurance of Civil Religion in Electoral Campaigns.* Ithaca, NY: Cornell University Press.

Chaves, M. 2011. *American Religion. Contemporary Trends.* Princeton, NJ, and Oxford: Princeton University Press.

Coser, L. 1960. "Durkheim's Conservatism and Its Implications for His Sociological Theory." In *Emile Durkheim 1858–1917*, edited by K. H. Wolff, 211–32. Columbus: Ohio State University Press.

Cowling, M. 1980. *Religion and Public Doctrine in Modern England.* Cambridge: Cambridge University Press.

Davie, G. 1994. *Religion in Britain since 1945. Believing without Belonging.* Cambridge: Blackwell.

Drury, S. B. 1997. *Leo Strauss and the American Right.* Houndmills: Macmillan Press.

Gamble, A. 1988. *The Free Economy and the Strong State.* Basingstoke: Macmillan.

Gane, M. 2006. *Auguste Comte.* London and New York: Routledge.

Hall, S. 1988. *The Hard Road to Renewal.* London: Verso

Hout, M. and C. S. Fischer. 2002. "Why More Americans Have No Religious Preference: Politics and Generations." *American Sociological Review* 67, no. 1: 165–90.

Jessop, B., K. Bonnett, S. Bromley and T. Ling. 1988. *Thatcherism: A Tale Of Two Nations.* Cambridge: Polity.

Judt, T. 2005. *Postwar: A History of Europe since 1945.* New York: Penguin.

———— 2010. *Ill Fares the Land: A Treatise on Our Present Discontents.* London: Penguin.

Lipset, S. M. 1962 [1955]. "Three Decades of the Radical Right: Coughlinites, McCarthyites and Birchers." In *The Radical Right. The New American Right Expanded and Updated*, edited by D. Bell, 373–446. Garden City, NY: Doubleday & Co.

———— 1996. *American Exceptionalism: A Double Edged Sword.* New York: W. W. Norton.

Manchester, W. and P. Reid. 2012. *The Last Lion: Winston Spencer Churchill Defender of the Realm, 1940–1965.* New York: Bantam.

Mannheim, K. 1936 [1929]. *Ideology and Utopia.* London: Routledge & Kegan Paul.

———— 1986 [1925]. *Conservatism: A Contribution to the Sociology of Knowledge.* London and New York: Routledge & Kegan Paul.

Nash, D. H. 2006. *The Conservative Intellectual Movement in America since 1945.* Wilmington, DE: ISI Books.

Nisbet, R. A. 1965. "Social Milieu and Sources." In *Emile Durkheim*, edited by R. A. Nisbet, 9–28. Englewood Cliffs, NJ: Prentice Hall.

———— 1967. *The Sociological Tradition.* London: Heinemann.

———— 1979. "Conservatism." In *A History of Sociological Analysis*, edited by T. Bottomore and R. A. Nisbet, 80–117. London: Heinemann.

Norton, A. 2004. *Leo Strauss and the Politics of American Empire.* New Haven: Yale University Press.

Parsons, T. 1963. "Christianity and Modern Industrial Society." In *Sociological Theory, Values and Sociocultural Change*, edited by Edward A. Tiryakian, 33–70. New York and Evanston: Harper Torchbooks.

Robin, C. 2011. *The Reactionary Mind. Conservatism from Edmund Burke to Sarah Palin.* Oxford: Oxford University Press.

Scruton, R. 1980. *The Meaning of Conservatism.* South Bend, IN: St. Augustine Press.

—— 2001. *England: An Elegy.* London: Random House.

—— 2012. "Nonsense on Stilts." In *Handbook of Human Rights*, edited by Thomas Cushman, 118–28. London and New York: Routledge.

—— 2013. *Our Church. A Personal History of the Church of England.* London: Atlantic Books.

Skocpol, T. and V. Williamson. 2013. *The Tea Party and the Remaking of Republican Conservatism.* Oxford: Oxford University Press.

Simmel, G. 2010 [1918]. *The View of Life.* Chicago: University of Chicago Press.

Sombart, W. 1976 [1906]. *Why Is There No Socialism in the United States?* New York: Macmillan.

Sorokin, P. 1956. *Fads and Foibles in Contemporary Sociology and Related Social Sciences.* Chicago: Henry Regenery.

Tanguay, D. 2007. *Leo Strauss: An Intellectual Portrait.* New Haven and London: Yale University Press.

Tiryakian, E. A. 1962. *Sociologism and Existentialism: Two Perspectives on the Individual and Society.* Englewood Cliffs, NJ: Prentice Hall.

——, ed. 1963. "Preface' to *Sociological Theory, Values and Sociocultural Change*, ix–xv. New York and Evanston: Harper Torchbooks.

—— 1973. "Sociology and Existential Phenomenology." In *Phenomenology and the Social Sciences*, edited by M. Natanson, 187–222. Evanston: Northwestern University Press.

—— 1978. "Emile Durkheim." In *A History of Sociological Analysis*, edited by T. Bottomore and R. Nisbet, 187–236. London: Heinemann.

—— 2013. "Introduction to the Transaction Edition." In *Sociological Theory, Values and Sociocultural Change*, edited by E. A. Tiryakian, vii–xxvi. New Brunswick, NJ: Transaction.

—— 2009. *For Durkheim. Essays in Historical and Cultural Sociology.* Farnham: Ashgate.

Tiryakian, E. A. and R. Rogowski, eds. 1985. *New Nationalisms of the Developed West.* Boston: Allen and Unwin.

Turner, B. S. 2014. "The Axial Age Religions: The Debate and Its Legacy for Contemporary Sociology." In *Sociological Theory and the Question of Religion*, edited by A. McKinnon and M. Trzebiatowska, 51–73. Farnham: Ashgate.

Weber, M. 1930 [1905]. *The Protestant Ethic and the Spirit of Capitalism.* London: George Allen & Unwin.

Wolfe, A. 2009. *The Future of Liberalism.* New York: Alfred A. Knopf.

Chapter 6

CONTEMPORARY CHANGES IN THE PROCESSES OF SOCIAL DIFFERENTIATION: TOWARD AN ANALYTICAL VERSION OF THE THEORY

Alfonso Pérez-Agote

Some sociologists apply the tools of historical sociology and genetics of concepts to attempt to strip away the universalistic and transhistorical nature of the notions and theories that were formed from the analysis of the historical processes of modernization affecting Western European societies. These concepts and theories can, therefore, be used as convenient instruments for examining any social reality, as they conserve their analytical powers while shedding their predictive nature.

Since Durkheim (1893) wrote his work on the division of social labor, sociology has held differentiation to be one of the underlying tenets of the theory of modernization. This theory has largely served as the skeleton for our discipline. The main aim of this chapter is to offer guidelines for analyzing certain changes in the realm of differentiation that are transforming contemporary Western European societies.[1] I will first highlight some elements in the theory of differentiation that are relevant to this task. I will then identify some of the primary processes in the differentiation of spheres, institutions and symbolic systems that occurred during what is termed the "modernization process." In the third and final section, I will seek to explain a number of contemporary changes in these differentiation processes.

Toward an Analytical Theory of Social Differentiation

According to Luhmann:

> [A]fter the collapse of the utopian beliefs in the future that guided Comte, Marx, and Spencer [...] classical sociology consolidated itself by means of a structural description of society. Differentiation was interpreted by Simmel and Durkheim and indirectly by Weber as a *result* of social development, and thus became a central theme of social theory [...] henceforth the *structural* theme of differentiation determined the view of *history*. Yet the structure did not take the place of process, as misleading polemics often assume, nor did it produce a static point of view that ignores dynamics and history. Rather, the description of contemporary society as highly differentiated forms was the hinge that mediated past and future. (Luhmann 1990: 413)

Subsequently, with Parsons the theory of differentiation adopts a theoretical coding from sociology, and with it a certain risk of ossification. However, some sociologists used this theory to offer an interesting ideal description of the historical evolution of several social institutions and an empirical analysis of various social realities. I will only recall here the works of Parsons (1964), Eisenstadt (1964, 1990), Bellah (1964), Geertz (1973) and the insightful re-examination of the theory of differentiation itself from a highly analytical and empirical approach in the compilation of Alexander and Colomy (1990).

The basic form of social differentiation, according to Luhmann (1990), is the separation of society in relation to its environment. Luhmann's reflection focuses on a society's physical environment, and thereby he seeks to address the ecological issues that are of such importance today. But it can also be a social environment composed of other societies. If we look at historical sociology, this has been fundamental for understanding the process whereby states were formed in Europe, to the point where we could speak of the European system of states (Tilly 1990). Here, the idea of political representation developed by Voegelin is very productive, as Luhmann himself recognizes (although he does not actually cite this author). According to Luhmann it is essential to distinguish two levels of differentiation:

> The level of the differentiated unit (society) must be distinguished from the level of its parts, each one differentiated from each of the others. [...] The distinction of levels is one of the many possibilities for treatment and logical refinement of the basic paradox of a *unitas multiplex*. Another possibility reintroduces the unit back into itself, as a part. This solution has been connected for a long time with the concept of "representation." [...] The distinction of levels helps us observe

and describe the differentiated system, whereas the solution of representation establishes a capacity to decide and act. (Luhmann 1990: 410)

Voegelin (1968) believes there are two ways of understanding political representation. One form—which he calls elementary—predominates in our social reality, consisting of a description—with varying degrees of strictness—of the institutions of representative democracy. However, used in a deeper sense—which he denotes as "representation in its existential sense" (of real existence) and equivalent to a more scientific conception—it refers to the specific articulation of the social reality in order to be able to act. This formulation is practically identical to the one subsequently used by Luhmann. This way of understanding political representation—of which the strictly democratic political representation is a specific form among other possible forms—is what interests us here as a means of exemplifying certain aspects in the theory of social differentiation.

Two dimensions are of interest in our analysis of the process of construction of contemporary European societies: the differentiation of a society in relation to its social environment—as formed by other societies—and the internal differentiation of society whereby its spheres, institutions and symbolic systems gradually become separate.

For Voegelin, political representation is the origin of the primary social differentiation, namely the internal organization for action. It is the birth of political society as the first form of social totality, transcending the previous segmentary social reality (segmented in terms of family or settlement). According to Voegelin, the same process that differentiates society from its surroundings gives rise to a party in its interior that is distinct from the rest of that society—for example a *rex* chosen to defend it from its enemy. Representation, in its more scientific sense, is therefore the historic moment when a representative appears who has the capacity to carry out an action that commits the whole society to constituting the foundation of that society as a totality. Voegelin provides an outline of the subsequent steps in Europe[2] through a series of stages of political representation, from "a first phase [in which] the king alone is the representative of the realm. [...] When articulation expands throughout society, the representative will also expand until the limit is reached where the membership of the society has become politically articulate down to the last individual and, correspondingly, the society becomes the representative of itself." This is the democratic moment of political representation (Voegelin 1968: 65–67). As can be seen, the political order articulates society and totalizes it as a political society.

The issue of representation in the deeper sense—understood as the moment of differentiation when action becomes possible because it is issued by an organ whose activity involves the whole of a social grouping—raises a series of aspects concerning totalization, centralization and possible forms of differentiation. Luhmann highlights four forms of differentiation that have proved effective in the process of social evolution: segmentary (equality between subsystems), center–periphery, stratified (inequality of rank between subsystems) and functional differentiation (inequality of functions, equality of rank) (Luhmann 1990: 423).

Some criticisms have been levelled at the theory of social differentiation as a notion that seeks to describe the historic process by proposing a succession of types. Luhmann sees segmentary differentiation as being the first differentiation, still egalitarian; social reality subsequently evolves from equality to inequality, until it attains the maximum difference when finally the unity of the system is achieved through a system of differentiation (Luhmann 1990: 423–25); in other words, through the division of labor. Luhmann (1977) devoted one work to the theoretical integration of the theories of systems and evolution. Voegelin (1968) was a further example of this evolutionary and universalizing spirit. Yet another significant manifestation of this universalization appears in the June 1964 issue of the *American Sociological Review*, with the work by Parsons (1964)—at that time at the height of his academic powers—entitled "Evolutionary Universals in Sociology"; and two related articles in the same issue: "Religious Evolution," by Bellah (1964); and "Social Change, Differentiation and Evolution" by Eisenstadt (1964). An interesting aspect of the evolutionary approach is signaled by Voegelin (1956), who asserts that society evolved from compact symbolic forms to differentiated forms (Voegelin 1956), a concept used later by Bellah in the article just cited.

The revolutionary vision of society is a direct participant of the desire to *transhistoricize* or universalize, which I am seeking to dismantle in order to avoid imposing theory on reality and prophesying the course of events. The objective is clear from my perspective: to make sociology a fundamentally analytical science. The dismantling of this universalizing trend began a long time ago, and originally stemmed from the interesting idea that, however differentiated a society may be, there are times when a re-enchantment occurs, such as an instant of religious fusion or a political revolution. Edward Tiryakian (1985a, 1994, 2009) is one of the great constructors of the theory of these processes of *dedifferentiation*, thus anticipating the return of mechanical solidarity. The aforementioned work by Alexander and Colomy was also a multilateral attempt to bring together works on the de-universalization of the theory of differentiation, as its editors explain in the preface: "Whereas the initial formulation of differentiation theory rested upon the identification of a master trend of change toward a greater institutional specialization, the current volume supplements the master trend with the backlash movements against differentiation. [...] The benign assessment of the consequences of differentiation, which stress adaptive upgrading and greater efficiency, is balanced by the recognition that differentiation often generates discontents" (Alexander and Colomy 1990: xiii).

The Differentiations of Modernization

The differentiation of the social unit from its social environment

In another work (Pérez-Agote 2006: Ch. 2), I have analyzed the classic Weberian notion of the state, and pointed out that in fact it was Weber (1978: 1056) who actually defined the modern national state when he said it was the community that demanded there be a monopoly on legitimate physical coercion, without mentioning that it could be the king who demanded it. However, I criticized his failure to discuss the necessary condensation of power—of violence—in a differentiated center. I also referred—in relation to the possible nonexistence of the element of *success*—to the difference between the objective dimension (the center that monopolizes physical violence over a physical territory) and the symbolic–subjective dimension (the community that has the monopoly over legitimacy) of the state: without objective elements there is no state (as in an earlier time or during war); and without the subjective elements the state exists, but lacks social legitimacy.

The Peace of Westphalia (1648) marked the establishment of a European system of states. This process of historical construction of the objective elements of the state (center of power with a monopoly over physical violence and a territory delimited by fixed borders) is, in terms of the theory of differentiation, the process of differentiation of a society from what I have called its social environment; in the European case, this is the clear differentiation of each state from the surrounding states in the region. This also simultaneously involves another process of differentiation that takes place in the interior of the territorial state in terms of a center of power as opposed to a periphery; in other words, a process of centralization of power within the territory of the state. The sweeping transformation of the military sphere allowed the creation of an army that was capable of imposing an internal monopoly over violence (internal peace) and preventing external forces from acting in the interior.

The Peace of Westphalia was a key moment in the foundational process of the system of European states. We could say that in terms of the theory of differentiation, what becomes established is each state in its objective elements. Each state is differentiated by its surroundings from other states. This foundational moment in which the state becomes separated from its surroundings can occur thanks to the military power accumulated by a king who is thus able to maintain internal peace (by defeating other possible military powers) and defend the borders. Tilly (1990: 103–7) very clearly explains the impact of the changes in the military sphere for the accumulation of this power by the king in a territory. In these first moments the state is, in effect, the army. As the state becomes separate from its surroundings, an internal differentiation also takes place: a clear separation between the king and the populace inhabiting the enclosed territory of the state. The emergence of the king's court plays a key role as a mechanism for concentrating military and political power in the king. In *The Court Society*, Norbert Elias (1983) perfectly describes the mechanisms by which the European monarchs ultimately leached power from the nobility. The nobility thus ceased to wield power based on its territorial possessions and gradually acquired it by virtue of greater closeness to the king, through the court. The king constituted the political sphere, and his dominance over his kingdom was hereditary. His subjects existed, but were not considered a political unit. The process whereby that remnant of social reality began to be viewed as a totality, as society, as the object of polity, would come later.

The differentiation between the political sphere and civil society: the relationship between both

Habermas (1978) showed us the historical birth of the possibility of envisioning a society—the historical birth of the fact that, progressively, from the private sphere of life a series of social groups might conceptualize the public dimension and society; the gradual substitution of an absolute order, the public sphere of which was the court, with a bourgeois order in which society conceives of itself and criticizes the politics of power. The public sphere is now no longer simple. It has become more complex, formed by the public sphere of political power, and the public sphere that emanates either from civil society or from the private sphere. Before this could occur, a series of social mechanisms were gradually generated whereby certain social sectors began to envisage the idea of society itself as being the ultimate object of politics. The hierarchical order of the two spheres slowly continued to invert until the dawning of the idea that power resides in the people: popular sovereignty. Returning to the theory of differentiation, the totalization of society is a political operation. When society is viewed as a totality, that is the object of politics, we see the political sphere as representing society. Voegelin is right: it is politics that generates the totality that sociologists call society.

Habermas has effectively described the emergence from the private sphere of the mechanisms that would shape the structure of communication between the public sphere and civil society, between the representatives and those they represent. First came the *salons*—nearly always presided over by women from high society and frequented by certain cultivated sectors of the aristocracy and the bourgeoisie—where literary criticism often strayed over the line into political criticism. Then came the *cafés*, which served as a similar stepping stone between the realms of literature and politics. Nor should we forget the *secret societies*, which were followed by the *periodical press* and finally *political parties*, as the central social channels for this communication (Habermas 1978: Ch. 2).

Religious and cultural homogenization and the differentiation among culture, religion and politics

Tilly (1990) established two principles to describe the historical process after Westphalia: the internal homogenization of each European state, and the progressive heterogenization among all of them. The process of cultural homogenization of the population occurs primarily in relation to the ethnic diversity of the inhabitants of the territory of the state. The national education system, the communications network, compulsory military service, are just a few of the important mechanisms for extending a national culture and language. Many years later, after the two world wars, the process of European cultural and religious homogenization will aim to integrate communities from international immigration.

Habermas schematically establishes two generations of nations in the interior of Western Europe. The first generation corresponds to the north and west of Europe and encompasses nations formed in the interior of previously established territorial states. In this case the nation exemplifies Nisbet's expression of "the offspring of the state" (Nisbet 1973: 164). The second generation comprises Germany and Italy. These were nations in search of a state (Habermas 1999: 81). In the more general case, in which the state precedes the existence of a national community (the case I have in mind when speaking of the process of modernization), one of its fundamental tasks is the cultural homogenization of all the different ethnic groups that live within the state's territory. This is the process that nationalizes the state and constitutes the nation (Pérez-Agote 2006: 2).

During the period of construction of the national democratic states, the separation between church and state was a core process of social differentiation, and one that was achieved with varying degrees of success in the different European states. The old principle, *cuius regio eius religio*, was the paradigmatic expression of the principle of internal cultural homogenization in the states. The advent of the Reformation meant that this maxim had to be applied in practice in order to produce the religious unification of the population under the religion of the sovereign. The subsequent process of democratization–nationalization of the state would make the idea of nation-hood necessary. This would serve as the new collective identity by which power would reside in substitution of the idea of the divine right of kings. It is in this later process that the state needed to become autonomous from religion and the Church. The idea of secularity lay at the heart of this question.

Another parallel process is the separation between culture and religion. This a slower and less-visible process than the one described above, as culture does not essentially depend on a social institution but is maintained and transformed by social actors under the influence of many institutions. Thus religion gradually became differentiated from the rest of the social institutions, and now is wholly differentiated.[3]

Contemporary Transformations of Social Differentiation

The loss of a clear differentiation between the state and its social environment: globalization and supranational unions

One of the features of modernization is that it was a political project, with the state as its fundamental agency (Albrow 1997: 200).[4] This entailed significant amounts of reflection and a certain predictability about the process. In modernity, the state enclosed the social logics in territorial terms and condensed them in the political logic *par excellence*, namely the state logic. This political logic also became burdened—in the strictest sense of the term—with the task of resolving the dysfunctions produced in other social spheres. The political sphere played a residual and compensatory role by managing anomie and transforming dangers into risks (Beck 1992).

The current crisis of the state will not lead to its disappearance, but to the weakening of its capacity to regulate internal social life. This implies the loss of the monopoly over internal control, the loss of its predominance over other logics. This crisis of predominance stems from the superimposition of new logics on the previous central logic. Europe is a part of the world that has lost its centrality in relation to the world it knew in the phase of modernization (Tiryakian 1985b). Moreover, globalization in Europe is now very advanced. In another work (Pérez-Agote 1999), I have outlined how we had built a supra-state political unity. Each society in the European Union has the option of turning to the corresponding state to defend itself from the political decisions of the Union. All the states have lost power, but not to the same degree. This is because not all states have the same amount of power in European institutions. This means that the interests of the citizens of some countries are better defended by their own state and by the EU than are others.

If we look at the formation of the European Union from a longer historical perspective, we can see it as the logical continuity of the historic process of concentration of power in Europe described by Tilly (1990). First came the concentration of power. The unformed, decentralized political structure of the feudal era evolved into a small number of enclosed territories, each with an exclusive center of power. We are currently in the process of creating a new European center, formed primarily by Germany.[5] The democratic legitimation still remains to be built. There is a democratic deficit, but the European process of concentration of power—of which the Peace of Westphalia was a cornerstone—continues its course (Pérez-Agote 1999).

The construction of the state also brought a delocalization of the decisions that affect the individual. These decisions had previously been taken at the local level, which was the place where the individual lived and the only one he or she knew—a closed, local social reality. Modernity meant, as pointed out by Thomas (1923), a profound weakening of the local community as the defining agency of the *situation*. Modernization brought a new centrality to the life of the individual, that is, the state. Local society continues to be the place where everything that happens affects the individual, but it is no longer the place where everything that affects her or him happens. There are things that affect her or him that happen far away, in the center of the state, or beyond. Modernization is therefore a process of breaking with the knowledge–affect equation, as local society begins to be exo-centered. However, nationalism as the vehicle for the dissemination of national ideas and sentiments progressively reasserts the emotional cohesion of the group, thereby recomposing the equation on a larger scale. In a modern society, everything that happens within my state affects me, everything that affects me happens within my state; I frequently only know what is happening within my state; and moreover, in political terms only what is decided within my state is legitimate.

But once again the equation between what the individual knows and what affects him is broken with globalization. Thanks to economic globalization the individual is unaware of where a large part of the decisions that directly affect him come from, as they occur in spheres of which he is not aware. However, thanks to cultural globalization he is able to learn about spheres of the world that do not affect his life. The balance between knowledge and affect is—at least for the time being—broken. Much of what affects him (economic and political decisions) he or she does not know, yet he/she knows many things that do not affect him or her. We only have to think of television. This imbalance constitutes a form of anomie. Internet browsing opens up new possibilities for relationships between knowledge and affect that are decoupled from territory. One of the defining logics of information technology is that of interconnection (Castells 1997, 1: 88). The morphology of the Internet—to which the logic of interconnection leads—facilitates the connection between individuals and agents of any type and demolishes the limits and borders clearly established by the territorialized logic of the state.

In terms of social differentiation the outlook is more complex. The state continues to be an important form, although it has lost a large part of its political decision-making capacity in substantive areas due to globalization and, as in the European case, supranational aggregation. Several levels of analysis are then worth pursuing from the standpoint of each national society: the internal level, and the position in both the supranational level in which it is immersed and the global level.

The crisis in the communication structure between the political sphere and civil society

The theory of social differentiation has often focused its attention on the processes of separation of the spheres, structures and institutions and neglected to explore the relationships established between these various elements. Differentiation does not necessarily mean the nonexistence of relations. When I reviewed the first differentiation of our current national European societies, I observed how the first moment of separation of a state from an environment of other states also entailed a process of internal separation between a center and its periphery. We then saw how the periphery proceeded to become structured as a civil society with a public–political dimension emanating from the private arena. This brought a change in the form of legitimation of political power, from the divine origin of power to power residing in the people, in the national community. This process implied the progressive constitution of a structure of relation and communication between the political sphere and the civil sphere, which constitutes the basis of the democratic system of government.

We can say today that in Europe this relation structure has become mired in an ongoing crisis. The political sphere has become increasingly autonomous from civil society, from the citizens themselves. Tables 6.1 and 6.2 show the low level of trust of Europeans and Spaniards[6] in particular, in their political institutions.

If we consider Spaniards, we can see that: (a) they have a much greater European awareness and identity than trust in European institutions; (b) their trust in these institutions is lower than the European average; (c) despite this they have much more trust in European institutions than in Spanish institutions; and (d) generally speaking, trust in Spanish institutions is practically nonexistent. A look at the Barometer[7] from the Centre of Sociological Research for July 2014 reveals the problem that most concerns Spaniards,

Table 6.1 European identity and trust of Spaniards and Europeans in European institutions

		(A) Feel they are a citizen of the EU	(B) Feel they are attached to the EU	(C) Trust the institutions of the EU	(D) The European Parliament takes into consideration the concerns of European citizens
Spaniards	Yes	75%	69%	38%	27%
	No	24%	31%	59%	69%
Europeans	Yes	63%	62%	43%	38%
	No	35%	36%	52%	54%

Source: European Elections 2014—Post-election survey.
http://www.europarl.europa.eu/aboutparliament/es/00191b53ff/Eurobarómetro.html?tab=2014_2

Table 6.2 Trust of Spaniards and Europeans in political institutions

		(A) In the European Union	(B) In their national parliament	(C) In their national government
Spaniards	Tend to trust	16%	8%	10%
	Tend not to trust	79%	89%	89%
Europeans	Tend to trust	31%	28%	27%
	Tend not to trust	56%	65%	68%

Source: Eurobarometer 2014.
http://ec.europa.eu/public_opinion/archives/eb/eb81/eb81_fact_Es_En.pdf

after unemployment,[8] rated at 54.8 percent: corruption, at 15.7 percent; and in third place, politicians in general, political parties and politics, 10 percent. In recent years, corruption has been gaining ground as an issue of concern to the public, and politicians and politics have gone from being part of the solution to being part of the problem. Table 6.3 shows data on the crisis in the communication structure in Spanish democracy.

This crisis of confidence in political institutions has become even more serious and now plays a leading role in the life of society because of the impact of the current economic crisis, which has now been under way for well over seven years. The high rates of general and youth unemployment (see note 8) in these years indicate how difficult it must be to have a normalized life (if it can be

Table 6.3   Some data on Spaniards' opinions, 2011 and 2013

- 90% of Spaniards think political parties should make some far-reaching changes.
- 19% think the two major parties (PP[9] and PSOE[10]) represent the interests of the majority of citizens.
- 85% think the EU acts more in the interests of Germany than of Europe as a whole.
- 66% are sympathetic to the 15M movement.[11]
- 81% think the 15M movement is right.
- 80% think the 15M movement addresses real problems.

Sources: Metroscopia, Social Climate in Spain. June 2011 and May 2013.

called that). High youth unemployment stands in stark contrast to the educational situation of young people. According to the OECD report on education, "Spain, where the educational level of the population is not very high, is one of the best placed countries for upward mobility, as 45% of its population aged between 25 and 34 have achieved a higher educational level than their parents; these figures are higher than in the OECD or the EU (37% and 39%) and than Finland (27%), Norway (25%) and Germany (20%)" (Ministerio de Educación, Cultura y Deporte 2012: 9). This strong upward educational mobility has come at considerable economic sacrifice by parents and has been supported by the personal endeavors of their offspring. The contrast between the substantial efforts made by individuals and families and the difficulty of entering the labor market has led to a widespread feeling among young people of an injustice perpetrated against them and their parents (Pérez-Agote and Santamaría 2008).

This highly frustrating structural situation, mutually reinforced by the lack of trust in the prevailing political institutions, was further exacerbated by the widespread epidemic of youthful political mobilization triggered by the "Arab Spring."[12] Although the underlying political and economic situations differ widely, this was a global epidemic. The segment driving the mobilization consisted of educated young people with difficulties joining the labor market and consistently involved a struggle for a democratic political system, one that addressed the real problems of the population, regardless of the regime.

In February 2011, a platform under the generic name of *Democracia Real Ya*[13] emerged on the social networks in Spain and began to agglutinate a whole series of movements and associations, primarily youth-oriented. This platform succeeded in organizing demonstrations in forty Spanish cities that took place on May 15 that same year.[14] This movement, called 15M, would go on to launch a powerful galvanization process in social and political life. Some of its aspects are significant from the point of view of social differentiation.

The *leitmotif* of the 15M is precisely the relationship between two spheres that have ceased to be interlinked: politics and civil society. This movement has two general objectives: first, to find a new way of being politically engaged in civil society; and, second, to overhaul political action in order to ensure that it is directed at resolving the real problems that affect the population. The movement has sought to impact two spheres: the political sphere (which has become independent of the sphere of civil society) and the sphere that has become accustomed to passively consuming politics through social media. This movement consists of a whole array of people, social networks, platforms, demands and actions that aim to re-establish the relationship between politics and society. The internal organizational spectrum has been very broad and has ranged from certain purely local social mobilizations that have aligned themselves with the 15M as a symbolic receptacle, and through to the formation of a political party (Podemos).[15] This has included organizations that became reinvigorated by joining the movement (PAH),[16] proto-parties (Partido X)[17] now looking to sponsor new mechanisms and forms for enabling ongoing citizen participation in conventional politics. It can be seen that one of the dilemmas constantly active in the process is the movement's relationship with conventional politics. Another dilemma is whether it is possible to maintain this symbolic general receptacle simply by using the social networks enabled by new communication technologies, or whether it will be necessary to enact certain rituals involving bodily contact in socially significant spaces in order to maintain the process. If this ritualized maintenance were to prove unnecessary, it would bring up the question as to whether a new form of differentiation is possible through the use of new communication technologies. A third dilemma stems directly from the growing interest in a type of mobilization that does not imply a center–periphery relationship, but rather the equality of all the participants.[18] Does this lack of a center, of an institutionalized leadership, involve a substantive increase in the need for territorialized rituals?

A movement of this nature undergoes intermittent periods of visibility and invisibility. The fundamental question is the relative symbolic unity of the movement and the maintenance of what could be seen as a breeding ground.

The crises in the differentiation of culture, religion and politics: A new form of secularity?

The two principles established by Tilly (1990) to define the transformation of European societies between the Peace of Westphalia and the late twentieth century—progressive internal cultural homogeneity of each state and heterogeneity between states—have been profoundly shaken in recent decades. The latest stage of homogenization involves the immigrant population that began to arrive in the 1950s. Attempts at integration were relatively unsuccessful and, particularly since the oil economic crisis of the 1970s, have created difficulties regarding entering the workplace for successive generations of immigrants. The heterogeneity between states is affected by the increasing cultural homogenization created by globalization. However, globalization not only homogenizes, it generates new international migrations that lead to a degree of internal heterogeneity in Western societies. Globalization produces two contradictory cultural logics: the "McDonaldization" of society (Ritzer 1996) coexists with and competes with the "cultural re-creation"[19] (Wieviorka 1998) of immigrant populations.

In the 1970s, the difficulties in entering the workplace experienced by young immigrants led them into conflict with the host society. They thus sought another social identity and other sources of self-esteem and social esteem, such as the culture, religion and languages of their original community. Religion became a religion of choice rather than of inheritance, but was by now divested of the wrappings of the original culture for these young people. It is worth noting that in spite of the dire economic situation in Europe, considerable flows of immigration have continued to arrive. For immigrants in general, religion offers an added societal value in terms of social refuge and a source of identity, self-esteem and pragmatic solidarity. The more severe the dysfunctions of public social mechanisms for integration in this population, for example, the education system, the labor market and the correspondence between them, the greater the immigrant need to achieve self-esteem and social esteem by their own means.

New migratory flows lead to the religious heterogenization of societies. Immigrant populations have not—at least not to the same extent as in Europe—undergone a process of differentiation of religion in relation to other spheres such as culture and politics. This difference in the level of differentiation of religion has on many occasions been, and continues to be, a source of sociocultural conflict. We can recall the controversy over the Islamic veil in France and the Stasi report of 2003, which recommended the prohibition in schools of "tenues et signes religieux" (Stasi 2003: 68). The report's only mention of the significance of the veil is that it may conceal "différentes significations. Ce peut être un choix personnel ou au contraire une contrainte." (Stasi 2003: 57). It is evident that the Stasi commission reached its conclusions from a single viewpoint, that of the autochthonous French population, which holds the veil to be a religious symbol. From a different cultural perspective in which there is no clear separation between culture and religion, and where there is no differentiated religion, the veil is a religious–cultural–family symbol, and on certain occasions can also even be said to be political. The commission took an ethnocentric stance based on the belief that France should be a culturally homogeneous society, and by 2003 it clearly was not.

In a democratic society that is no longer culturally homogeneous and yet maintains a dominant religious tradition, the separation between church and state can be approached differently. A case in point is Spain, where the process of subjective secularization has come very late—in relation to France, for example—and very fast. The separation between the Catholic Church and the state started with the transition to democracy (1975–78) and was a fraught process. A substantial immigrant contingent has arrived since the beginning of this century,[20] highlighting a new religious diversity that increasingly uses religion as a mechanism for community integration and identity, particularly in the most recent economic crisis that began around 2007. Without a solid tradition of separation of church and state, with the Catholic Church still retaining considerable political power, and with the arrival of contingents of non-Catholic populations, the state has, through its changing governments, followed a pragmatic model of relations with the new religious confessions. Steps have been made to recognize them legally and collaborate with them, particularly through the Ministry of Justice and the Fundación Pluralismo y Convivencia (Pluralism and Coexistence Foundation)[21] set up by the ministry—the work of which foundation has been highly effective[22] in spite of its very meager resources.

European societies have been relatively[23] homogeneous from the religious point of view. Today, however, a sector of their populations (with immigrant origins but by now largely national) professes religious confessions other than the historically dominant ones. For this segment, religion plays an important role in the social integration of the community. These religious groups appear to need economic and political support to conduct their religious activities. This is even more so when the labor market, the fundamental mechanism for social integration, is becoming ever more disengaged from state control because of the globalization of the economy. Attention is definitely beginning to focus on the issue of the separation of church and state in Europe.

There are other places where this issue has been addressed by political means. For example, Gérard Bouchard and Charles Taylor promoted the idea of "open secularity" in a report commissioned by the prime minister of Quebec. These two authors consider the most fundamental of the four principles of secularity to be the moral equality of people and the freedom of conscience and religion. The other two have become open to interpretation: the principle of separation of church and state and the neutrality of the state in relation to religions and deeply held secular beliefs (Bouchard and Taylor 2008: 135–36).

As we have seen, international migration in Europe has destroyed the seemingly cultural homogeneity of its societies, which in turn means the differentiation between culture and religion has ceased to be a common feature of Europe as a whole. And the ultimate consequence of this is that the differentiation between politics and religion also ceases to be an absolute and general feature of society. Yet the differentiation between religion and politics has opened up another potential crisis. The Western European Christian churches—and in particular the Catholic Church—have reacted strongly to a number of laws passed by European legislatures since the 1970s. These laws concern ethical and intimate issues, such as the family, marriage, reproduction, life. In recent research work edited by Dobbelaere and Pérez-Agote (2015) the responses of the Catholic Church to this type of law in five countries were compared. Among these, Belgium and France are the two societies with the highest level of subjective secularization and the greatest separation between politics and religion. At the other extreme are Portugal and Italy. Spain is at an intermediate point. However, very recently we have witnessed the militant reaction of the French Catholic Church to same-sex marriage, a completely unexpected development given the French church's historical conformity with the law of 1905 enshrining the absolute separation of both institutions (Béraud and Portier 2015).

There is no doubt that political intervention in issues described as bioethical has aroused intense philosophical debate over the question of whether religion should step into the public arena with regard to the regulation of such matters. Here, I wish only to point out that European secularity has replicas that come from religion, but also from rationalist philosophical positions. For a sociologist, the particularly interesting aspect of all of this is that the issue has been raised and is now the subject of debate, which indicates the loss of clarity of differentiation between religion and politics.

Conclusion

A large number of changes in social differentiation appear to be arising. I have attempted to extract the evolutionary and transhistorical dimension from the theory of differentiation. I have merely touched on that ever-present dimension in all those realities, that of a return—momentary or, less commonly, long-term—to dedifferentiation (Tiryakian 1985a), a "return to mechanical solidarity" (Tiryakian 1994). These are moments or processes—religious or revolutionary (Tiryakian 2009)—in which the differentiation from the social environment can be seen in its purest state.

We have found differentiations in modernity that have been plunged into crisis. To a certain extent globalization represents the rupture of the primary or basic differentiation, that of social unity, or—subsequently—of society in relation to what I have called its social environment: the crisis of the state as the loss of the monopoly of the final political logic of society. Of course other differentiations can be seen on the horizon in terms of the formation of a single global society. We can envisage this possibility through the route of the formation of a single global state, which is unlikely to be easy, given that it requires an alterity that may be either exterior or interior. We may recall that George W. Bush attempted to define Islam as such an enemy. This calls to mind the route of the emanation from a center as opposed to the global periphery. But there is also the other aspect, defined by Albrow (1997) as "performative citizenship," of citizens in search of a global state they themselves are trying to build. But as a defensive reaction, we also see the retrenchment—as the best way of safeguarding European interests at the global level—of the European Union. This paradoxically leads to the retrenchment of the center–periphery relationship in the interior of the Union.

The differentiation between religion and politics in European societies is being compromised by the strengthening of the traditional religious institutions with respect to laws relating to intimacy (Dobbelaere and Pérez-Agote 2015), as well as by the "arrival" in society of new religious confessions among immigrant populations. This latter aspect is fueled by the difficulties in the functioning of the public mechanisms for social integration and the increasing search by young immigrants for their sources of self-esteem. Serious tensions are already becoming evident, pointing to the need to rethink the idea of secularity. We have also seen that the national population is no longer homogeneous in terms of its culture and religion. Large parts of our society no longer regard religion as an institution that is separate from culture, making it even more difficult to apply the modern idea of secularity and the separation of religion from politics. The state is constrained to protect the mechanisms of integration belonging to that population (i.e., imported confessions), and even more so when the state has lost the capacity to control the mechanisms governing the labor market.

One aspect of this theory that has been highlighted and often overlooked is that the differentiation of spheres and institutions should not allow us to forget their interrelationships. In this chapter we have seen how the long road towards the separation of the political sphere and civil society has been interlinked with that of the institutionalization of their relations, and how this modern structure of communication between them is today profoundly under threat. We have also seen how, in today's civil society, another communication structure—different from the modern one, but with subtle and complex relationships with conventional politics—is struggling to become institutionalized under a new form.

Notes

1 I use these societies as a core reference, as sociology emerged as a science to analyze the changes they were undergoing at the time.
2 Of course we can find political totalizations—representations—in earlier periods and regions many miles away from the above-mentioned social and historical context. Voegelin himself gives examples.
3 Later on I will discuss the most recent revisions of the notion of secularity. Secularity was a generalized mobilization—with the active collaboration of the social sciences—to expel religion from the territory of political legitimacy (Pérez-Agote 2014).
4 It was Edward Tiryakian who recommended that I read this fascinating work.
5 France also seeks to be part of this center. The case of the United Kingdom is also interesting because of its distance from the center of Europe and its closeness to the United States. I cannot explore these issues here in greater depth. What I am interested in signaling is that Europe is certainly a network—the least structured of structural forms—of states, but a more powerful structure is gradually being overlaid on that network, a structure that connects these states in terms of center–periphery. Luhmann clearly asserts that "the different forms of system differentiation are not necessarily mutually exclusive" (Luhmann 1990: 424).
6 I have particularly chosen Spain because of the severity of the crisis it has undergone, and because this country has seen the rise of a protest movement against this autonomization; and also because I was fortunate enough to observe the founding moments of that movement with Professor Tiryakian in the Puerta del Sol square.
7 http://www.cis.es/cis/opencm/ES/1_encuestas/estudios/ver.jsp?estudio=14099
8 In 2007, the unemployment rate that had hovered around 8% began to shoot up, and by 2011 had almost tripled. Today, in September 2014, it stands at around 24%, and around 54% for the under 25s: http://www.datosmacro.com/paro/espana
9 The strongest right-wing party.
10 The strongest socialist party.
11 http://www.movimiento15m.org
12 On 17 December, 2010 a young 26-year-old Tunisian set himself on fire and was burnt alive. This was the symbolic trigger for this epidemic.
13 http://www.democraciarealya.es
14 http://sociedad.elpais.com/sociedad/2011/05/11/actualidad/1305064806_850215.html
15 This organization became increasingly centralized to ensure efficiency, while attempting to conserve the reference to a new way of doing politics in direct and constant communication with civil society, without forming part of a separate caste. http://podemos.info
16 http://afectadosporlahipoteca.com
17 http://partidox.org
18 Podemos has transferred this rule by accepting the proposal presented by Pablo Iglesias over the one presented by Pablo Echenique, as it was less centralizing than the other and won in October 2014.
19 In Kivisto (2014: 61–87) we see the forms of re-creation of the ecclesiastic organization by the immigrant population, often very closely aligned with the organizational forms of the autochtonous confessions.
20 This has risen from less than 2% of the foreign population to over 12%, in only around ten years.

21 www.pluralismoyconvivencia.es
22 Most notably by the Observatory on Religious Pluralism in Spain: www.observatoriore-ligion.es
23 Relatively, because there are nonreligious and anti-religious forms; although we also need to consider the transformation of a country with a Catholic religion into one with a Catholic culture (such as France and Spain). This is equivalent to saying that religious pluralism does not predominate historically.

References

Albrow, M. 1997. *The Global Age: State and Society beyond Modernity*. Stanford: Stanford University Press.

Alexander, J. C. 1990. "Core Solidarity, Ethnic Out-Groups, and Social Differentiation." In *Differentiation Theory and Social Change: Comparative and Historical Perspectives*, edited by J. C. Alexander and P. Colomy, 267–93. New York: Columbia University Press.

Alexander, J. C. and P. Colomy, eds. 1990. *Differentiation Theory and Social Change: Comparative and Historical Perspectives*. New York: Columbia University Press.

Beck, U. 1992. *Risk Society: Towards a New Modernity*. London: Sage.

Bellah, R. 1964. "Religious Evolution." *American Sociological Review* 29, no. 3: 358–74.

Béraud, C. and P. Portier. 2015. "'Mariage pour tous': The same-sex marriage controversy in France." In *The Intimate: Polity and the Catholic Church*, edited by K. Dobbelaere and Pérez-Agote, 55–91. Leuven: Leuven University Press.

Bouchard, G. and C. Taylor. 2008. *Fonder l'avenir: le temps de la conciliation: rapport abrégé*. Commission de consultation sur les pratiques d'accommodement reliées aux différences culturelles. *Rapport final, Québec: Gouvernement du Québec*. http://collections.banq.qc.ca/ark:/52327/bs66285

Castells, M. 1997. *La era de la información. Economía, sociedad y cultura. Vol.1 La sociedad red*. Madrid: Alianza.

Dobbelaere, K. and A. Pérez-Agote, eds. 2015. *The Intimate. Polity and the Catholic Church*. Leuven: Leuven University Press.

Durkheim, E. 1893. *De la division du travail social: étude sur l'organisation des sociétés supérieures*. Paris: Félix Alcan.

Eisenstadt, S. N. 1964. "Social Change, Differentiation and Evolution." *American Sociological Review* 29, no. 3: 375–86.

Eisenstadt, S. N. 1990. "Modes of Structural Differentiation, Elite Structure and Cultural Visions." In *Differentiation Theory and Social Change: Comparative and Historical Perspectives*, edited by J. C. Alexander and P. Colomy, 52–87. New York: Columbia University Press.

Elias, N. 1983. *The Court Society*. New York: Pantheon Books.

Geertz, C. 1973. *The Interpretation of Cultures*. New York: Basic Books.

Habermas, J. 1978. *L'Espace Public. Archéologie de la Publicité Comme Dimension Constitutive de la Société Burgeoise*. París: Payot.

Habermas, J. 1999. *La Inclusión del Otro. Estudios de Teoría Política*. Paidós: Barcelona.

Kivisto, P. 2014. *Religion and Immigration: Migrant Faiths in North America and Western Europe*. Cambridge: Polity Press.

Luhmann, N. 1977. "Differentiation of Society." *Canadian Journal of Sociology* 2, no. 1: 29–53.

——— 1990. "The Paradox of System Differentiation and the Evolution of Society." In *Differentiation Theory and Social Change: Comparative and Historical Perspectives*, edited by J. C. Alexander and P. Colomy, 410–40. New York: Columbia University Press.

Ministerio de Educación, Cultura y Deporte. 2012. *Panorama de la Educación. Indicadores de la OCDE. Informe español*: http://www.mecd.gob.es/dctm/inee/internacional/ panorama2012.pdf?documentId=0901e72b81415d28

Nisbet, R. A. 1973. *The Quest for Community*. New York: Oxford University Press.

Parsons, T. 1964. "Evolutionary Universals in Society." *American Sociological Review* 29, no. 3: 339–57.

Pérez-Agote, A. 1999. "Globalización, Crisis del Estado y Anomía. La Teoría Social Visita Europa." In *Globalización, Riesgo, Reflexividad: Tres Temas de la Teoría Social Contemporánea*, edited by R. Ramos Torre and F. García Selgas, 73–103. Madrid: Centro de Investigaciones Sociológicas (CIS).

——— 2006. *The Social Roots of Basque Nationalism*. Reno: University of Nevada Press.

——— 2014. "The Notion of Secularization: Drawing the Boundaries of its Contemporary Scientific Validity." *Current Sociology*, no. 62, 886–904.

Pérez-Agote, E. and E. Santamaría. 2008. *Emancipación y Precariedad en la Juventud Vasca: Entre la Anomia Funcional y el Cambio Cultural*. Vitoria-Gasteiz: Gobierno Vasco.

Ritzer, G. 1996. "The McDonaldization Thesis: Is Expansion Inevitable?" *International Sociology* 11, no. 3, 291–308.

Stasi report. 2003. "Commission de Reflexion sur l'application du Principe de Laïcité dans la République." *Rapport au Président de la République*, December 11. http://www. ladocumentationfrancaise.fr/var/storage/rapports-publics/034000725/0000.pdf

Thomas, W. I. 1923. *The Unadjusted Girl*. Boston: Little & Brown.

Tilly, C. 1990. *Coercion, Capital, and European States, AD 990–1990*. Oxford: Blackwell.

Tiryakian, E. A. 1994. "Revisiting Sociology's First Classic: *The Division of Labor in Society* and Its Actuality." *Sociological Forum* 9, no. 1: 3–16.

——— 1985a. "On the Significance of Dedifferentiation." In *Perspectives on Macro-Sociological Theory*, edited by S. N. Eisenstadt and H. J. Helle, 118–34. London and Beverly Hills: Sage.

——— 1985b. "The Changing Centers of Modernity." In *Comparative Social Dynamics: Essays in Honor of Shmuel N. Eisenstadt*, edited by E. Cohen, M. Lissak and U. Almagor, 131–47. Boulder, CO: Westview Press.

——— 2009. "From Durkheim to Managua: Revolutions as Religious Revivals." In *For Durkheim: Essays in Historical and Cultural Sociology*, 189–202. Burlington: Ashgate.

Voegelin, E. 1956. *Orden and History, vol. I.* Baton Rouge: Lousiana State University Press.

——— 1968. *Nueva Ciencia de la Política*. Madrid: Rialp.

Weber, M. 1978. *Economía y Sociedad*. Mexico: Fondo de Cultura Economica.

Wieviorka, M. 1998. "Le Multiculturalisme est-il la Réponse?" *Cahiers internationaux de sociologie* 105, no. 1: 233–60.

Chapter 7

CONSIDERATIONS ON GLOBAL STUDIES

Roland Robertson

Every society known to history is a global society, every culture a cosmo-logical order; and in thus including the universe within its own cultural scheme [...] the people accord beings and things beyond their immedi-ate community a definite place in its reproduction. (Sahlins 2000: 489)

1

Edward Tiryakian, to whom this book is dedicated, is a prime example of a global sociologist (Cohen and Kennedy 2007). One of the very first things that Ed ever uttered to me was "have passport, will travel." In the forty years or more that I have known him, his activity has most certainly conformed to this maxim; although my first (indirect) encounter with the work of Tiryakian was my reading of the book that he edited in honor of Pitirim Sorokin, *Sociological Theory, Values, and Sociocultural Change* (1963, 2013). As a newly appointed soci-ologist at the University of Leeds in England and in a context in which theory and works deriving from countries other than England were relatively mar-ginal, this volume struck me immediately as the kind of work I hoped to do myself. The range of Ed's interests—and my interactions with him concerning these over this long period—in large part constitutes the basis for much of what follows, not least the currently highly problematic relationships between and among regional, area, comparative, international and global studies, as well as civilizations. In addition, Ed and I have also shared a long-standing concern with the condition of disciplinarity. These are the kinds of interest that form the basis for this present, celebratory chapter. Indeed, what follows could use-fully be regarded as a continuation of the general conversation that has been occurring between Edward Tiryakian and myself since we first met.

I propose to identify the major problems involved in defining—or, better, characterizing—the field of global studies, giving particular attention to the following. I begin by making a brief statement concerning my own academic-intellectual path to global studies (Robertson, 2012a). Second, I focus upon the relationship between global studies and the more specific topics of globalization and glocalization (Robertson, 2012b). Third, I reflect upon the inevitably unstable field of global interrogation and its connection to the theme of disciplinarity; taking a glance at the relationship between global and comparative studies—emphasizing the all too frequent conflation of these two perspectives. Fourth, I will argue that the precise word, *global*, is becoming increasingly inadequate, considering the rapidly growing significance of space exploration and theorization about this topic, not to speak of the significance of contemporary science fiction and its overlap with "real" science. In fact, some cosmologists would now claim that the entire issue of cosmology and astronomy raises the question as to the degree to which fact and fiction merge.

The present chapter is partly based upon a presentation that I made at a conference held at the University of California, Santa Barbara, in 2012. It also draws on an interview of myself conducted by Paul James and Manfred Steger during the same conference, this being part of a project that they were conducting and that was subsequently published in the journal, *Globalizations* (2004). The conference itself was held under the aegis of the UCSB program titled Global and International Studies. The conjunction of these two words, global and international, indicates much about the history and present state of what is now often, but by no means unproblematically, called global studies.

In my own case what is particularly relevant is that, upon my arrival at the University of Pittsburgh in the fall of 1967, I was informed that shortly before there had been established a center for international studies that was one of the first, if not the very first, such center in the United States. However, for much of my period of nearly forty years in Pittsburgh I was an increasingly firm advocate of either changing the name of the center so as to substitute "global" for "international," combining these two words, or giving prominence to global studies as part of the center. However, I was increasingly disappointed with the resistance to my ideas on the part of the center's leadership; even though there was, after some years, a concession that consisted of what might well be called an empty box within the center, labeled global studies. This meant that the center continued to maintain its original title, the University Center for International Studies (UCIS), and with no apparent content in "global studies." However, about two years after I left Pittsburgh in 1999 a global studies program was, in fact, initiated within UCIS and became designated as a center within the latter in 2010.[1]

It should be added at this point that many of my meetings with Ed occurred upon the occasion of his numerous visits to Pittsburgh in his role as a member of the Board of Visitors of UCIS. However, to the best of my recollection, Ed and I rarely, if ever, discussed the topic of the absence of a global center or at least a special focus on global studies within the latter. I suppose that there was a tacit understanding that this was a topic that should be kept to one side during our numerous conversations. It is also worth mentioning that, during much of the period of Ed's regular visits to Pittsburgh, he was the head of a much smaller center for international studies at Duke University, his home institution, one that I also visited. I must emphasize that even though the following concentrates upon my own path to and conception of global studies, it is at the same time an illustration of the ways in which two friends and colleagues have followed two different, but complementary and overlapping trajectories.

2

The course of my own career has frequently involved my having to deal with the often-perceived tension between international and global studies. At the center of this tension has been the view that processes of globalization have undermined the nation-state, whereas I have consistently maintained that the latter has been a *core feature* of globalization itself. Therefore, in my perspective, by definition the nation-state cannot be undermined by globalization. Global is a much more inclusive term than is international. In other words, the idea of internationality is subsumed by that of globality. More specifically, international relations (IR) are in my perspective but one of the four major components of what I call the *global* field (Robertson 1992: 25–31; see also Robertson and Chirico 1985). I define and still define the global field as consisting in the following: the nation-state; individual selves; the system of societies (IR); humanity.

The question as to how we define the field of global studies raises the issue of whether it should be regarded as an academic discipline as such, rather than a focus or field of study. Many people have maintained that global studies is interdisciplinary, but I have consistently objected to this; primarily on the grounds that the very idea of interdisciplinarity actually often consolidates—indeed, unintentionally or otherwise, celebrates—disciplinarity. At its worst, interdisciplinarity involves people from particular so-called disciplines spending much time announcing where they are "coming from" rather than directly addressing the problem(s) ostensibly at hand. In fact, many so-called interdisciplinary discussions amount to little more than announcements and celebrations of particular disciplines. At least this was the circumstance until quite recently and in some quarters still is. A particularly striking example of an organization that fruitfully mixes membership of different disciplines without heralding any kind of disciplinarity, is the American Society for the Study of Religion, my membership of which was promoted and sponsored by Ed Tiryakian.

If we must consider global studies as a kind of academic field, in the institutionalized academic sense, it is best if we consider it as crossdisciplinary, postdisciplinary or even antidisciplinary. In fact, the first and second of these are presently in use in a few institutions of higher education, and quite often in publications. However my own preference—if we are indeed to stay in the "disciplinary game"—is to characterize global studies as being *transdisciplinary*; meaning that this field of investigation transcends other extant disciplines and that it is, so to speak, beyond disciplines or, alternatively, is an all-inclusive (or "higher") field of study (Robertson 1996).

However, it must be emphasized that, like many other such programs, UCIS at the University of Pittsburgh was, when I was there, not so much international in its focus as it was at, least in a weak sense, comparative. More specifically, the center largely consisted in a set of area, or regional, studies such as Asia, Western Europe, Eastern Europe and Latin America. In fact, there was very little attention paid to international relations per se, even though specific individuals within particular area study programs were indeed primarily concerned with international affairs. Moreover, it was clear that Asian studies, with a particular focus on Japan and China, was much more concerned with cultural issues than it was with, for example, the program for Latin American studies. Latin American studies was much more likely to be concerned with political or economic issues. In any case, there was very little direct comparison of the different area studies or of their overall rationale, at least from the 1960s to the 1990s. Specifically, the structure of the center had very little that would facilitate comparison between the functioning of different area studies. In fact, it is intriguing, at least retrospectively, to speculate on the reason for the substantive foci of different programs of study.

It must be strongly emphasized that here I have been speaking of my own experience and observation of the Pittsburgh circumstance from the late 1960s until 1999, when I left the University of Pittsburgh. Thus, in this respect I have only been sketching a particular configuration of what I see as a not-untypical program in the general area of what was at that time, "international" studies. The very title of the Santa Barbara program—Global and International Studies—illustrates the manner in which "global" began to overcome "international." In fact, there has been a remarkable increase in the use of the term "global" in the last decade or so. Indeed, the adjective global has now become virtually an intellectual *brand*. It is a somewhat unfortunate feature of Western academia that most schools of thought or university sectors have been, or are rapidly becoming, branded. Indeed, it is not infrequently said that if one cannot identify oneself as being part, or preferably an instigator, of a school of thought, one is unlikely to become "famous."

One of the very first occasions upon which I employed the concept of globality was (somewhat paradoxically) in 1983 at a conference of the Pennsylvania Council of International Education that had strong links with UCIS, the title of my lecture being "Interpreting Globality." This was subsequently published in *World Reality and International Studies* (Robertson 1983).

A small number of members and affiliates of the University Center for International Studies at Pittsburgh were also associated with what was then called the International Society for the Comparative Study of Civilizations (ISCSC) (US), in which Ed Tiryakian intermittently participated. The link between UCIS and civilizational analysis is, or at least was, important for two main reasons. First, it raises the issue of the relationship between international studies and civilizational studies and, second, it brings to the surface the paramount question of the relationship between civilizational studies and what has been called, at least in recent years, global studies.

The fact that Samuel Huntington's highly influential article "The Clash of Civilizations?" was published in 1993, and that Huntington himself was a specialist in political and international affairs, has greatly contributed to the confusion surrounding the idea of civilizational studies. In fact, Huntington himself showed little interest in or knowledge of what had been known throughout the century as the study of civilizations. Through much of the twentieth century, the study of civilizations had been a well-established intellectual focus— indeed, for some a separate discipline, Arnold Toynbee and Oswald Spengler having been among the early major practitioners. For readers of such a journal as *Foreign Affairs* (where Huntington's article was published) the very idea of intellectual discourse with respect to civilizations appeared to come "out of the blue" (Huntington 1996). Hence, much of the enormous attention to and controversy surrounding Huntington's argument—an argument that was largely concerned with the question as to the pattern of international relations after the (old) Cold War. Briefly put, Huntington maintained—in spite of some acknowledgment of the considerable number of civilizations—that the civilizational clash of which he spoke was centered on the relationship between a Judeo-Christian West and an Islamic "Rest." I invoke the Huntington debate only because it then drew attention away from "genuine" civilizational analysis although, whatever one may think of the Huntington thesis, it has certainly played a large part, not merely in intellectual debate, but also in the whole sphere of *Realpolitik*. In any case, the area of civilizational analysis and discourse was to play a large part in my own shift toward a genuinely, and more or less comprehensive, global perspective. It almost goes without saying that Edward Tiryakian's recent work has focused a great deal on the analysis of civilizations. In any case, this is made clear in the list of Ed's publications at the end of this volume.

3

Regardless of the preceding observations, we must surely avoid the temptation to conceive of global studies as (yet) another discipline, however inclusive. In this connection it is necessary to interrogate the relationship between the study of globalization per se and the much wider field of global studies, emphasizing that upon occasion I, as well as some of my colleagues and some of my former graduate students, have been accused of conflating the two. This has been particularly the case with respect to the almost constant repetition of this fallacious contention by Jan Nederveen Pieterse (e.g. Pieterse 2013), even though I am certainly committed to the view that the analysis of globalization/glocalization processes is at the core of global studies.

I have consistently maintained that globalization is multidimensional, although I should add that I regard the two *most general* features of globalization to be (global) connectivity and (global) consciousness (Robertson 2011 and forthcoming). Of these two, however, the issue of consciousness has been greatly neglected. In fact, many still seem to regard globalization as more or less to be defined by global connectivity—indeed what some now call hyperconnectivity. In contrast, I regard global consciousness as relatively autonomous and *analytically* independent of connectivity. Moreover, there is also the analytical question of global culture.

Global consciousness is related rather closely to what in other contexts one might well call global culture or, indeed, the global imaginary. As defined by Manfred Steger in his *The Rise of the Global Imaginary* (2008), the global imaginary has a much more ideological connotation than the more general concept of global culture. While very appreciative of the usefulness of "global imaginary," I not only prefer the notion of culture but also regard it as more adequately expressive of a form of consciousness. This I explain in the first chapter of *Global Culture: Consciousness and Connectivity* (2016).

Such themes as global imaginaries, global culture and antisystemic movements were of particular relevance at the time of my beginning to think seriously about the present chapter. The theme of *The Economist* for June 29–July 5, 2013 was "The march of protest," under which rubric recent nationwide as well as transnational protests against "the system" were examined. Such transnational developments have accelerated since that time, not least because of the social media and related means of electronic communication.

In addressing what was announced as "anger around the world," attention was paid specifically to Turkey, Brazil, Greece, France, China, Saudi Arabia and Russia—to which might be added a large number of other countries, including South Africa, India, Spain and Portugal. This general development might well be viewed as a kind of outcome of the activities of the "Occupy Movement" that appeared in 2012 in the United States and the United Kingdom. It is of more than passing interest that the cover of the relevant issue of *The Economist* situated the eruptive trends of 2013 as the culmination of the "march of protest" that began in 1848 with the outbreak of revolution across much of Europe. This was continued through the widespread events (mainly in, but not confined to, North America and Europe) to the demise of the so-called Soviet Empire in 1989, as well as the world-shaking events in Tiananmen Square in China. However, since the rapid and disturbing increase in the tensions centered upon, but not confined to, the Ukraine, between Russia and the West—particularly with respect to Russia's annexation of Crimea, its incursion into the eastern part of Ukraine, and its apparent "threats" to the Baltic states and other parts of the old Soviet Union, the entire circumstance has become increasingly intractable. Moreover, the extremely complex situation in Syria and Iraq, at the center of which has been the rise of so-called ISIS, not to speak of the spread of the activity of Al-Qaeda and its various affiliates, has intensified the entire situation in the Middle East, Eurasia and northern and central Africa.

My own first ventures into the general field with which I am dealing here were, in fact, a combination of sociology and international relations. This mixture came about primarily through my collaborations with the late Peter Nettl, who in the mid-1960s was a colleague in the Department of Social Studies at the University of Leeds. Nettl was a political scientist and historian who had just completed a highly praised biography of Rosa Luxemburg, while I was a sociologist with particular interests in religion, politics and socio-cultural change. Having decided to give a joint paper titled "Industrialization, Development or Modernization," at a conference at the University of Manchester in 1965, we embarked upon a project that resulted in the book *International Systems and the Modernization of Society* (1968). The principal feature of these two closely connected publications was our decision to conceptualize modernization as a general process of catching-up with what were regarded as more "advanced" nation-states. This was, again, an issue in which Ed Tiryakian was intimately involved. In any case, this meant that Nettl and I brought together the comparative and the international approaches to the study of societies. More specifically, we synthesized the issue of relations between societies and the "everyday" comparison of societies. In itself, this marked a move beyond the disciplinary convention to regard societal analysis and the study of international relations as almost separate endeavors. This stance was later to form the basis of my own conception of the global field.

At this point it might well be fruitfully emphasized that, quite separately, Immanuel Wallerstein took, or was about to take, a somewhat parallel path—moving from the study of development or modernization to the study of the world as a whole. From this point on, my own work was characterized by a continuing attempt to synthesize what had been—and still are, although to a much lesser extent—considered to be more or less separate disciplines. Nettl tragically died in an airplane crash in the fall of 1968, but I continued to work and publish on the same lines upon which we had collaborated, although I veered more in the direction of a focus on religion and culture than would probably have been the case had we been able to continue our collabora-tion. In fact, much of my own work was to analyze what I later came to call globalization—even later, glocalization—from within the intersection of the sociology of religion and the sociology of culture. Here it should be said that during the period in question both religion and culture were low down the totem pole of disciplines or subdisciplines of the social sciences. This was in great contrast to the present circumstance, in which culture and religion are two of the major foci of the social sciences, in spite of what is presently called the new atheism. In this sociological turn toward culture and religion, Tirya-kian's endeavors have paralleled or overlapped with my own.

To retrace my steps somewhat, I should refer to a paper that I gave with JoAnn Klepin (subsequently Chirico) in 1980 at Syracuse at the annual meet-ing of ISCSC, titled "The Modern Emergence of Concern with the Human Condition: A Working Paper." Among other features of this as yet unpublished paper was the emphasis upon the absence of concern in sociology and most other disciplines with the issue of humanity, in spite of a rapidly increasing interest in the theme of human rights. Specifically, we focused upon what we called "humanitic" (as contrasted with humanistic) themes. A central feature of the elaborated program was the insistence upon the ways in which, as the world became very problematically "united" (*as opposed to unified*), conflicts of various kinds would arise. This, we claimed, would largely be centered upon "the increasing relativization of everything." The idea of relativization has continued to inform my work ever since, including more recently the relativ-ization of Planet Earth.

A useful indication of this could be found in a paper that I published titled "From Secularization to Globalization" (Robertson 1987). Much more impor-tant, however, was the paper that I coauthored with JoAnn Chirico in 1985, titled "Humanity, Globalization and Worldwide Religious Resurgence," *Socio-logical Analysis* 46 (3). (It might be remarked here that this paper was rejected by a number of other journals!) The article brought together, in a much more systematic manner than had been published before, the themes of international relations (or what Parsons called the system of modern societies); the study of individual societies (or nation-states); individual selves; and what has become the increasingly vital theme of humanity and, indeed, post-humanity.

4

Two of the most basic issues involved in attempting to delineate the sphere of global studies are its scope and its historical length. In other words the issues of comparison and comparativity, on the one hand, and history and historicity, on the other, are pivotal in any project endeavoring to define this sphere. One should also emphasize that any form of delineation does not have to be static. Indeed, I would go further and maintain that global studies is/are and should be, in a condition of "permanent revolution"—and that this characteristic is essential to any declaration as to the novelty and innovatory status of global studies. In this particular sense, any answer to the question as to what is meant by "global studies" must inevitably be met by the response that it is basically indefinable or, perhaps less controversially, in a (welcome) state of continual flux. This thesis may well remind some of Nietzsche's contention that any phenomenon that has a history cannot, nor should be, securely defined.

At this stage, the discussion might well be illustrated by Mark Mazower's book, *Governing the World: The History of an Idea* (2012). Mazower explores the history of international governance from 1815 until the present. This book is an important case study that I have chosen more or less randomly. Quite apart from the book's intrinsic value, it is of particular relevance here because it touches briefly on the subject of globalization, but is mainly concerned with ideological conflicts, or what Steger calls "global imaginaries," and such crucial issues as the standard of civilization (Robertson 1992: 115–37). In fact, nothing could demonstrate better than Mazower's book the "slippage" between the study of globalization and global studies in general. I say this partly because the phrase *global studies* is not mentioned in the entire book, even though it is obvious that the book itself might well constitute pivotal reading in any course on global studies. *Governing the World* does not by any means confine itself to the study of international relations; therefore, the book is not easily classifiable in conventional disciplinary terms. (Mazower holds the positions of professor of World Order Studies as well as professor of history, at Columbia University, New York.)

Another example, or case study, is *A World Connecting: 1870–1945*, edited by Emily Rosenberg (2012). In spite of its relative inattention to what I have called global consciousness, this book does not even include "globalization" in its index. This, in a book over eleven hundred pages in length, with five sections by different authors, and covering such a wide range of topics as global empires, migrations, commodity chains and transnationality. Here again, but in a somewhat different way, one finds the kind of book that might well be central to a program in global studies, but also to a course on globalization.

A third case study is provided by Robert Rydell in his *All the World's a Fair* (1984). This makes absolutely no mention of the concept of globalization (nor, certainly, glocalization) nor even any mention of global or globality. This book is a study of imperial visions that were shown in American international expositions in the period 1876 through 1916. Clearly, these discussions of eight exhibitions, or expositions, in a number of US cities, set out to demonstrate that these occasions, attended by nearly a hundred million visitors, and with participants from a wide variety of countries, were manifestations of American hegemonic projects—including the fact that the fairs served as reminders of the belief that, in the United States, the people were sovereign. On the other hand, Rydell insists that the (not so subliminal) message of the fairs in general was the proposition that America was culturally and racially superior to the rest of the world. In fact, Rydell's book stands in the tradition of exhibiting that in one country the leaders could show, by displaying what we would now call "global variety," that their country was, paradoxically, superior to others.

The latter was, in fact, a trope that had begun well before this period, with the first steps in showing that one demonstrates one's superiority by exhibiting the power and influence to show great variety and difference. It would, of course, be remiss to omit mention of the irony of holding these exhibitions at a time when racial and ethnic relations in the United States were particularly heinous. It must, however, be emphasized that many of the "ethnological" displays of peoples regarded as racially inferior were endorsed by major anthropologists, who thereby lent scientific credibility to existing negative racial stereotypes. Again, in a somewhat paradoxical way, this openness to the world was, and still is, the flip side of American insularity. The world is there to be gazed upon and, by and large, not to be visited or directly experienced.

As I have previously remarked, the idea that global studies is, or are, to be equated with the study of globalization is a shibboleth. However, a bridge between the two may well be found via the concept of glocalization. In my own work over the past twenty years or more I have increasingly employed the concept of glocalization as transcending the distinction between the local and the global (e.g., Robertson 1994, 1995, 2014a, 2014b). This has been done largely as a way of stressing the significance of heterogeneity in contrast to the dominant tendency for many globalization theorists to emphasize homogeneity (at least until very recently). Glocalization enables us to both synthesize and transcend sameness and difference. Specifically, global phenomena always have to be applied or implemented "locally." Moreover, what may be called glocality enables us to bring together systematically comparative and global perspectives. This confluence is necessitated, particularly in view of the fact that in many global studies programs virtually no distinction is made between comparative and global analyses.

The bridge between globalization and global studies may consist in the fact that glocalization—and its relation, glocality—highlights and directly addresses sociocultural difference. In this respect both globalization, when expressed as glocalization, is much closer to the typical themes dealt with in global-studies programs—largely because it avoids the strictly temporal connotations of globalization, and particularly because the purely temporal connotation of globalization intensifies the tendency to think of it as a homogenizing process.

Global studies has many parallels with cultural studies (not to speak of substantive overlaps). A similar problem arises with respect to the difference, if any, between cultural studies, cultural sociology and the sociology of culture. Here again we confront the problem of demarcation, a problem that is partly intellectual but largely administrative. Moreover, each of the "disciplines" or "subdisciplines" should and must be regarded as bases of power creation, meaning that they are often rhetorically constructed so as to create new academic–administrative sites, upon which power may be generated. Here it might be remarked that there has recently come into existence a field of study called "synthetic biology," a field that apparently brings back together perspectives that had previously become separated from each other. Something like this may well happen in the intellectual orientations with which I am dealing here. Indeed, I will be advocating precisely this kind of synthesis, while acknowledging that the administrative and disciplinary barriers to such remain formidable.

As I have previously remarked, many programs, books and other pronouncements in so-called global studies try to convey the idea that adding one society to another makes it more global—or, indeed—in itself global. One can readily see this practice in the increasing use of the subtitle to books: "a global perspective." This, in fact, overlaps considerably with the common practice in contemporary advertising that involves such phrases as "the new global style," "global opulence," "global tones" (cosmetics), "global grilling" (food), "global interiors" (home furnishings), and so on. The proximity of such phrases as "a global perspective" and the use of a phrase like "global style" illustrate the ways in which branding is to be frequently found within everyday commercial, as well as purely intellectual, contexts (Lury, Franklin and Stacey 2000).

When all is said and done, the line between globalization and global studies is, to say the least, by no means clear-cut. What is exceedingly clear is that while global studies is much broader than globalization/glocalization—that is, more inclusive—nevertheless, globalization/glocalization must surely be its pivotal, not to say fundamental, concept. Often, even when globalization is not explicitly mentioned in a particular article or book, it is very frequently there by default.

However, particularly in the light of developments in anthropology, on the one hand, and even more important, astronomy and astrophysics on the other, we must now take a much more serious and skeptical look at the very concept of the global. Nevertheless, as interest in what was long ago called the great chain of being (Lovejoy 1936) has been revived, and particularly the place of man (in the generic sense of the latter) in this "chain" in relation to what lies beyond this planet, we should now reconsider what we mean by "the global." Most importantly, we must thoroughly confront the fact that the globe, or Planet Earth, has been *relativized*. It is most unfortunate that the entire issue of the relation of Copernicus, Galileo and their successors to the almost obsessive concern with Planet Earth in the study of globalization has been so grossly neglected. I say this in full awareness of the increasing significance of such issues as climate change, global warming and, more generally, sustainability (not to speak of much current talk of the end of the world as we know it). The recent work by such people as Adam Frank, particularly in his *About Time* (2011) has brought the entire problem of the double meaning of cosmology into sharp focus. The content of Frank's book is well illustrated by its long subtitle: *From Sun Dials to Quantum Clocks, How the Cosmos Shapes Our Lives—and We Shape the Cosmos*. The issue with which Frank is particularly concerned is clear in his main question: What happened before the "Big Bang?" Posing this question requires him/us to dwell on the issue of consciousness or, to put it another way, "personal time and cosmic time have been linked from the earliest origins of culture" (Frank 2012: xviii).

Retrospectively, we must now recognize that students of globalization and, indeed, of global studies, have been guilty of a great neglect of what has been called "cosmic society" (Dickens and Ormrod 2007). Invocation of the latter should not be interpreted as a complete stamp of approval, since Dickens and Ormrod came to think of space exploration and potential colonization of other planets as an extension of "normal" imperialism and what they call the "humanitization of outer space." In contrast, in addition to Adam Frank, one should also invoke the work of such writers as Nagel (2012), Evans (2014), Unger and Smolin (2015) and Nancy and Barrau (2015). These authors attempt to combine anthropological thought with astronomical thought, or philosophical thought with physical thought; and thus they bring completely new light to the study of globality. In this sense, we can now better appreciate the double meaning of cosmology, which is well expressed by Frank's question concerning what happened before the "Big Bang." As he says, "personal time and cosmic time have been linked from the earliest origins of culture" (Frank 2012: xviii); and, he also remarks that we invented culture and in doing so we invented ourselves.

5

In the preceding I have discussed various aspects of what has come to be called global studies. However, I have not in any way attempted to be exhaustive or all-encompassing. Moreover, I have periodically connected my arguments to the work of Edward Tiryakian, although only in a relatively skeletal way. Much more substantive themes are addressed by other chapters in this volume. It should also be said that in various parts of the world there are now programs in, or schools of, global studies, not to speak of organizations with that same title. To take but one example, in Russia what in the West is called global studies is there called "globalistics." In fact, this term covers much more intellectual ground than does global studies. However, if we come to one of the more important points of the present chapter, I must emphasize once again that global studies is certainly not identical to the study of globalization. A casual glance at various programs of global studies associations in different countries would more than substantiate this claim.

Note

1 It should be emphasized that UCIS supported me in various ways throughout the period 1968–97.

References

Cohen, R. and P. Kennedy. 2007. *Global Sociology*. London and New York: Palgrave Macmillan.

Evans, G. R. 2014. *First Light: A History of Creation Myths from Gilgamesh to the God-particle*. London and New York: I. B. Tauris & Co. Ltd.

Frank, A. 2011. *About Time: From Sun Dials to Quantum Clocks, How the Cosmos Shapes Our Lives—and We Shape the Cosmos*. New York: Free Press.

Franklin, S. L. C. and J. Stacey. 2000. *Global Nature, Global Culture*. London: Sage.

Huntington, S. 1993. "The Clash of Civilizations?" *Foreign Affairs* 72, no. 3: 22–49.

Huntington, S. 1996. *The Clash of Civilizations and the Remaking of World Order*. New York: Simon & Schuster.

James, P. and M. B. Steger. 2004. "A Genealogy of 'Globalization': The Career of a Concept." *Globalizations* 11, no. 4: 417–572.

Lovejoy, A. O. 1936. *The Great Chain of Being: A Study of the History of an Idea*. New York: Harper & Row.

Mazower, M. 2012. *Governing the World: The History of an Idea.* London: Penguin Books.

Nettl, J. P. and R. Robertson. 1968. *International Systems and the Modernization of Societies: The Formation of National Goals and Attitudes.* New York: Basic Books.

Pieterse, J. N. 2013. "What Is Global Studies?" *Globalizations* 10, no. 4: 499–514.

Prinz, J. J. 2012. *Beyond Human Nature: How Culture and Experience Shape Our Lives.* London: Allen Lane.

Robertson, R. 1983. "Interpreting Globality." In *World Realities and International Studies Today*, 7–20. Glenside: Pennsylvania Council on International Education.

———— 1987. "From Secularization to Globalization." *Journal of Oriental Studies* 26, no. 1: 28–32.

———— 1992. *Globalization: Social Theory and Global Culture.* London: Sage.

———— 1994. "Globalisation or Glocalisation?" *Journal of International Communication* 1, no. 1: 33–52.

———— 1995. "Glocalization: Time–Space and Homogeneity–Heterogeneity." In *Global Modernities*, edited by M. Featherstone, S. Lash and R. Robertson, 25–44. London: Sage.

———— 1996. "Globality, Globalization and Transdisciplinarity." *Theory, Culture and Society* 13, no. 4: 127–32.

———— 2011. "Global Connectivity and Global Consciousness." *American Behavioral Scientist* 55, no. 10: 1336–45.

———— 2012a. "Early Academic Approaches to Global Studies." In *Encyclopedia of Global Studies*, edited by M. Jurgensmeyer and H. Anheier. London: Sage. DOI:http://dx.doi.org/10.4135/9781452218557.

———— 2012b. "Civilization(s), Ethnoracism, Antisemitism, Sociology." In *Antisemitism and the Constitution of Sociology*, edited by M. Stoeltzer, 206–45. Lincoln and London: University of Nebraska Press.

———— 2014a. "Situating Glocalization: A Relatively Autobiographical Intervention." In *Global Fields and Local Variations in Organizations and Management: Perspectives on Glocalization*, edited by G. S. Drori, M. A. Hollerer and P. Walgenbach, 25–36. London: Routledge.

———— 2014b, ed. *European Glocalization in Global Context.* London: Palgrave Macmillan.

Robertson, R. and J. Chirico. 1985. "Humanity, Globalization and Worldwide Religious Resurgence: A Theoretical Exploration." *Sociological Analysis* 45, no. 4: 219–42.

Robertson, R. and D. Buhari-Gulmez, eds. 2016. *Global Culture: Consciousness and Connectivity.* Farnham: Ashgate.

Rosenberg, E. S., ed. 2012. *A World Connecting: 1870–1945.* Cambridge, MA: Harvard University Press.

Rydell, R. W. 1984. *All the World's a Fair: Visions of Empire at American International Expositions, 1876–1916.* Chicago: University of Chicago Press.

Sahlins, M. 2000. *Culture in Practice: Selected Essays.* New York: Zone Books.

Steger, M. B. 2008. *The Rise of the Global Imaginary: Political Ideologies from the French Revolution to the Global War on Terror.* Oxford: Oxford University Press.

Tiryakian, E. A., ed. 1963. *Sociological Theory, Values, and Sociocultural Change: Essays in Honor of Pitirim Sorokin.* New York: The Free Press of Glencoe.

————, ed. 2013. *Sociological Theory, Values, and Sociocultural Change: Essays in Honor of Pitirim Sorokin.* New Brunswick, NJ, and London: Transaction Publishers.

Unger, R. M. and L. Smolin. 2015. *The Singular Universe and the Reality of Time: A Proposal in Natural Philosophy.* Cambridge: Cambridge University Press.

Chapter 8

HONORING EDWARD TIRYAKIAN AS A METASOCIOLOGIST: A METACONCEPTUAL ANALYSIS OF PROSUMPTION AND RELATED CONCEPTS

George Ritzer

Ed Tiryakian may not have thought of himself as a meta-analyst, or of what he was doing as meta-analysis, but he, and a very large proportion of his work, fit under those headings. At times, his meta-analytical orientation was quite clear in work on such topics as the "metacultures" of modernity (Tiryakian 1996); the presuppositions of macrosociology (Tiryakian 1992); and the sociology of sociology (Tiryakian 1971). Much more often he did this kind of analysis more implicitly in, for example, his work on sociology in general (Tiryakian 2001), on a wide range of sociological theorists (especially Emile Durkheim), sociological schools (Tiryakian 1986, 1979) and theoretical integration and synthesis (Tiryakian 1990).

While I have not done a great deal of meta-analytic work in recent years, I will return to it in this essay as a way of paying tribute to Ed. This essay will also serve as a way of extending in some new directions my recent work on what might be thought of, in Ed's terms, as a neo-modern concept: prosumption. This concept is meant to subsume the clearly modern concepts of production and consumption. I begin by outlining my thinking on prosumption. In the process, I will be doing a kind of meta-analysis—*metaconceptual analysis*—that I and others have not previously differentiated from other, better-known forms of meta-analysis (especially, metatheory, metamethods, metadata analysis). Tiryakian (1981), himself, has done such metaconceptual work—for example, in his essay on Weber's "iron cage" metaphor.

That is not to say there is any shortage of work in sociology and many other fields devoted explicitly to such conceptual analysis (e.g., Bulmer 1979). Best-known, at least at one time and in certain circles, was some of the early work of Raymond Boudon (1968), which dealt, in part, with *explication de texte*. This is defined as "the identification of the current uses of a term in different traditions and the specification of its meaning based on its common dimensions" (Hamlin, forthcoming). While work on *explication de texte* was not done under the heading of meta-analysis, that is clearly what was being undertaken in such work. More generally, meta-analysis and, in particular, metaconceptual analysis, have been inherent aspects of sociology since its inception.

In line with Boudon's sense of *explication de text*, the main objective here will be to look at some of prosumption's most important cognate terms with the objective of better specifying the meaning of the concept of prosumption.

Clarifying the Concept of Prosumption

There is little or no ambiguity about what is meant by production and consumption,[1] but what is prosumption? The process of prosumption involves the interrelationship of production and consumption where it becomes difficult, if not impossible, to clearly and unequivocally distinguish one from the other.[2] As we will see, it is hard to avoid using the terms production and consumption, especially because the term prosumption itself involves a fusion of those two concepts. However, when production and consumption are mentioned in this essay we are dealing with them as extreme types, or moments, in the overarching process of prosumption.

In the future we need to go even further and get away as completely as possible from thinking in terms of, and using the concepts of, production and consumption. This is because production *always and in all settings* involves consumption (Marx, among others, acknowledges this but does not emphasize it in his work on nineteenth-century capitalism) and, conversely, consumption *always and in all settings* involves production. This is especially clear in work on the media,[3] as well as on, among other domains, brands and branding (see below). In other words, production and consumption have always been prosumption processes or, to put it another way, prosumption is a hybrid that always involves a mix of production and consumption. *There is no such thing as either pure production (without at least some consumption) or pure consumption (without at least some production); the two processes always interpenetrate.* This is the case which-ever one—production or consumption—seems to predominate in any par-ticular setting and at any given point in history. Even if they did not have the concept, sociologists, social theorists and other students of society should have *always* focused on prosumption. At best, production and consumption should have been treated as special limiting cases of prosumption, as "ideal types" (Weber 1949 [1903/1917]: 90). As ideal types, pure production and consumption do not exist in the "real world" economy, but they may be useful in helping us to analyze it. However, even that accords production and consumption too much importance since, from the point of view of this discussion, they are merely types, albeit extreme types, of prosumption.

From the perspective of this conceptual discussion of prosumption, production and consumption are what Ulrich Beck (2001) called "zombie concepts." In Beck's work the nation-state in the age of globalization is such a concept. That is, the nation-state continues to "live on," to survive, as a concept in the contemporary context, even though it is of reduced importance and being undermined by global processes (e.g., terrorism, the flow of drugs) that it cannot control and that, in some cases, increasingly control it. The nation-state is one of the "living dead" that litter the social and conceptual landscape. The concepts of production and consumption were of questionable utility even in the heydays of producer and consumer capitalism, but they are clearly zombie concepts today in what can be called "prosumer capitalism" (Ritzer forthcoming). They have always served to obscure the more fundamental process of prosumption, and that is clearly a far greater problem in prosumer capitalism in which the process is increasingly obvious and omnipresent.

Thus, to the degree that we continue to think in terms of production and consumption, we need to conceptualize both as subtypes, and in terms, of prosumption. Rather than thinking as we normally do in terms of production and consumption, we should think—we should have *always* thought—in terms of "prosumption-as-production" (p-a-p) and "prosumption-as-consumption" (p-a-c). It is these concepts (*not* production and consumption) that constitute the two ends of the prosumption continuum (see Figure 8.1) that lies at the base of this discussion and analysis. It is at the midpoint of that continuum that p-a-p and p-a-c are more or less evenly weighted—where a "balanced" form of prosumption exists. Had social thinkers thought in terms of, and operated with, such a continuum they would not have erred wildly in thinking, mainly in either-or terms, of production (e.g., Marx 1967 [1867]) and consumption (e.g., Baudrillard 1998 [1970]), or in labeling societies as either producer or consumer societies. The fact is that *all* economic processes and societies *always* involve a mix of production and consumption. In that sense,

p-a-p	Balanced Prosumption	p-a-c
Prosumption-as-Production		Prosumption-as-Consumption

Figure 8.1   The prosumption continuum

p-a-p	**Balanced Production & Consumption**	p-a-c
Production & Consumption Phases		Consumption & Production Phases

Figure 8.2   The prosumption continuum with phases of production and consumption

"pure" production and "pure" consumption are theoretical possibilities, but they are empirical impossibilities. Rather, we need to think in terms of differences in degrees and types of prosumption.

Although they are usually seamlessly intertwined, we also need to distinguish between the "consumption" and "production" phases[1] of p-a-p, as well as of p-a-c (see Figure 8.2). The utility of this distinction, as well as of the prosumption continuum more generally, will be clarified in the ensuing discussion.

P-a-p involves those (typically thought of as workers) who consume what is needed in order to be able to produce goods, services and so forth, with what they have consumed. In this, we are distinguishing between the time during, and the process in which, a p-a-p consumes and produces. It takes a p-a-p[5] time and energy both to produce and to consume during the prosumption process. For example, while putting hubcaps on a car in the assembly process, it takes time and energy to put the hubcaps on (the production phase), but also to retrieve them from where they are stored (the consumption phase). This distinction seems trivial, but it is important to the general conceptualization of prosumption.

P-a-c involves those (usually seen as consumers) who produce what is needed in order to be able to consume goods and services. Here, the distinction is between the time during, and the process in which, p-a-cs produce and consume. As with p-a-ps, it takes p-a-cs time and energy to produce and consume. For example, while eating in a fast-food restaurant, it takes time and energy not only to eat the food (consume it), but also to produce the meanings associated both with the fast food restaurant and the meal eaten. More importantly, in order to consume the meal p-a-cs must increasingly engage in physical tasks such as lining up to order their food, carrying their trays to their table, and pouring their soft drinks. The "work" done by p-a-cs is of increasing importance in prosumer society.

While the models presented in Figures 8.1 and 8.2 are applicable to all types of societies and social institutions, the major focus here is its applicability to the economy, specifically the contemporary capitalist economy, as it exists in the developed world. In that context, we are interested in prosumption in material brick-and-mortar settings (e.g., IKEA, McDonald's, banks with ATMs), its predominance in the digital world (e.g., Wikipedia, eBay and its Stubhub, Craigslist, Expedia, Facebook, blogs, citizen journalism), as well as its most recent manifestations in business (e.g., Uber, Airbnb), which seamlessly link the material and digital worlds. While prosumption is ubiquitous in contemporary capitalism—as it has been at all times and in all economic systems (Ritzer 2014)—its crucial importance and its centrality on the Internet, as well as the latter's connection to the material world, which is serving to elevate it from obscurity to, arguably, a defining economic concept of our age (Ritzer, Dean and Jurgenson 2012).

In general, the prosumption that takes place on digital, especially social media, sites (in addition to Facebook, examples include Twitter, Snapchat, Pinterest, Foursquare), lies toward the middle of the prosumption continuum; little that takes place there can be mistaken for anything approaching extreme p-a-p or p-a-c. We are more likely to find activities that lie closer to those polar alternatives in the material world. P-a-p is more the norm in factories and offices while p-a-c is more likely to predominate in malls and fast-food restaurants.

It seems as if a clear distinction is being made here between the material and the immaterial (especially the digital), but it is important to understand that no such clear differentiation exists in the "real" world. On the one hand, all material realities have innumerable immaterial aspects. For example, many meanings are associated with the daily trip to and from work. A similarly wide range of meanings and feelings are associated with a shopping trip to, say, Wal-Mart. In addition, many other feelings and emotions are likely to be associated with specific work-related tasks and encounters with coworkers or with particular products purchased or in dealings with cashiers.

On the other hand, it is also the case that a range of material realities are associated with our digital experiences, especially the computers, tablets and smartphones that are needed for those experiences. Then there are the material realities (a rise in the stock market) that lead to a visit to a digital site (where stocks can be purchased), as well as the material consequences of such a visit (the addition of shares of stock to one's portfolio). Of great recent importance in this context is the increasing interpenetration of the digital and the material made possible by mobile technologies such as smartphones and tablets. For example, Foursquare is an app used on smartphones and tablets that allows us to let others know where we are physically (e.g., a bar, a location in the mall) and to provide them with information and feelings about those locations. It also allows others to proceed to those locations, perhaps to meet us, if they so choose, as well as to express their views about those locations or on meeting us at one of them. The lending of money on Zopa, renting domiciles on Airbnb, and the offering of car rides on Uber are all made possible by computers, the Internet and smartphones.

What all of this points to is the fact that we need to avoid the material–digital or, more generally, the material–immaterial, dualism in thinking about prosumption in any kind of setting. In fact, prosumption itself overcomes another dualism, that of production and consumption. Indeed, all of these distinctions are modern binaries that prevent us from a more accurate conception of the social and economic worlds. Jurgenson (2012) has aptly critiqued the tendency toward "digital dualism" in thinking about the digital world of the Internet as somehow entirely different from the material, offline world. Similarly, we need to avoid the "Internet-centrism" that plagues much of the analysis of the Internet. The Internet needs to be seen as imbricated in the material world, and vice versa, creating an "augmented reality" (Jurgenson 2012). Uber, among others, well illustrates the idea of augmented reality. Another good example is "showrooming," whereby people shop on their smartphones while they are shopping in department stores (Clifford 2012).

Returning to Figure 8.1, p-a-p involves what we have traditionally thought of as "producers" (but conceived of here as *both* producing and consuming workers; as those who must inevitably consume various goods and services in the process of production). P-a-p is clear in Marx's work and is the primary meaning associated with the concept of prosumption by most analysts. As a result of Marx's (and that of many others) prioritization of production, work on p-a-p, and on prosumption more generally, tends to have a productivist bias.[6] However, to Marx, producers (that is the proletariat) must consume a variety of goods and services in order to produce. For example, workers must consume raw materials, tools and machines, the services provided by many others, as well as their own labor time. There can be no production without consumption in the factories of interest to Marx. Indeed, it is safe to say that there can never be any production without consumption.

However, it is important to accord similar, if not equal, weight to p-a-c (prosumption-as-consumption). (By the way, it needs to be made clear that p-a-ps and p-a-cs often involve the same people who both produce and consume, often at more or less the same time.[7]) To the degree that it has been recognized, at least implicitly, p-a-c has been subordinated to p-a-p because of an overwhelming productivist bias. As we have seen, just as p-a-ps (prosumers-as-producers) must consume, p-a-cs (prosumers-as-consumers; or "producing consumers") must produce (Dujarier 2014) or work (Rieder and Voss 2010). This has always been the case (at the minimum, p-a-cs must produce some of the meanings associated with what it means to be consumers, what they consume, where they consume it, and the process by which they consume it). However, the production associated with consumption is especially important in the case of contemporary prosumption. This is true in various ways and in a variety of venues.

The most obvious of these venues are the increasing number of material settings in which p-a-cs must now not only consume, but also must do work performed at one time by paid employees. In her typology of "consumer work," Dujarier labels this "self-service work." P-a-cs "work" in such settings as fast-food restaurants: serving as waiters, buspersons, and in the case of the drive-through window as waste collectors, taking their garbage with them and then disposing of it (Ritzer 2015); banks: depositing and withdrawing money at ATMs rather than having that work done for them by bank tellers (Ritzer 1995); supermarkets: wandering the aisles, checking prices on scanners throughout the markets, loading up their wagons, and increasingly working as clerks on self-checkout lines as they scan their own purchases and as baggers of those purchases; department stores, where p-a-cs are increasingly largely on their own to find what they are looking for because fewer and fewer paid employees are being hired to help them; and perhaps most notably and interestingly in IKEA where, in addition to engaging in many of the activities described above, p-a-cs sometimes put together their own purchases (e.g., the Billy bookcase).

All "consumption" and "consumption settings" demand immaterial work, but this work is required more than ever in the newer and more elaborate "cathedrals of consumption" such as megamalls, cruise ships, theme parks and casino-hotels (Ritzer 2010). These are created to be spectacular and to be defined as such by those who frequent them (Debord 1977). While much of the basis for those definitions is provided by the sites themselves (great size, a multitude of attractions, a spectacle), those who visit them must often have those definitions in mind and be able to refresh and even enhance them during their visit. The cathedrals of consumption need such definitions and redefinitions in order to attract the large numbers of visitors they require to be profitable and, more importantly, to keep them coming back over and over, as well as to interest others in visiting these sites. This is an example of collaborative coproduction, Dujarier's second type of consumer work.[8]

The importance of immaterial work is especially obvious at media events, especially today's mega-events. Potential audience members (Bruns 2008; Smythe 1977, 1981), especially "fans" (Jenkins 2006), engage in immaterial work before, during and after such events. The centrality of immaterial work by audience members has come to be increasingly recognized by media scholars (Jenkins, Ford and Green 2013). At one time those who studied the media tended to see audiences as passive consumers of the content being produced and promulgated by the media. However, that view has long been rejected and replaced by a view of the audience as, in the terms of this analysis, actively producing (defining, interpreting, etc.) content as they consume it (for more on this, see below). The same point is made about brands. Brand meanings are not simply produced by marketers and advertisers, but they are actively produced by the very people who consume branded products (Arvidsson 2005).

Prosumption: A Metaconceptual Analysis

Beyond the work on prosumption, we have seen the creation and flowering of work on a wide range of concepts in a number of different fields that seek to get at the essence of this development broadly conceived. While there are significant differences among them, they all serve to break down binaries as well as to reject the binary thinking that has served to inhibit the development of many disciplines in the modern era. Several of these bodies of conceptual work are explored below (including some by sociologists) with the objective of investigating their relationship to the concept of prosumption and examining to what degree they help clarify sociological thinking on that concept.

As pointed out earlier, there are several extant versions of metasociology, including metatheory, metamethods and metadata analysis. In any case, this essay makes the case for the addition of metaconceptual analysis. The goal in such work is to analyze a variety of related or similar concepts in a number of fields in order to clarify the nature of a concept in a given field. In this case, the goal of the metaconceptual analysis is the clarification of the concept of prosumption.

In terms of my earlier work on meta-analysis (specifically metatheorizing) (Ritzer 1991), we will engage here specifically in Mu,[9] or meta-analysis (in this case metaconceptual analysis) as a means of attaining a deeper understanding of the concept of prosumption. There are four subtypes of Mu (internal–intellectual, internal–social, external–intellectual, external–social). In this essay we mainly undertake an external–intellectual form of metaconceptual analysis in looking at ideas largely outside of sociology and their implications for attaining a better understanding of the sociological concept of prosumption. However, we will also look at some work within sociology in an internal–intellectual analysis. Due to space limitations we will not concern ourselves with social factors (either internal or external) although, obviously, the external–social factors (i.e., the expansion of, and social changes in, prosumption sites, especially on the Internet) are of huge importance for the development of work on the concept of prosumption.

Perhaps the oldest idea related to prosumption, going back a century or more, but gaining centrality in the 1950s, is "do-it-yourself" (DIY) (Watson and Shove 2008). This idea, common in many fields (e.g., business-oriented consumer research) and in the social world, is that without outside help, especially professional, people consume (e.g., raw materials) and produce on their own. In that sense, DIY clearly overlaps with the concept of prosumption. In addition, the process of DIY itself has expanded greatly in recent years with the development of businesses that make DIY easier (e.g., Home Depot) as well as the Internet, where people have little choice but to do it themselves. While the concept is of considerable interest, it is flawed from the point of view of this discussion because, like many other ideas in the modern world, it has a "productivist bias" with its emphasis on doing (producing) things and largely downplaying the consumption aspect of the process (Ritzer and Slater 2001).

The concept of the "craft consumer" obviously avoids that bias, at least to some degree, by seeming to foreground the consumer even though the term "craft" comes first and emphasizes a particular kind of more skilled production (Campbell 2005). Thus, the craft consumer can be seen as a skilled DIYer, as well as a kind of prosumer. Thus, the concept does emphasize both production and consumption, although it accords undue emphasis on the skilled character of production. In fact, for prosumption to take place, its productive aspects need not involve a high degree of skill and, in most cases, often involves work requiring little or no skill.

The concept of the "pro-am" deals with *am*ateurs who work up to *pro*fessional standards, for example, citizen-scientists in astronomy (Leadbetter and Miller 2004). While this idea also has a productivist bias, Leadbetter and Miller are not focally interested in either production or consumption, but rather in the status (mostly amateur) of those involved. Pro-ams can be seen as prosumers: for example, amateurs in astronomy are considered capable of collecting (consuming) information on the heavens and producing highly professional research on what they find. However, the issue of whether a prosumer is a professional, an amateur, or some combination of the two (a pro-am) is of little utility in advancing our understanding of prosumption. Further, both professionals and amateurs, as well as those who combine those statuses, engage in prosumption.

As is obvious from the title and thrust of this essay, my personal favorite in this conceptual realm is the term *prosumption*, coined not by a sociologist, but by the futurist Alvin Toffler (1980; Toffler and Toffler 2006). Toffler was a popular thinker without a disciplinary home, but influential in many fields. Interestingly, even though the concept of prosumption was central to his work, it got little attention for several decades. It tended to get lost in all of the focus on Toffler's broader, sexier and futuristic idea of "future shock." However, the last decade has witnessed a significant body of work dealing with, or using, the idea of prosumption.

The term prosumer is preferred to many others because even though it seems to privilege *pro*ducer over con*sumer* ("pro" comes before "sumer"), it potentially gives equal weight to both; it could have just as easily been labeled "conducer." Toffler undoubtedly chose prosumer—and probably did not even consider a term like conducer—because of his own productivist bias. Thus, in spite of our effort to use it in a more balanced way, prosumption does seem, at least in a formal, terminological sense, to prioritize production.

Avery Bruns (2008) created concepts—produser and produsage—that have been particularly influential in media studies. While he does not explicitly use the idea of a productivist bias, that ultimately is why he rejected adopting Toffler's term prosumer and substituted the produser. What especially rankled Bruns was the subordination of the consumer to the producer in Toffler's terminology and work, as well as in much of the recent reconceptualization of, and work on, the topic. To Bruns, the use of the consumer in the term prosumer imparts a passive sense since, historically, the consumer has been seen as largely passive in the face of the more active producer. Hence, Bruns replaces the consumer with the more active user in the concept of the produser. Thus, Bruns's concept of the produser has more balance between producer and user (consumer) than the prosumer concept, but it sounds odd to most ears and, as a result, has been influential mainly in its home discipline—media studies.

Bruns is building on a very active tradition and wide body of work in media studies that focuses on the audience (and fans) as active producers of media events. An important theoretical source of this work is deCerteau's (1984: 34) romantic and powerful image of consumers as "unrecognized poets of their own affairs" and as "trailblazers in the jungles of functionalist rationality." They are accorded considerable power and independence as "poets" and "trailblazers," but we must not forget that they are operating within the constraints of structures that are in accord with, and the product of, functionalist rationality.

Of central importance in this tradition in media studies is the work of Stuart Hall (Hall et al. 1980), especially his distinction between the concepts of *encoding and decoding*. Broadcasting structures such as those associated with television emit "encoded" messages that are embedded in specific programs. However, to have an effect, these programs and their meanings must be "decoded" by the audience. In other words, the audience must do interpretive work in order to understand the meanings of a TV program and for those meanings to have an effect on them. Indeed, the objective fact of TV discourse and the subjective interpretive work of the audience cannot be clearly separated from one another; they are dialectically related. Thus, Hall rejects the idea, associated with the Frankfurt School, of the power of the media and their control over the audience.

To Dallas Smythe (1977: 3) "all non-sleeping time of most of the population is work time." Included in the "work" done during this period is "essential marketing functions for the producers of consumers' goods" (Smythe 1977: 3). Advertisers are seen as buying the marketing services of the audience. Audiences work for advertisers by creating the demand for products. They "learn to buy particular 'brands' of consumer goods, and to spend their income accordingly" (Smythe 1977: 6). In so doing, they "complete the production process of consumer goods" (Smythe 1977: 6).

Henry Jenkins (2006) developed the concepts of *participatory culture* and *convergence culture*. Participatory culture is one in which fans (a main concern in Jenkins's work) are not mere spectators but active participants; fandom is a specific form of participatory culture. He defines convergence culture as the place where the power of the media producer and the media consumer interact unpredictably (Jenkins 2006). His primary interest is to counteract the idea of the passive media spectator with the ideas of spectators performing work and as consumers engaged in active participation. This is especially the case with new technologies empowering audiences who are demanding the right to participate.

While all of the above conceptualizations are in the social sciences, or influenced by them, similar perspectives have emanated from other disciplines, especially business. The concept of *co-creation* is closely related to the idea of prosumption (Prahalad and Ramaswamy 2004a, 2004b). The creators of this idea are business professors who, not surprisingly, look at this process from a business perspective. As a result, there is no hint of a critical perspective in their sense of co-creation. In fact, the use of the term "creation" implies in their work a positive view of the process for *both* businesses and their customers. Both parties—producers and consumers—are seen as being creators of the co-creation process. Also implied is the idea that both parties are, or at least can be, equally creative in the process. This is traced to "the emergence of connected, informed, empowered and active consumers" (Prahalad and Ramaswamy 2004a: 6). Such consumers are involved in every phase of business and, as such, they co-create (and co-extract) value.

Closely related to the idea of co-creation is another concept from the field of marketing—*service-dominant logic*. The central figures in work on this idea are Stephen L. Vargo and Robert F. Lusch (2004, 2008). They put their work in the context of what they describe as a paradigm shift from a focus on goods-centered systems to those that center on services. Furthermore, while goods and services were in the past treated as distinct from one another, they put the provision of goods in the context of service provision. That is, goods provision involves services of various kinds. For our purposes the key to this argument is the distinction between the positions of customers in these two systems. In goods-centered systems customers are defined as *operand resources* who are "acted on to create transactions with resources." In contrast, in service-centered systems customers are *operant resources* and as such are "active participants in relational exchanges and coproduction" (Vargo and Lusch 2004: 7). The idea that customers are active participants and coproducers brings us very close to the ideas of co-creation (Vargo and Lusch explicitly link their thinking on this to Prahalad and Ramaswamy's work) and prosumption.

Tapscott and Williams (2006) define *Wikinomics* as the "art and science of collaboration" (Tapscott and Williams 2006: 18). The term *collaboration* implies prosumers, since it is they who are collaborating. In addition, Tapscott and Williams operate with an explicit conception of the prosumer. In fact, Chapter 5 is entitled "The Prosumers." Another key and similar term in *Wikinomics* is *peer production*, and this makes it clear that the authors are focusing on the prosumption-as-production end of the prosumption continuum and have little to offer on prosumption-as-consumption.

They correctly argue that the Internet is crucial in this development, especially the transition from Web 1.0 to Web 2.0. While most of what took (takes) place on Web 1.0 was "produced" by those in control of the sites (e.g., Yahoo), Web 2.0 is "about the communities, participation, and peering" (Tapscott and Williams 2006: 19). To put it another way, people were largely passive on Web 1.0, but are active participants on Web 2.0. The book is loaded with many examples of websites, circa 2005, that are characterized to a large degree by prosumption (Flickr, YouTube, googlemaps, Craigslist), as well as activities that inherently involve prosumption such as remixing and mashups.

While collaboration is central to Tapscott and Williams, Botsman and Rogers (2010) focus on *collaborative consumption*. Collaborative consumption overlaps to a considerable degree with a sharing economy (see below), although it also includes transactions with economic gain such as rental, since it involves a search for alternatives to purchasing goods and services. Collaborative consumption includes sharing, lending and swapping. Botsman and Rogers include under this heading both profit-making (e.g., Zipcar, acquired by Avis in 2013) and nonprofit (Freecycle) examples.

Sharing implicitly involves prosumption, with those producing sharing with those consuming; producers and consumers often change roles in the process of sharing. Rifkin (2014) sees the sharing economy as a harbinger of a hoped-for amelioration of the excesses of capitalism, if not as an alternative to that economic system. However, it is difficult to ignore the power, resilience and adaptability of capitalism. Two recent examples demonstrate that it may be the alternatives to it that are in jeopardy, rather than capitalism itself. In Belk's (2014) terms the sharing systems analyzed by him—Zipcar and Couchsurfing—involve "pseudo-sharing," since commercial interests masquerade as communal sharing and intervene in, if not dominate, the process, and profit from the sharing process.

Belk (2014) argues that sharing is being transformed into *pseudo-sharing* by, among other things, the profit-making organizations that have found a way to make money from the sharing economy—such as those discussed in the last few paragraphs. He sees sharing as a *communal* alternative to private owner-ship and profit making. "True sharing" is not about making money, but about "helping and making human connections" (17), or "Money profanes the shar-ing transaction and transforms it into a commodity exchange" (19). When profit motivation is involved, we are talking about pseudo-sharing. The key is intention—do those involved intend to share communally or to exploit shar-ing in order to earn a profit? As Belk (11) puts it: "Pseudo-sharing is a business relationship masquerading as communal sharing."

In sum, in contrast to true sharing, pseudo-sharing involves "egoistic motives, expectations of reciprocity and lack of a sense of community" (16). Inverting this, true sharing is then altruistic, done without an expectation that it will be reciprocated, and those involved have sense of community. The latter involves "sharing in" versus "sharing out," which lacks community and mutu-ality. Sharing in is key because it is "likely only in true sharing" (17). Sharing out stands somewhere between true- and pseudo-sharing.

While Belk's work is critical of pseudo-sharing, it is animated by a roman-tic Archimedean point of true sharing. He clearly hopes that his readers will see the light, back away from pseudo-sharing systems and involve themselves more in true sharing.

Peer-to-peer (P2P) lending sites, such as Zopa, are based on prosumers shar-ing money; that is, lending money to one another, perhaps switching time and again between being borrowers and lenders. However, as P2P lending has grown in importance, large financial, profit-making institutions have become increasingly involved. Further, their participation is not always clear to those interested in borrowing money. This institutional involvement threatens to drive out individual investors interested in lending money, thereby subverting the process of sharing that lies at the base of all P2P systems. Of course, if they are aware of the participation of these institutions, prosumers retain the ability to reject their offerings and to borrow only from other prosumers.

What Have We Learned?

The issue is: What have we learned from this metaconceptual analysis, this "explication" of the concept of prosumption, as well as of a number of simi-lar terms in a number of disciplines: do-it-yourself, craft consumer, pro-am, produser and produsage, encoding and decoding, participatory and conver-gence culture, co-creation, service-dominant logic with operand and operant resources, collaboration, peer production, collaborative consumption, sharing, pseudo-sharing and peer-to-peer?

Above all, meta-analysis of this array of related concepts makes it clear that a set of profound social changes has occurred in recent decades, and that scholars in various disciplines, often in isolation from one another, are struggling to conceptualize and get a better handle on the implications of those changes. The diversity of these changes in many different areas of the social world makes it difficult to fully understand those implications. Furthermore, the underlying social changes in the digital, and especially the material, world are ongoing, and all efforts to understand and conceptualize them are doomed at this point to be, at best, provisional. However, we can at least glean a variety of more specific lessons, albeit also provisional, from this conceptual work:

- no single concept is as yet hegemonic across disciplines, but at the moment prosumption is the most promising and widely accepted term;
- there is no such thing as a "pure" producer or consumer;
- analyses of prosumption must be wary of overemphasizing either production (as does DIY, craft consumer) or consumption (as does collaborative consumption); indeed they should desist from using those terms;
- prosumers can be active, passive or anything in between;
- prosumers can be creative or uncreative;
- prosumption applies to the actions of a single individual taken on his or her own without outside help;
- prosumption can also be applied the actions of two or more individuals in interaction with one another;
- prosumers can be professionals, amateurs, or some combination of the two (pro-ams);
- prosumption does not necessarily say anything about skill levels; prosumers can range anywhere from the unskilled to the highly skilled;
- analyses of prosumption can offer insights into the full range of processes that exist on the prosumption continuum, but can also focus on a specific aspect of the process and point on the continuum;
- analyses of prosumption can range anywhere from being highly positive to highly critical of the process, although the process itself is neutral—the judgments are more about how it is affected by a particular social and economic context, especially capitalism;
- prosumption can lead to positive outcomes (e.g., the sharing economy), but its positive potentialities can be, and often are, subverted.

Perhaps the most general point is that the tendency to make binary conceptual distinctions, especially that between producer and consumer, is a thing of the past. This is in large part because of a growing recognition of the always-active role of the p-a-c (consumer) as well as a wide range of social changes that are making the p-a-c more active than ever, and those actions are more efficacious than ever. They have the ability to empower the p-a-c as never before, but there are larger forces, especially those associated with capitalism, that limit, co-opt and likely will seek to denude the prosumers of their powerful potential.

Notes

1 Although, as implied above, they will be redefined here in the context of the following discussion of prosumption and the prosumption continuum.
2 Prosumption can therefore be seen as a postmodern concept that overcomes the modern tendency to create binaries (Saussure 1994).
3 Media studies have long been dominated by the view that the focus of work on the media needs to be on *both* the production of content by the media as well as the consumption, definition and interpretation of that content by its consumers (the audience).
4 While the traditional terms of production and consumption are employed here for the sake of simplicity and clarity, these phrases should also be seen as being subsumed under the heading of prosumption.
5 Throughout this chapter I will use p-a-p (prosumption-as-production) and p-a-c (prosumption-as-consumption) to designate prosumption processes and p-a-ps (prosumers-as-producers) and p-a-cs (prosumers-as-consumers) for those who engage in those processes.
6 Quite astoundingly, a recent conference and resulting edited volume on the Internet and social media continued to operate with a productivist bias and to focus almost exclusively on "digital labor" (Scholz 2013).
7 However, production and consumption in the process of prosumption can also be separated in time (and space). For example, farmers may harvest part of their crops for their own immediate use, but also may store, can or freeze some of it for later use. Shoppers may do the same things with many of the products they prosume.
8 Her third type is "organizational work" involving the production of practical responses to organizational contradictions, such as compensating for badly organized work.
9 The other types are Mp—methatheorizing as a prelude to theory development and Mo—metatheorizing as a source of perspectives—metatheories—that overarch sociological theory. These would need to be rethought in terms of the broader arena of meta-analysis.

References

Arvidsson, A. 2005. "Brands: A Critical Perspective." *Journal of Consumer Culture* 5, no. 1: 235–58.
Beck, U. 2001. "Interview with Ulrich Beck." *Journal of Consumer Culture* 1, no. 1: 261–77.
Belk, R. 2014. "Sharing Versus Pseudo-Sharing in Web 2.0." *Anthropologist* 18, no. 1: 7–23.
Botsman, R. and R. Rogers. 2010. *What's Mine Is Yours: The Rise of Collaborative Consumption.* New York: Harper Business.
Boudon, R. 1968. *The Uses of Structuralism.* London: Heinemann.
Bruns, A. 2008. *Blogs, Wikipedia, Second Life, and Beyond: From Production to Produsage.* New York: Peter Lang.
Bulmer, M. 1979. "Concepts in the Analysis of Qualitative Data." *The Sociological Review* 27, no. 1: 651–77.

Campbell, C. 2005. "The Craft Consumer: Culture, Craft and Consumption in Postmodern Society." *Journal of Consumer Culture* 5, no. 1: 23–42.

Clifford, S. 2012. "Browsing While Browsing." *New York Times*, 10 March, B1, B4.

Debord, G. 1977. *Society of the Spectacle*. Detroit: Black and Red.

deCerteau, M. 1984. *The Practice of Everyday Life*. Berkeley: University of California Press.

Dujarier, M-A. 2014. "The Three Sociological Types of Consumer Work." *Journal of Consumer Culture*, published online April 8, doi: 10.1177/1469540514528198

Hall, S., D. Hobson, A. Lowe, and P. Willis. 1980. *Culture, Media, Language*. London: Unwin Hyman.

Hamlin, C. L. forthcoming. "Boudon, Raymond (1934–2013)." In *The Wiley-Blackwell Encyclopedia of Sociology*, 2nd ed, edited by G. Ritzer. Malden, MA: Wiley-Blackwell.

Jenkins, H. 2006. *Convergence Culture: Where Old and New Media Collide*. New York: NYU Press.

Jenkins, H., S. Ford and J. Green. 2013. *Spreadable Media: Creating Value and Meaning in a Networked Culture*. New York: NYU Press.

Jurgenson, N. 2012. "When Atoms Meet Bits: Social Media, the Mobile Web and Augmented Revolution." *Future Internet* 41, no. 1: 83–91.

Leadbetter, C. and P. Miller. 2004. *The Pro-Am Revolution: How Enthusiasts Are Changing Our Economy and Society*. London: Demos.

Marx, K. 1867 [1976]. *Capital: A Critique of Political Economy*, Vol. 1. New York: International Publishers,

Prahalad, C. K. and V. Ramaswamy. 2004a. "Co-creation Experiences: The Next Practice in Value Creation." *Journal of Interactive Marketing* 18, no. 1: 5–14.

Prahalad, C. K. and V. Ramaswamy. 2004b. *The Future of Competition: Co-creating Unique Value with Customers*. Boston: Harvard Business School Press.

Rieder, K. and G. Gunter Voss. 2010. "The Working Customer: An Emerging New Type of Consumer." *Journal Psychologie des Alltagshandelns/ Psychology of Everyday Activity* 3, no. 1: 2–10.

Rifkin, J. 2014. *The Zero Marginal Cost Society; The Internet of Things, The Collaborative Commons, and the Collapse of Capitalism*. New York: Palgrave Macmillan.

Ritzer, G. 1991. *Metatheorizing in Sociology*. Lexington, MA: Lexington Books.

———— 1995. *Expressing America: A Critique of the Global Credit-Card Society*. Newbury Park, CA: Pine Forge Press.

———— 2010. *Enchanting a Disenchanted World: Revolutionizing the Means of Consumption*. Thousand Oaks: Pine Forge Press.

———— 2014. "Prosumption: Evolution, Revolution, or Eternal Return of the Same?" *Journal of Consumer Culture* 14, no. 1: 3–24.

———— 2015. *The McDonaldization of Society*. 8th ed. Thousand Oaks: Pine Forge Press.

———— Forthcoming. "Prosumer Capitalism." *Sociological Quarterly*.

Ritzer, G., P. Dean and N. Jurgenson. 2012. "The Coming Age of the Prosumer." *American Behavioral Scientist* 56, no. 1: 379–98.

Ritzer, G. and N. Jurgenson. 2010. "Production, Consumption, Prosumption: The Nature of Capitalism in the Age of the Digital 'Prosumer.'" *Journal of Consumer Culture* 10, no. 1: 13–36.

de Saussure, F. 1994. *Course in General Linguistics*. New York: McGraw-Hill.

Scholz, T., ed. 2013. *Digital Labor: The Internet as Playground and Factory*. New York: Routledge.

Smythe, D. 1977. "Communications: The Blindspot of Western Marxism." *Canadian Journal of Political and Social Theory* 1, no. 1: 120–27.

Smythe, D. W. 1981. "On the Audience Commodity and Its Work." In *Media and Cultural Studies: Keyworks*, edited by M. G. Durham and D. M. Kellner, 253–79. New York: Blackwell.

Tapscott, D. and A. D. Williams. 2006. *Wikinomics: How Mass Collaboration Changes Everything.* New York: Portfolio.

Toffler, A. 1980. *The Third Wave.* New York: William Morrow & Company.

Toffler, A. and H. Toffler. 2006. *Revolutionary Wealth.* New York: Doubleday.

Tiryakian, E. A. 2001. "Some Challenges for Sociology in the New Era." In *New Horizons for Sociological Theory and Research*, edited by L. Tomasi, 315–36. Aldershot and Burlington: Ashgate.

——— 1996. "Three Metacultures of Modernity: Christian, Gnostic, Chthonic." *Theory, Culture and Society* 13, no. 1: 99–118

——— 1992. "Pathways to Metatheory: Rethinking the Presuppositions of Macrosociology." In *Studies in Metatheorizing in Sociology*, edited by G. Ritzer, 69–87. Newbury Park, CA: Sage.

——— 1990. "Exegesis or Synthesis? Comments on 50 years of The Structure of Social Action." *American Journal of Sociology* 96, no. 1: 452–55.

——— 1986. "Hegemonic Schools and the Development of Sociology." In *Structures of Knowing: Current Studies in the Sociology of Schools*, edited by R. C. Monk, 417–41. Lanham, MD: Rowman and Littlefield.

——— 1981. "The Sociological Import of a Metaphor: Tracking the Source of Max Weber's 'Iron Cage.'" *Sociological Inquiry* 51, no. 1: 27–33.

——— 1979. "The Significance of Schools in the Development of Sociology." In *Contemporary Issues in Theory and Research: A Metasociological Perspective*, edited by W. E. Snizek, E. R. Fuhrman and M. K. Miller, 211–33. Westport, CT: Greenwood Press.

——— 1971. "Introduction to the Sociology of Sociology." In *Phenomenon of Sociology*, edited by E. A. Tiryakian, 1–15. NJ: Irvington Press.

Watson, M. and E. Shove. 2008. "Product, Competence, Project and Practice." *Journal of Consumer Culture* 8, no. 1: 68–89.

Weber, M. 1949 [1903/1917]. *The Methodology of the Social Sciences.* New York: Free Press.

Chapter 9

DANGEROUS NOUNS OF PROCESS: DIFFERENTIATION, RATIONALIZATION, MODERNIZATION

Hans Joas

My objective in this essay[1] is pretty clear from its title. It is to sound the alert about dangerous nouns of process, nouns that lead sociologists astray whenever they try to use them to place their analyses of the contemporary world on a historical foundation. These nouns of process also exercise a detrimental effect beyond the boundaries of sociology when other scholars, such as historians, see them as a source of theoretical guidance that is already well-tried in the social sciences. To explain the sharp tone of my warning, I must begin with a fairly detailed historical retrospective. We have to go back to the relationship between sociology and history during the period when the former was getting off the ground, paying special attention to the role of the topic of religion in this process.

Sociology has a number of roots as an independent academic discipline. It has absorbed: philosophical ideas, sometimes with anthropological underpinnings, about the nature of human social relations; enquiries into social problems of social reformist intent (on poverty, alcoholism, criminality, divorce); attempts to analyze the modern world; and models for systematizing the mass of historical and ethnological knowledge generated by the nineteenth century. When all goes well, the fusion of these disparate strands produces brilliant writings of broad interdisciplinary resonance. When things go awry, the discipline often threatens to disintegrate into its constituent elements, into disciplinary subcultures that have little to say to one another and that feel greater rapport with neighboring subjects than with their originary discipline.

If we go by university curricula, however, we do at least find a fair degree of internal cognitive stability within the discipline of sociology, in two respects. A specific canon of empirical methods of data collection and data analysis enjoys undisputed status. For many people, then, the discipline's professional identity consists chiefly in these methods. But there is also consensus with respect to classical sociological theory. Throughout the world, sociologists unanimously agree that sociology's core canon is centered on the work of two authors, namely Max Weber and Emile Durkheim, and a good knowledge of both is an absolute prerequisite for membership in the disciplinary community.

This fact can, however, easily blind us to the improbability of this theoretical canon. In all the countries in which sociology emerged, these canonical authors were mentioned only peripherally during the discipline's first few decades. Not only that, but much of Weber's writings consisted of scattered fragments or failed to enter the canon at all, and there is an endlessly complex relationship between these two "gospels," which by no means tell the same story. All efforts to expand the canon and make Adam Smith, Karl Marx, George Herbert Mead or Georg Simmel canonical in the same way remain controversial. And while modern sociological theory certainly features a corridor of shared themes, it is by no means a fixed paradigm.

I mention all this because it is vital to clarify a point without which we can have no hope of evaluating the nouns of process that dominate sociology. What I have in mind is the fact that the writings of both Weber and Durkheim exhibit two characteristics that do *not* apply to sociology as a discipline. Both authors were concerned with social phenomena throughout human history, and the topic of religion was central for both of them. In other words, two scholars who espoused a universal historical approach, and for whom the history of religion was a central part of this universal history, became the classical figures of a discipline to which these two characteristics do not apply. Sociology narrowed its focus to the point where it became the "study of the present," a process lamented by later disciples of the classical figures, such as Norbert Elias, while being given programmatic status by others, such as Anthony Giddens. And sociology increasingly pushed its subdiscipline, the sociology of religion, to the margins. To the extent that scholars still pursued it at all, it had very little prospect of shaping the discipline as a whole.

The state of affairs described above sounds paradoxical. Is this a case of a discipline betraying its founders? But if so, why does it continue to value them at all, going so far as to retrospectively declare—in an increasingly strident way—Weber and Durkheim its founders? The key to this paradox is, I think, obvious. Sociology is losing its historical perspective and marginalizing religion, while at the same time canonizing authors and texts to which these two characteristics do not apply, because the classical figures' theories themselves foster this development. They do so in two respects. First, their theories contain assumptions about progressive secularization, which means nothing other than that religion is becoming increasingly less important. Second, they entail assumptions about specific features of modernity as an entirely novel historical formation to which, supposedly, much of that which has always applied throughout history no longer applies. The latter characteristic can lead to a simplistic dichotomous perspective (*Gemeinschaft* or community versus *Gesellschaft* or society, mechanical versus organic solidarity, traditional versus modern society). It may also be extended to include three phases (Chicago School: "reconstruction") or divided up in a sophisticated way (Parsons' "pattern variables") (Joas 1993: 14–51; Joas and Knöbl 2009). But the common ground is the assumption of a fundamental break with all previous history as a new age dawns, an age for which the term "modernity" has increasingly taken hold. This modernity without religion thus becomes the object of sociology. In essence, this means that now sociology only needs to show an interest in religion as a condition for the emergence of this modernity. And this explains the key role played by Weber's essay on the Protestant ethic and also Durkheim's theory of the transformation of the division of labor and of law.

I risk being misunderstood here. I am well aware that the writings of the two classical figures contain elements that defy this description. Weber's theorem of "disenchantment" is really more an analysis of demagification, and is not identical with any simple thesis of secularization. Durkheim's mature theory of religion can also be seen as an approach to analyzing sacralization of all kinds, even the sacralization of secular content such as the nation or human rights. I shall return to this topic later. For now I merely want to highlight the fact that simple recourse to the classical figures must remain unsatisfactory as long as we fail to eliminate those of their assumptions that prompted the development of sociology as the study of a religion-free modernity.

The crisis of secularization theory has now endowed this question with profound contemporary relevance. Even those who continue to adhere to the notion of a causal relationship between modernization and secularization—such as Steve Bruce, Ronald Inglehart, Pippa Norris and Detlef Pollack—will concede that they are now in the minority, that within the social sciences more scholars now reject than embrace the thesis of secularization. Of course, this does not mean that we can now simply reverse the thesis of secularization. To critique the assumption that modernization necessarily leads to secularization is not to dispute that secularization has occurred in many European and a small number of non-European societies. It means finally making a serious attempt to explain this fact. In the same way, skepticism about the explanatory power of the theory of functional differentiation in no way entails a naive call for societal dedifferentiation. But it does imply that, in light of the historical developments of the twentieth and early twenty-first centuries, we should ask whether those canonized theories derived from the classical figures are truly capable of explaining these developments. This cannot be a matter merely of applying differentiation theory historically and seeing what happens, or of determining how contemporary historical research fits into this framework. Instead we must reflect historically upon the phenomenon of differentiation theory itself and make it compete with alternatives.

Such a critique of the theory of functional differentiation is not, of course, in its infancy—quite the opposite. As early as 1984, in his spirited book *Big Structures, Large Processes, Huge Comparisons*, Charles Tilly referred to the notion of advancing functional differentiation as a "pernicious postulate" (1984: 43–53). He readily conceded that in the nineteenth century a whole range of processes of social change made it seem plausible to apply the concept of differentiation sociologically, a concept that had been gleaned from biological models of evolution. The specialization of labor, the construction of state bureaucracies, the spread of commodities markets and the proliferation of societies and associations all seemed to point in the same direction. These processes appeared to confirm a general law of social change, a law, moreover, that stated that this change was progressive in some way or another. The theory that emerged in the late nineteenth century almost died out again between the world wars—although not without triggering a number of skeptical and ironical reactions. It then resurfaced around 1960 with great intensity when Talcott Parsons began to build his search for a theory of social change around this idea, which he had previously tended to reject. Wolfgang Knöbl, in his outstanding history of modernization theory (2001), has shown just how much this maneuver was in fact a kind of pre-emptive defense of the postwar theory of modernization when it came to face its first crisis.

Tilly, then, did not dispute that processes of functional differentiation occur. But he emphasized that there is also a wealth of concurrent processes that would be better described as processes of dedifferentiation. His examples are processes of linguistic standardization in connection with nation-state formation, the development of a mass market in consumer goods and the agglomeration of small territories to form nation-states. Neither term—differentiation or dedifferentiation—is an appropriate means of describing other key processes of social change such as progressive capital concentration or the diffusion of world religions (of the kind we observe today in the tremendous global expansion of Christianity and Islam). What is more, processes of differentiation in one location—Tilly's example is the European shoe industry in the nineteenth century—often lead to processes of dedifferentiation in another place, in this case the shoe-importing countries.

But if this is correct, then there is clearly a pressing need to clarify the logical status of the theory of functional differentiation. Does it aspire to describe individual processes of social change or social change as a whole? Does it seek to go beyond description and provide explanations? In other words, does calling a phenomenon a "differentiation process" explain its causes and progress over time? To what extent is the theory of functional differentiation normative? In other words, does it not only describe or perhaps even explain a developmental trend but identify it as desirable as well? In fact, there is no doubt that the theory often entails significant normative content and, because of this, its exponents frequently perceive the critique of its explanatory power as a quasi-totalitarian call to eliminate existing forms of differentiation. Is the term differentiation chiefly meant to indicate a state of affairs or an increasing degree of distinction between functional systems?

As mentioned earlier, there have been debates on all these questions among the theory's supporters and critics for decades. I myself have collated (for a book) the unresolved questions associated with this topic: concerning processes of differentiation and their causes, effects, agents, impediments, tempo, contingencies and normative evaluation (Joas 1997: 223). Parsons's students and their students in turn, have given creative answers to all these questions. It is impossible to provide an exhaustive account here, so I will content myself with the observation that the theory underwent gradual "liberalization" in the United States as scholars (most notably Shmuel Eisenstadt, Edward Tiryakian, Robert Bellah and Jeffrey Alexander) increasingly opened it up to action theoretical explanations. This initially led to the abandonment of the theory's explanatory aspirations and then even of the label "(neo-)functionalist," while German sociology came to be dominated by Niklas Luhmann's radicalized functionalism, a theory that can view every social phenomenon as contingent except one, namely the very process of progressive functional differentiation. While in the first case there is a risk of shapelessness, in the second case we find a dangerous noun of process of the most extreme kind.

Durkheim and Simmel are the classic reference authors for this theory of functional differentiation. But Max Weber injected another dangerous noun of process into the sociological canon, namely that of progressive "rationalization." It is surely beyond dispute today that we cannot really reconstruct Weber's work in light of this concept. Dirk Kaesler (2006: 199) makes it abundantly clear that Weber did not *start out* with an intuitive sense of a "universal historical process involving the rationalization of all spheres of life in all cultures and at all times," but instead *subsequently* hit on the idea of using this concept to unite his disparate studies on bureaucratization, industrialization, intellectualization, the development of rational enterprise, capitalism, specialization, objectification, methodization, disciplining, disenchantment, secularization and dehumanization. But there is a huge question mark over the plausibility of this retrospective self-systematization, over whether it can be correctly understood as the "unintended product of his many individual pieces of research" (as Kaesler puts it), or even as a "discovery" (Schluchter

1991: 102), or whether we might make better use of Weber's work by eschewing the notion that these discrete processes are subprocesses of an overarching rationalization.

Here I will mention just two reasons for my skepticism about the overarching processual notion of "rationalization." First, there are clearly radical differences between rationalization in the sense of an increasing orientation towards profit-making principles and, for example, rationalization in the sense of theologians' intellectual systematization of religious content. It makes no sense at all, in my opinion, to use the same term for both processes—unless one assumes that there is some kind of causal relationship between them. But this—my second reason—makes sense only if we assume the existence of a specific process of rationalization within a particular culture over very long periods of time: in other words the development of "occidental rationalism." I shall illustrate what disturbs me so much about this with reference to a single statement by Weber. In his study of Hinduism, in connection with a discussion of the caste system and the limits to commensality associated with it, Weber mentions the famous dispute between Peter and Paul in Antioch and writes:

> The elimination of all ritual barriers of birth for the community of the eucharist, as realized in Antioch, was, in connection with the religious pre-conditions, the hour of conception for the occidental "citizenry." This is the case even though its birth occurred more than a thousand years later in the revolutionary *conjurationes* of the medieval cities. (Weber 1958: 37, slightly modified translation)

In a narrowly logical sense, Weber is of course correct: no medieval urban bourgeoisie is without a shared Communion. But it is far from obvious that we should look for the origin of this prerequisite in an event in religious history that occurred a thousand years earlier. This ascribes to very long-standing religious traditions a role that might also be played by contemporary social configurations. It is true that Weber attributes no determinative power to these traditions. But he treats them as either facilitators or impediments to such an extent that it would be fair to say that he underestimates religions' adaptability. The notion of the development of occidental rationalism is underpinned by specific assumptions about the West's enduring uniqueness and about features common to all "rationalization"—assumptions that, in my opinion, are becoming increasingly implausible today in light of the tremendous economic rise of East and South Asia. Questions concerning the connection between religion and the rise of an acquisitive bourgeoisie in Europe are surely too narrow for the needs of a historical-comparative sociology of religion, and may in fact be fundamentally misconceived.

Even more than in the work of Weber himself, which of course features many productive internal inconsistencies, this lurking danger arises when his work is rendered consistent, when it is thoroughly systematized. Wolfgang Schluchter has probably done more than anyone else in this vein, and in his work on occidental Christianity—whose epigraph happens to be the above-quoted statement from Weber—Weber's analysis of medieval "community religiosity" in its sectarian or sect-like form is forced to help prepare the ground for ethical rationality and thus the spirit of the Reformation and the development of modern capitalism (Schluchter 1991: 382). As impressive as this systematization is, it is also highly one-sided. It would have been possible to adopt a quite different perspective, one that portrayed this form of Christianity as one in its own right, one that could be picked up on later in a wide variety of ways and that already showed affinities with various contemporary phenomena.

"Rationalization," Weber's dangerous noun of process, has exercised a tremendous influence on analyses of the contemporary world, an influence even greater than the notion of functional differentiation, which has remained a largely academic concept. Weber's own tragic perspective, the communist–utopian eclipsing of Weber in György Lukács's conception of reification and its elimination through a Leninist-led revolution, the return of tragic resignation in the "dialectic of Enlightenment" envisaged by Horkheimer and Adorno, the more optimistic attempts to open up these ideas in Habermas's concept of communicative rationality and Touraine's notion of "subjectivization"—all of this has done much to gear the intellectual self-understanding of the last few decades to this dangerous noun of process. With the exception of Touraine's work, there was very little space left for religion in this analysis of modernity, because here religion was robbed of its vigor by the thesis of progressive "disenchantment," visions of its utopian eclipse or the rationalist conception of an intensifying "linguistification of the sacred."

The third dangerous noun of process that I would like to flag here is "modernization." Sometimes it is actually quite harmless. This is so if we merely mean economic growth and the productivity-increasing effects of scientific research. From this point of view there has always been modernization, and its scale and tempo are simply empirical questions. We can then refer, for example, to the modernization of agrarian technology in the high Middle Ages, without associating this with any great theoretical claims. But the term is used far more often in the sense of a transition to a specific era called "modernity." This, however, infects the term with all the problems associated with the concept of modernity. The term modernity, of course, suffers from a notorious lack of definition with respect to its precise timing (from 1492 to 1968) and, much like the term functional differentiation, from a blurring of empirical and normative claims. Even more significant, so-called modernization theory too conceives of processes such as bureaucratization, democratization and secularization as subprocesses that are closely linked with one another, rather than being relatively independent processes that, while certainly featuring a wide range of mutual dependencies, essentially generate a field of tension rather than a holistic process.

I shall say no more at this point about the dangers of this third noun of process (see Joas 2014a: 63–77). The more pressing issue is what the outcome would be if my warning were heeded. For some people, the theory of functional differentiation is, for example, so constitutive of the identity of sociology (or: a specific variant of rationalization theory is so constitutive of the identity of critical theory) that they fear foregoing these theorems would mean annulling all theoretical claims, leaving us with nothing but historiography itself, the study of history in all its contingency.[2] So I feel an obligation at least to outline the basic ideas of a theoretical alternative that has eliminated the dangerous nouns of process, and to derive from this alternative theory a number of statements concerning the history of the relationship between religion and politics.

Given what I have said so far, the shortest route to this objective is to briefly indicate how we might draw on the classical sociological figures of Weber and Durkheim if we are aware of the dangers of these nouns of process and distance ourselves from the notion of a religion-free modernity that rests upon them. I shall limit myself to two comments about each of these thinkers, one relating to their understanding of religion and the other to their understanding of modernity.

At the time of his early death, Weber's thinking was clearly still in flux, and we might speculate as to whether he himself would have continued to adhere to all of those ideas that were later canonized. This speculation is nourished by newly available material such as Gangolf Hübinger's edition of Weber's 1920 lecture on the sociology of the state, held just a few weeks before his death, and a newspaper article on a lecture given by Weber in Vienna in 1917.[3] Here as elsewhere, Weber underlines the supposed uniqueness of the occidental city and concludes his description of the modern forms of political domination by highlighting the city and the "kind of politics and economic policy that were first developed by it" as the "third indispensable historical component of the modern forms of political domination alongside the "rational bureaucratization of the monarchical military states and of rational capitalism." The point I want to make here is that while the military state, capitalism and urban self-government are all qualified here as "rational," Weber can in no way be thinking about a coherent principle. What he has in mind must instead be a configuration characterized by profound internal tensions. The term rationality, so it seems to me, tends to conceal this tension rather than elucidate it. At a certain point, Weber's action theoretical analytical aspirations and the assumption of a universal historical process of rationalization are bound to come into conflict. The internal logic of state action within the modern nation-state or within a postnational constellation, the internal logic of economic action in various institutional forms of capitalist economy and the internal logic of more or less democratic self-government are not identical with one another.

My second comment relates to Weber's understanding of religion. This has a cognitivist or intellectualist slant whenever he regards the issue of theodicy as fundamental to all religion. As I see it, the dynamics of religious experience and their interpretation are more fundamental than issues of meaning and justice, and these dynamics generate the framework within which such issues can be explored in the first place. After his shift towards the topic of ecstasy and, above all, in his brilliant "Intermediate Reflections" (*Zwischenbetrachtung*), Weber developed a schema for the competition between experiences of ecstasy (or self-transcendence) that is crucial to any analysis of the "tensions between world and religion." In his hands, however, this schema immediately turns into the thesis of the competition between the internal tendencies of cultural spheres, a thesis on which readings beholden to differentiation theory could later build. This makes theories of rationalization and differentiation seem quite compatible, virtually crying out to be linked together. But it would also be possible to remain on the level of action and experience without making any assertions about the internal logic of cultural spheres. From this angle the conflicts between different approaches to experiences of self-transcendence (through religion, art, eroticism, violence, intoxication, etc.) appear as problems of individuals and collectivities and as balancing acts performed by institutions—without any transhistorical trajectory towards disenchantment.

If we draw in parallel on Durkheim and also begin—at least tentatively—by parenthesizing the assumptions of differentiation theory, we discover that he was a pioneer of the theory of dynamic processes of sacralization.[4] The point of his classical work on the elementary forms of religious life is to be found in this theory, not in the reduction of religion to the function of social integration. It is also because of this theory that his essay of 1898 could serve as the jumping-off point for a sociology of human rights as the modern sacralization of the person. But, as with Weber, we cannot adopt Durkheim's theory in any simple way. No matter how brilliant his theory of sacralization is, it has serious shortcomings, which are clearly bound up with Durkheim's laicist political intentions. In a nutshell: in contrast to Weber, Durkheim failed to recognize the emergence of an ethicized religion of redemption in the "Prophetic Age" as a fundamental turning point and, therefore, presented modern sacredness, including secular sacredness, as similar to the structures of tribal religion.

In Durkheim's work, far more than in Weber's, the notion of modernity is molded by the concept of functional differentiation. Durkheim interprets the problems of his era as essentially bound up with the switch to this new mode, as temporary anomie. But this means that, in much the same way as later modernization theory, his theory can only comprehend the totalitarianisms of the twentieth century as deviations from the path of modernization. There can be no "totalitarian modernity" within this construction—which demonstrates the latent normativity of the notion of modernity.

This point is bound up with a particular understanding of religion in the sense that within Durkheim's one-dimensional concept of sacralization there is no way to distinguish examples of sacralization within a totalitarian framework—the sacralization of nation, race, class, party, *Führer*, revolution—from sacralization with a transcendent dimension. As a result, in his work he conjoins universalism and secularism, while failing to grasp both the risk of secularist anti-universalism and the potential of religious universalism.

My brief remarks and the theoretical alternative I have mentioned thus have two key ramifications. First, skepticism about the dangerous nouns of process prompts us to begin one level of abstraction lower than do theories of functional differentiation, rationalization and modernization. Like Charles Tilly and other major representatives of historical sociology, what I have in mind are historically specific processes on the level of the organization of economy and politics, although I advocate a far broader action theoretical foundation than those scholars who work essentially with models of rational action. Analyses of the social configurations located between institutionally embedded processes remain captive, however, to the notion of a religion-free modernity if they fail to incorporate the dynamics of always-arising new instances of sacralization, the "fact of ideal formation," as I call it (Joas 2013: 102). The notion of linear processes of secularization or disenchantment must be replaced by analysis of the interplay between sacralization and desacralization, by study of the migration of the sacred, while "functional differentiation" and "rationalization" must give way to analysis of open processes involving an interplay between institutionalized logics of action. The dynamics of sacralization, too, ceaselessly ensure new upheavals and the emergence of new institutions.

What approach to the relationship between religion and politics can we derive from this theoretical alternative? I shall restrict myself to three brief remarks. To begin we must consider the first historical phase of the "differentiation of religion and politics." I am referring here to what Karl Jaspers called the Axial Age (and Max Weber the Prophetic Age). However we evaluate the exact religious character of this Axial Age, it is beyond dispute that the desacralization of political rule, but also of the structures of social inequality, were part and parcel of it. In brief: with the emergence of notions of transcendence in ancient Judaism and among the Greeks, Chinese, Indians and perhaps Iranians, it became impossible to deify rulers as such. The ruler can now be measured against divine or other transcendent postulates and forced to justify himself. This critique of rulers introduces a novel dynamic into the historical process and breaks with the framework of archaic statehood. For our purposes it is particularly important to note that the Axial Age, as the first phase in the desacralization of political rule, applies not just to the history of Europe but to that of other places as well. In other words, the potential to criticize rulers is present in all religions that were the direct or—like Christianity and Islam, indirect—products of the Axial Age breakthrough. What Jaspers shows us is that, rather than the other of occidental rationalism, the non-European world was a field of tension featuring competing universalisms and anti-universalisms (Bellah 2011; Bellah and Joas 2012; Joas 2014b).

Second, exponents of the idea that European history has for a long time been exceptional are keen to highlight the "Investiture Controversy" as a first step towards the separation of state and religion. Yet it is astonishing how little serious attention sociologists have paid to the first major attempt at a sociology of Christianity, namely Ernst Troeltsch's *The Social Teaching of the Christian Churches* (1981 [1912]: 229). In Troeltsch's work the Investiture Controversy appears as a consequence of the Gregorian church reforms that inevitably culminated in the total "the freedom of the Church from the State," which means in a kind of theocracy. "The dogma of the universal episcopate requires as its complement the dogma of theocracy." Troeltsch even interprets Thomas Aquinas as expounding a moderate form of theocratic thought. Separation of Church from state, yes—but this "did not mean the separation of the State from the Church" (234). I think we would struggle to express this distinction in the idiom of differentiation theory.

There is a vast gulf between the theocratic project, however successful or unsuccessful it may be, and a learning history in which, on the basis of religious motives, religion itself forgoes coercion or coercive support from the state. But this is a learning history that has in fact taken place. This is the history of religious freedom and the history of its contribution to the emergence of human rights. It is the history of the sacralization of the believing individual as such or of all individuals, whether believers or nonbelievers. As I see it, we cannot understand the history of human rights as the history of secularization, rationalization or differentiation, but only as a novel form of sacralization, namely that of the person.

I began this essay with a brief look back at the relationship between sociology and history in the early days of sociology and, against this background, I have tried to convey the key requirements for a contemporary sociology that is beginning to dip into the universal historical research that was once so crucial to Weber and Durkheim. It seems to me that there are five such requirements. This new sociology must renounce the fetishization of a homogenous modernity; premises drawn from secularization theory; and what I would call an occidental-centrist worldview. It must be sensitive to historical contingency and must formulate its stance on normative issues in light of the "fact of ideal formation." In order to do all this, this sociology must jettison certain borrowings from the natural sciences and relinquish the notion of progressive functional differentiation as a master trend of history.

My observations here have a religious intent as well as a scholarly one. The notion of religion as a cultural sphere with the same status as all the others, or as a functional system in analogy to all the others, is itself secularistic. Religion has specific characteristics, but these do not consist in a cultural specialization in the religious dimension. If they take their faith seriously, believers and their social organizations must inevitably make claims regarding the organization of all cultural spheres and functional systems. This is not a call for religious fundamentalism or integralism, since I have faith in the religious learning history of respect for other value systems and forms of belief and the insight into the functional logic of societal subsystems. But the pathos of universalist religion and, it should be noted, universalist secular thought as well, does not fit neatly into the worldview of progressive functional differentiation. The scope, degree and trajectory of this process must themselves be measured against ideals of conduct and of how the world should be organized, ideals of both a religious and secular nature.

Notes

1   This text is a translation of an article originally published in 2012, *Umstrittene Säkularisierung Soziologische und historische Analysen zur Differenzierung von Religion und Politik*, ed. Karl Gabriel, Christel Gärtner and Detlef Pollack, 603–22. Berlin: Berlin University Press.

2   I would like to point out here that I have British sociologist of religion David Martin to thank for the term so central to this essay. His work certainly suffers no lack of theoretical content (see Martin 2011).

3   Max Weber, *Allgemeine Staatslehre und Politik (Staatssoziologie)*, ed. Gangolf Hübinger (Tübingen: Mohr, 2009) (MWG III/7); Max Weber, "Probleme der Staatssoziologie. Bericht der Neuen Freien Presse" (Vienna), October 26, 1917, in: Weber, *Herrschaft*, ed. Edith Hanke (Tübingen: Mohr, 2005) (MWG I/ 22–4), 745–56, here 755.

4   Edward Tiryakian has made substantial contributions in this vein in his studies of Durkheim. These can be found in an extremely useful collection: see Tiryakian 2009.

References

Bellah, R. 2011. *Religion in Human Evolution*. Cambridge, MA: Harvard University Press.

Bellah, R. and H. Joas, eds. 2012. *The Axial Age and Its Consequences*. Cambridge, MA: Harvard University Press.

Joas, H. and W. Knöbl. 2009. *Social Theory*. Cambridge: Cambridge University Press.

Joas, H. 1993. *Pragmatism and Social Theory*. Chicago: University of Chicago Press.

———— 1997. *The Creativity of Action*. Chicago: University of Chicago Press.

———— 2014a. "The Age of Contingency." In *Faith as an Option: Possible Futures for Christianity*, 63–77. Stanford: Stanford University Press.

———— 2013. *The Sacredness of the Person*. Washington, DC: Georgetown University Press.

———— 2014b. *Was ist die Achsenzeit? Eine wissenschaftliche Debatte als Diskurs über Transzendenz*. Basel: Schwabe.

Kaesler, D. 2006. "Max Weber." In *Klassiker der Soziologie*, Vol. 1, 5th ed., edited by D. Kaesler.

Knöbl, W. 2001. *Spielräume der Modernisierung*. Weilerswist: Velbrück. 191–214. Munich: Beck.

Martin, D. 2011. *The Future of Christianity*. Farnham: Ashgate.

Schluchter, W. 1991. *Religion und Lebensführung*, Vol. 1. Frankfurt/Main: Suhrkamp.

Schluchter, W. 1991. *Religion und Lebensführung*, Vol. 2. Frankfurt/Main: Suhrkamp.

Tilly, C. 1984. *Big Structures, Large Processes, Huge Comparisons*. New York: Russell Sage Foundation.

Tiryakian, E. A. 2009. *For Durkheim. Essays in Historical and Cultural Sociology*. Farnham: Ashgate.

Troeltsch, E. 1981 [1912]. *The Social Teaching of the Christian Churches*. Chicago: University of Chicago Press.

Weber, M. 2009 (MWG III/7). *Allgemeine Staatslehre und Politik (Staatssoziologie)*, edited by G. Hübinger. Tübingen: Mohr.

Weber, M. 2005 (MWG I/ 22–4) "Probleme der Staatssoziologie: Bericht der Neuen Freien Presse" (Vienna), October 26, 1917. In: Weber, *Herrschaft*, edited by E. Hanke, 745–56. Tübingen: Mohr.

Weber, M. 1958. *The Religion of India: The Sociology of Hinduism and Buddhism*. New York: The Free Press.

Chapter 10

MODERNIZATION AS SOCIAL BECOMING: TEN THESES ON MODERNIZATION

Piotr Sztompka

Modernization, as a crucial type of macrosocial change, is an ambiguous and contested concept. Like the idea of social change itself, modernization is treated in two opposite ways in sociological theory. One characteristic of evolutionism, or developmentalism, dominant in classical nineteenth-century social thought, puts emphasis on its inevitable unilinear course and single final destination. Another characteristic—emerging from the critique of determinism, fatalism and finalism—assumes contingency, multilinearity and open-endedness of modernization. It looks at modernization as a possibility rather than a necessity, as an achievement rather than a fate, and claims that whether this possibility is achieved depends on the actions, decisions and choices of the members of society plus the conducive circumstances for mobilizing and facilitating such actions. The contingent character of these actions and circumstances produces various trajectories and outcomes of modernization, in other words multiple modernities.

I take the latter perspective and in this chapter will attempt to apply to the analysis of modernization my general theory of social becoming as put forward in two books in the 1990s: one, a monograph by Polity Press, Cambridge (Sztompka 1991), and another a textbook of the sociology of social change by Blackwell, Oxford (Sztompka 1993). This very general model of social becoming has a number of implications that have been hinted at or formulated here and there in the rich literature on modernization. I propose to put these implications together in a synthetic picture by means of ten theses on modernization. Each could be elaborated separately, but here I will present a list, a sort of agenda for future research.

- **Thesis 1. Modernization is the particular implementation of social becoming.** Therefore, the inspiration for the theory of modernization can be found in one of the most important sentences in the history of sociology: "Men make their own history, but they do not make it as they please, only in circumstances given to them, encountered and inherited from the past generations" (Marx 1964, 1968). Applied to modernization, "making history" means that the process results from the transforming potential of human agency, understood as a synthetic force ascribed to a society as a whole. Such a transforming potential emerges as a combined product of three factors:

  (a) The quality of the actors, their endowment (e.g., pro-modern motivations, aspirations, beliefs, relevant knowledge). An interesting ideal type of a modern personality as a prerequisite for modernizing actions was proposed by Alex Inkeles and David Smith (1974). They mention such traits as: readiness for new experience, openness and tolerance for a variety of opinions and beliefs, treating time as a precious resource, planning the future, optimism and activism. Key to shaping such personalities are socialization and education.
  (b) Structural circumstances opening the field of opportunities for modernizing actions (e.g., level of technology, economic regime, cultural values and rules). Key to shaping pro-modern structures are institutional reforms, and wise policies.
  (c) The inherited shape of society produced by our predecessors in the earlier phases of cumulative social becoming. Here, the key is respect, cultivation and continuation of indigenous tradition.

The combination of these three types of determinants facilitates or hinders modernizing praxis: choices and decisions undertaken by human actors—individual, or collective, or authoritative (governmental decisions, legislation). And it produces various routes of modernization with its multiple outcomes.

- **Thesis 2. Is there one modernization or many?** All three components of the model—(a) personalities of the members of society, (b) economic, political and cultural institutions, and (c) inherited traditions—are contingent and variable. Therefore the idea of multiple modernities, put forward most forcefully and elaborately by Shmuel Eisenstadt (2003), Bjorn Wittrock (2000), Johan Arnason (2000) and others is clearly implied by the model of social becoming. It leads to the relativization of modernizing processes, in which so-called Western (or Euro-American) modernity appears as just one of the historical trajectories and outcomes of the process of modernization. The ethnocentrism of the early theorists of modernization—Talcott Parsons (1966), Daniel Lerner (1958), Marion Levy (1966)—is excluded by the logic of our model.

- **Thesis 3. Is the impact of multiple modernities equal, or are some versions dominant?** The corrective factor is the process of globalization, as grasped by Roland Robertson (1992), Manuel Castells (1996–98) and many others, and which has allowed the influence of Western modernity to spread to other parts of the world because of the hegemonic, expansionist power—economic, political, military, cultural—of leading centers of modernization, and the popular appeal of technological novelties, mass culture and consumerism. But the epoch of conquest and colonialism with imposed Westernization is over. Apart from its own, original civilizational area Western modernity is no longer accepted wholesale, but only selectively. In the era of globalization multiple modernizations merge.

- **Thesis 4. Is not such dominance and hegemony pushing toward the uniformization and homogenization of the modernizing processes—proverbial McDonaldization (Ritzer 2004)—refuting the claim of multiple modernities?** The answer is no, because modernity is a multidimensional condition—economic, political, cultural, religious, mental—wherein various dimensions may appear in multiple configurations and permutations. And the globalization and imposed homogenization in line with the Western syndrome of "capitalism plus democracy plus individualism plus secularization" evokes defensive reactions to preserve unique, indigenous formats of modernization responding to local traditions and circumstances and incorporating only some elements of Western modernity. Such alternative scenarios of globalization and modernization are, for example, discussed by Ulf Hannerz under the labels of hybridization, creolization or mutual adaptation (Hannerz 1996). The mark of modernization should be an open and enriching dialogue with other modernizations.

- **Thesis 5. If there are many trajectories of modernization, how do we know that in concrete cases we witness authentic, true modernization?** Is there any common denominator? Are there any universal criteria of modernization? This is perhaps the most difficult question, and the answer cannot be given on purely factual grounds. It must invoke valuations and ideological convictions, refer to philosophical anthropology and ethics.

For me modernization is not a value, or a goal *per se*, but the means, an instrument for making more people happier, living a more full and dignified life. More concretely, it means the access for ever more members of society to the growing opportunities for the realization of human potential.

I accept the romantic and optimistic, rather than cynical and pessimistic, image of a human person. I believe there are three crucial human potentials (a) creativeness, inventiveness, innovativeness; (b) reason and reflexivity; and (c) impulse of community, craving for embeddedness in rich, satisfying moral bonds with others, such as trust, loyalty, reciprocity, solidarity and sympathy. Similar claims are phrased by a number of authors: for example, Erich Fromm, contrasting being-syndrome with having-syndrome (1979); Ralf Dahrendorf, focusing on life-chances, in his language, the combination of "options and ligatures" (1979); and Norbert Elias, emphasizing civility, gentleness and recognizing the dignity of others in everyday interpersonal contacts (2000 [1939]).

- **Thesis 6. Must the natural human drives always be realized?** The answer is no because, as implied by the model of social becoming, there must be conducive structural circumstances mobilizing the people for modernizing praxis.

  There are some preconditions for human self-realization, three of which are, for me, the most important: (a) some level of technological and economic development ensuring comfort and prosperity; (b) widely available education, including ethical and aesthetic formation, and providing the people with what I call "civilizational competence," that is, necessary skills to effectively use the technological, economic and cultural opportunities that modernization offers (Sztompka 1993a); (c) cultural institutions providing easy access to higher forms of art and culture, raising sensitivity and enriching experiences. Neither of these three preconditions emerge spontaneously—they require political vision, political will, and effective implementation. Building structural and institutional fields allowing people to engage their full potentialities is the task of enlightened leadership, cultivating the project of modernization. Modernization must involve both the reforms from above and the mobilization of the people. Somewhat parallel observations can be found in the work of Charles Tilly (1978), Meyer Zald and J. McCarthy (1988), Aldon Morris (1992) and others proposing the "resource mobilization theory" of social movements.

- **Thesis 7. Does modernization mean complete social change and absolute novelty?** No, modernization must be linked with the traditions of a given society, its unique social memory, cultural heritage, religious or ideological creeds. These traditions provide intellectual and moral resources for modernizing action, both for the authorities using the wisdom of generations for rational reform and for the people who, in the rootedness and continuity with the past, find existential security in the time of chaos and change. The emphasis on the importance of tradition may be found in the work of Edward Shils (1981) or, again, Shmuel Eisenstadt (2003). The optimum course of modernization is some historically and culturally determined mix of innovation, novelty with social memory and tradition.

• **Thesis 8. Is modernization a synonym for progress, bringing only the beneficial changes, the betterment of societies and improvement of human condition within societies?** The answer is no. Fetishization of modernity is a mistake. Our world is so constructed that every benefit has a price and entails some cost. As the famous saying has it: "There is no free lunch."

Among the indisputably progressive achievements of modernization one may list: the growing length of life, health, comforts and hygiene, technological inventions making life easier and more attractive, expanding social capital, raising level of education and awareness, and so forth. But, already the classical theorists of modernity have been aware of side effects, dysfunctions and pains of modernization. Marx raised the theme of alienation (Ollman 1975), Durkheim of anomie (1972), Weber of the iron cage of bureaucracy (1947), Toennies of the lost Gemeinshaft (2001 [1926]), Simmel of the hypertrophy of stimuli and impressions in the urban life (2009), Ortega Y Gasset of degradation of mass culture (1993) and Jurgen Habermas of the colonization of the life world by the bureaucratic systems (1989). Later writers, as well as leaders of social movements, raised the theme of wars and genocide with the recent scourge of terrorism, ecological destruction, depletion of natural resources, pollution and, recently, climate change. All these refer to concrete adverse consequences of historically specific modes of modernization and, in any estimates of the success of modernization, an ambivalent balance of functions and dysfunctions must always be taken into account.

But at a more general level, modernization as such means a comprehensive, rapid and often unexpected social change. The fetishization of change as inherently good is a mistake. Change is often progressive, but not necessarily so, and it also incurs costs. Again, the ambivalent balance must be considered. To refer to negative consequences of change I, together with Jeffrey Alexander and others (Alexander, Eyerman, Giesen, Smelser and Sztompka 2004), have proposed the concept of trauma, and particularly cultural trauma. By this we understand the painful experiences of disruptive social change because of the breaking of continuity, routines, accustomed modes of everyday life, earlier strategies of adaptation, strongly internalized beliefs and rules, revising cherished memories. At the cultural level, such trauma may become widespread, reaching the status of shared and constraining "social fact *sui generis*" in the sense given to this concept by Emile Durkheim (1964), and in effect paralyzing activism. Traumas of modernization seem to be a common phenomenon in modern society, perhaps more unstable than earlier ones, pervaded with radical mutability and accelerated change, some on the revolutionary scale. Thus, a new challenge is not only to modernize but to relieve the traumas of modernization and effectively cope with them.

- **Thesis 9. Is the course of modernization smooth and gradual?** The evolutionist and developmentalist tradition of Auguste Comte and Herbert Spencer, as well as all proponents of the sequential stages of growth, would respond in the affirmative. For them, societies move as if on a single escalator, at the same speed, along the same path and constantly upward, driven by a constant impulse toward structural and functional differentiation. But, from the perspective of social becoming, the answer is no.

Whether influenced directly or only indirectly by dialectics and revolutionary logic of change of Hegelian and Marxian provenance, the picture of modernization incorporates antagonisms, conflicts and struggles, resulting in contingent, variable routes and outcomes. The reason for this is that human society is never homogenous, but always divided between groups with different interests, aspirations, horizons and ideologies. Hence, the question "modernity for whom?" becomes relevant. It happens that benefits of modernity—economic, political or cultural goods—are never equally distributed. They fulfill the interests and aspirations of some groups—for example, modernizing elites, middle classes, professionals— while costs of change, deprivation and trauma of all sorts, the "bads," burden other groups, for example: unqualified working class, peasantry, dwellers in poorer rural areas. Modernization may also uproot cherished traditional ideas, creeds, customs and ways of life, and evoke clashes at this level. Hence, modernization often encounters conservative contestation; it becomes the focus of conflict that may lead to stagnation, blocks, backlash or even—to use the concept as it was couched by Edward Tiryakian—prolonged dedifferentiation (1976). The conflict-ridden and permanently contested nature of modernization is strongly emphasized by Shmuel Eisenstadt, who summarizes his analysis with a sentence by Polish philosopher Leszek Kolakowski, who says that modernization is on "endless trial" (Eisenstadt 2003).

• **Thesis 10. Can the future of modernization be extrapolated from present trends or, rather, may we expect some qualitative turns?** In view of the complex dialectics of modernization, is the prediction of the future at all possible? The heritage of evolutionist or developmentalist approaches with their inclination toward prophecies, was influential in the heydays of futurology, in various theories of postindustrial society or of systems convergence. In contrast, the theory of social becoming implies the activist and dialectic image, with no assured future. To foresee where the contingent and open-ended process of modernization will lead seems impossible. But with some probability and risk, one may, with Ronald Inglehart, venture the prediction of a major cultural and ideological turn from the current focus on material and survival values such as economic prosperity, abundant consumption and hedonistic experiences, toward higher, more spiritual concerns, or "postmaterialist values," such as harmony with nature, health and fitness, peace and security, aesthetic sensitivity and so on (Inglehart and Welzel 2005).

Of course, the condition of their ascendance is the continued economic growth, and satisfying, of fundamental survival or mundane needs of large segments of the human population. We are far from that, and whether it is at all attainable is far from certain. But similar intuitions, or perhaps dreams about new, higher levels of needs and values have been expressed by numerous scholars coming from completely different disciplines or theoretical traditions: psychologist Abraham Maslow, with his hierarchy of psychological needs (1968); cultural anthropologist Bronislaw Malinowski, with his sequence of necessary social functions (1969); sociologist Pitirim Sorokin in his cyclical theory, with a prophecy of the next idealistic epoch after a long rule of hedonistic materialism (1937).

Perhaps, just perhaps, this convergence of views may be a source of hope that further modernization of the human society will not necessarily just mean more and more cars, bigger and bigger cities, higher and higher buildings, richer and richer shopping galleries, more and more crowded beaches, quicker and quicker computers and jets, more and more pixels in the cameras and applications in the mobile phones, louder and louder rock concerts, more and more amusing TV programs—but something more ambitious.

But the theory of social becoming assumes that hopes are not enough. To make the hopes come true, action and struggle are necessary. As Antonio Gramsci puts it: in the social world, predicting means acting for the embodiment of prediction (1988). Perhaps the next phase of modernization will witness the conflicts and fights about its own deeper, humanistic meaning.

References

Alexander, J., R. Eyerman, B. Giesen, N. Smelser, P. Sztompka. 2004. *Cultural Trauma and Collective Identity*. Berkeley: California University Press.

Arnason, J. P. 2000. "Communism and Modernity." *Daedalus*, Winter: 61–90.

Castells, M. 1996–98. *The Information Age*, Vols. I, II and III. Oxford: Blackwell.

Dahrendorf, R. 1979. *Life Chances*. Chicago: University of Chicago Press.

Durkheim, E. 1964. *The Rules of Sociological Method*. New York: Free Press.

Durkheim, E. 1972. *Selected Writings*, edited by A. Giddens. Cambridge: Cambridge University Press.

Eisenstadt, S. N. 2003. *Comparative Civilizations and Multiple Modernities*, Vols. I and II. Leiden: Brill.

Elias, N. 2000 [1939]. *The Civilizing Process*. Oxford: Blackwell.

Fromm, E. 1979. *To Have or to Be?* London: Sphere Books.

Gramsci, A. 1988. *Antonio Gramsci: The Reader*, edited by D. Forgacs. New York: Shocken Books.

Habermas, J. 1989. *On Society and Politics*, edited by S. Seidman. Boston: Beacon Press.

Hannerz, U. 1996. *Transnational Connections*. London: Routledge.

Inglehart, R. and C. Welzel. 2005. *Modernization, Cultural Change and Democracy*. Cambridge: Cambridge University Press.

Inkeles, A. and D. Smith. 1974. *Becoming Modern*. Cambridge, MA: Harvard University Press.

Lerner, D. 1958. *The Passing of Traditional Society*. Glencoe, IL: Free Press.

Levy, M. 1966. *Modernization and the Structure of Societies*. Princeton, NJ: Princeton University Press.

Malinowski, B. 1969. *A Scientific Theory of Culture and Other Essays*. New York: Oxford University Press.

Marx, K. and F. Engels. 1968. *Selected Works*. Moscow: Progress Publishers.

Marx, K. 1964. *Selected Writings*, edited by Tom Bottomore. New York: McGraw Hill.

Maslow, A. A. 1968. *Toward a Psychology of Being*. New York: Van Nostrand.

Morris, A., ed. 1992. *Frontiers in Social Movement Theories*. New Haven: Yale University Press.

Ollman, B. 1975. *Alienation: Marx's Conception of Man in Capitalist Society*. Cambridge: Cambridge University Press.

Ortega y Gasset, J. 1993. *Revolt of the Masses*. New York: Norton.

Parsons, T. 1966. *Societies: Evolutionary and Comparative Perspectives*. Englewood Cliffs, NJ: Prentice Hall.

Ritzer, G. 2004. *The McDonaldization of Society*. Thousand Oaks: Pine Forge Press.

Robertson, R. 1992. *Globalisation: Social Theory and Global Culture*. London: Sage.

Shils, E. 1981. *Tradition*. Chicago: University of Chicago Press.

Simmel, G. 2009. *Sociology: Inquiries into the Construction of Social Forms*. Leiden: Brill.

Sorokin, P. 1937. *Social and Cultural Dynamics*, vols. I-IV. New York: American Book Company.

Sztompka, P. 1991. *Society in Action: The Theory of Social Becoming*. Cambridge: Polity Press.

——— 1993. *Sociology of Social Change*. Oxford: Blackwell.

——— 1993a. "Civilisational Incompetence." *Zeitshrift fur Soziologie*, no. 2, 85–95.

Tilly, C. 1978. *From Mobilization to Revolution*. Reading, MA: Addison-Wesley.

Tiryakian, E. A. "On the Significance of De-differentiation." In *Macro-sociological Theory*, edited by S. N. Eisenstadt and H. J. Helle, 118–34. Beverly Hills: Sage.

Toennies, F. 2001 [1926]. *Community and Civil Society*. Cambridge: Cambridge University Press.

Weber, M. 1947. *The Theory of Social and Economic Organization*. London: Routledge.

Wittrock, B. 2000. "Modernity: One, None or Many?." *Daedalus*, Winter: 31–60.

Zald, M. and J. McCarthy. 1988. *The Dynamics of Social Movements*. Lanham, MD: University Press of America.

Chapter 11

RELIGION AND EVOLUTION

John Simpson

Robert Bellah's *Religion in Human Evolution: From the Paleolithic to the Axial Age* was published by Harvard University Press in September 2011 (Bellah 2011). Bellah's death in July 2013 made it the last book he wrote and published during his lifetime. Based on more than two decades of reading and research plus discussions with his *Habits of the Heart* coauthors (Bellah et al. 1985) and others (Bellah 2011: xxv–xxvii). *Religion in Human Evolution* marks the final flourish of Bellah's notable scholarly career.

To him we owe such things as his analysis of religion and the turn to modernity in nineteenth-century Japan (Bellah 1957); a twentieth-century version of the idea of civil religion and its use in understanding American society (Bellah 1967: 1–21); an elaboration of the idea of symbolic realism (Bellah 1970); and his widely cited article, "Religious Evolution" (Bellah 1964: 358–75).[1] These and many other items constitute a major oeuvre among scholars and researchers in the sociology of religion coming of age professionally in the mid-twentieth century.[2]

Religion in Human Evolution has been described as Bellah's magnum opus (Wolfe 2011: 1). There is no doubt that it is a book that displays a sweep of learning and an effort to organize literatures ranging over the social sciences, the humanities and the physical and life sciences. In the first part the reader is asked to consider cosmology and evolution according to Bellah. In the second part he lays out tribal and archaic religion as precursor types and then moves on to the civilizations of the Axial Age: Ancient Israel, Ancient Greece, China in the Late First Millennium BCE and Ancient India.

While not described as such, a Guttman-like progression characterizes Bellah's description of religions, from tribal to those of the Axial Age. New things appear, but nothing is lost. Tribal religion—the earliest type—is undifferentiated from the society in which it is expressed. Archaic religion entails the appearance of differentiated religious symbol systems and cultic practices, and the entwinement of meaning (god) and power (king) in stratified societies (rulers and ruled). In the Axial Age, the idea of transcendence and immanence occurs along with the force of critique that, via observation from a standpoint (usually preserved in writing), can support the persistence of imminent good or the need for change.

Where *Religion in Human Evolution* contains a large amount of information compared with the compact and tightly written earlier article (Bellah 1964: 358–74), the general form of the argument, though embellished in the recent book, resembles the earlier article. There, Bellah identified and described five ideal typical stages of development in religious evolution: primitive, archaic, historic, early modern and modern. The Guttman-like frame is not applied to those categories.

In both the book and the article, Bellah eschews the strongly held notion of the nineteenth and twentieth centuries that social progress can be identified with evolution. But what does he mean by evolution? In both the book and the 1964 article, Bellah refers to the appearance of new stages of religion, and he places them under the aegis of evolution in the title he gives each publication. Yet it is arguable—indeed, strongly deniable—that evolution falls into the same category as change. Evolution is a type of change, but a type of change that is different from any other. That claim will be elaborated in this chapter.

Is Bellah's use of the term *evolution* justified? And, if so, should his work in *Religion in Human Evolution* be supported as a template for research on religion and human evolution? Above all, does the traditional working assumption of sociologists that the human body–brain can be treated as a substructural platform that need not be taken into account in doing theory and research remain tenable, today?

In what follows, I lay out several brief sketches of portions of the work of four well-known scholars, two historic and two contemporary figures. These propaedeutic sketches provide an entry into the difference between evolutionary models and models of development and change, and in a preliminary way touch on the relationship between contemporary biology and the construction of social theory. The selected figures, their texts and the topics addressed are:

- Johann Wolfgang von Goethe (1748–1832), *Die Metamorphosis der Pflanzen (The Metamorphosis of Plants)*, 1790. Development in a pre-Darwinian context.
- Charles Darwin (1809–82), *Origin of Species*, 1859. The elements of Darwin's view of evolution and their role in the contemporary neo-Darwinian consensus.
- John Tyler Bonner (1920–), *The Evolution of Culture in Animals*, 1980. The biology of cultural evolution.

- Robert Bellah (1927–2012), *Religion in Human Evolution: From the Paleolithic to the Axial Age*, 2011. A reviewer's view of Bellah's challenge to Darwin.

Goethe

Some readers may be surprised to find Johann Wolfgang von Goethe "batting leadoff" in a chapter entitled "Religion and Evolution." Goethe was a poet, playwright and novelist whose life and career spanned the eighteenth and nineteenth centuries. His literary immortality is due in part to the dramatic stage play, *Faust*, and its role in underwriting German Romanticism. Faust's contract with the Devil (Mephistopheles) is a staple of Western high culture. The Devil granted Faust (a man of science) anything he wanted during his lifetime in exchange for Faust's soul at death.

Perhaps, the most accomplished writer of post-Reformation North German letters, Goethe was also an estate manager, civil servant and diplomat. And in the latter part of his career he pursued scientific studies. Among other things,[3] he published *Die Metamorphosis der Pflanzen* (1790).[4] One might ask: What is the relevance, today, of a text in the field of biology written before the Darwinian–Wallacian/Mendelian/Crick–Watsonian/Human Genome revolutions that transformed the science of life into what we know, today?

Its value lies in Goethe's explication of his method for the examination of plant growth and the conclusions he reaches when the external visible features of an object have been examined and described, but the internal process underlying the production of those features is beyond the senses. Goethe accurately and beautifully describes the development of the plants he observes. But how does growth and development come about? What are the processes beneath the surface that are invisible to the naked eye?

Here, Goethe fills in with an imaginary (a trope that lies at the heart of Romanticism) that is taken as real. An irreverent critic might attribute the following argument to Goethe: What you do not see is open to speculation, and the more ingenious your logic, the more beautiful your language—indeed, the more beautiful and poetic your language and the more you are able to embed the good in your speculation—the more convincing you will be until you reach the point at which people believe and think this is the way it is, irrespective of the fact that they see none of that which they believe is true.

Goethe thought there were two cognitive faculties involved in his method: Understanding, or rational thinking, that is the instrument of science used in the examination of the visible (the empirically available); Reason (identified above as speculation) used to access the invisible heart, or mind, of nature wherein lies the source of the *how* of the observed development of the living organism.

> The Understanding will not reach her [the heart, or mind, of nature]; man must be capable of elevating himself to the highest Reason, to come into contact with the Divinity, which manifests itself in the primitive phenomena (*Urphänomenen*), which dwells behind them, and from which they proceed. (Goethe 2009: 111)

Further insights into what Goethe called "his method" are gained by considering his description of events on the time line of a growing plant. He writes:

> At first I will tend to think in terms of steps, but nature leaves no gaps, and, thus, in the end, I will have to see this progression of uninterrupted activity as a whole. I can do so by dissolving the particular without destroying the impression itself. (Goethe 2009: 105)

The appearance of stems, leaves, flowers, and so forth may be glimpsed by the observer as steps, but in reality they are manifestations of continuous activity that can be put together as a series visualized in memory to form an ideal whole.

As living things, plants evolve by human selection or natural selection. Goethe's metamorphosis is neither of those things. Rather it is a description of the visible features of a plant as it moves from a dormant form (seed or equivalent) to maturity. Were Goethe to describe the stages of the development of the offspring of a plant and note similarities and differences with its parent(s), he would be venturing beyond development and into the stuff of evolution.

By the same token Bellah's ideal typical stages in religious evolution lack the *how* of transformative passage from one stage to another. Stages are not explicated in terms of parent–offspring relationships, nor is it clear how sociocultural change from one religious stage to another is achieved. Bellah's stages, in other words, are not evolutionary outcomes. Some other model is required to understand religious change as an evolutionary event.

Darwin[5]

Darwin wanted to understand the existence of varieties within species and the vast array of species within plant and animal forms of life. For example, there are many varieties of birds within the species of birds and many species within the form of life we call the animal kingdom. His conclusions regarding those distinctions as put forward in the first edition of *On the Origin of Species* (1859) were formed over a long period of observation, reflection, writing and agonized consideration of possible repercussions from those whose assumptions (taken for granted at the time) would be violated by his conclusions.

The making of Darwin into a public figure and Victorian celebrity, something that his novel views thrust upon him, began with the five-year voyage of HMS *Beagle*. The *Beagle* was a Cherokee-class 10-gun brig-sloop of the Royal Navy, refitted as a survey barque. The mission was to conduct hydrographic surveys of the Atlantic and Pacific coastal waters of Latin America and nearby archipelagos, observe and record geology and gather and study specimens of flora and fauna.

For observing and describing geological formations and undertaking field studies of plants and animals, the services of a gentleman naturalist were sought: someone who could pay his own way, knew the literatures and scientific procedures of geology and natural history and, also, could offer appropriate company to the master of the vessel, Captain Robert FitzRoy.[6] Darwin was identified as the ideal person for the job. The ship left port on December 27, 1831, returning five years later, having circumnavigated the globe.

Darwin brought back to England a trove of material that would occupy him for the rest of his life: specimens that constituted one of the world's great collections of the flora and fauna of Latin America and adjacent islands, and a library of notebooks and diaries containing an extensive record of what he observed and what he thought about what he observed during the voyage. These were published in 1839 as *The Voyage of the Beagle*.

Origin of Species was published in 1859, 23 years after the *Beagle* returned to England. Why the delay? For a long time there was no pressure to publish. Darwin neither needed the money from the sale of a book nor did he need to enhance his reputation as a natural historian. No "blockbuster" had to be written.

Also, Darwin was concerned with getting the facts that would appear in a book in support of his arguments, correct and exactly stated. He believed that the more facts he adduced the less deniable his arguments would be against a charge of speculation—not realizing, perhaps, that a few favorable facts and an absence of counterfactuals presented a level of proof against speculation that a large number of repeated facts did not, and would require less expenditure of time and effort.

Finally, Darwin feared that the publication of a book explicitly identifying natural processes, and not divine action, as the origin of living things would lead to public violence. This was not a figment of his imagination. Darwin's father was a friend of J. B. Priestley, the free-thinking Dissenter and scientist who discovered oxygen. Soon after the French Revolution, Priestley described his political letters published in 1790 as "grains of gunpowder" (Johnson 2012: 12). He favored reforms in England similar to those that had occurred in France, and he was not alone. On the other side, numerous "Church-and-King" organizations vigorously opposed the French

Revolution. On July 14, 1791, Bastille Day, Priestley's home was burned and his books and scientific paraphernalia destroyed by a "Church-and-King" mob. Still fearing for his life, Priestley emigrated to New York in 1794. The fate of Priestley was embedded in the collective memory of the Darwin family (Johnson 2013: 56).

In the 1850s Darwin was not the only English architect and builder of theories—a philosopher, as used then—attempting to develop an explanation for change and variation in the empirical world of living and once-living things. Among others was Herbert Spencer (1820–1903), a polymath who laid out a general theory of evolution (Blute 2010: 5–7). Spencer thought that the common path across the biological and physical worlds was cumulative progressive development manifested in increasing specialization and complexity and fueled in the biological world by competition and conflict for resources (Malthus 1798). Only the fittest survived. "Survival of the fittest" was a phrase coined by Spencer, and Darwin used it in the 1869 edition of *Origin of Species* with the meaning of better designed for an immediate, local environment.

As Darwin worked on *Origin of Species* in the 1850s he knew that his views differed from Spencer's. Darwin saw natural selection as the key to understanding variation in species. He had no interest in cumulative progressive development á la Spencer. He rejected a singular interpretation of Lamarck's position (Spencer did not) that acquired phenotypical characteristics could be inherited by the offspring of the acquiring organism. And he added a principle to his transformational armamentarium that he called "divergence," whereby variation in a species can occur because organisms take advantage of a previously unexploited resource in their living space (Browne 1980: 53–89).

At various points in the 1850s Darwin was urged by his friends to publish. *Origin* was turning into a lengthy magnum opus, and they were fearful that Darwin would be "scooped" on natural selection. In June 1858 he received a manuscript posted from the Dutch East Indies and written by the naturalist, Alfred Russel Wallace. It contained Wallace's account of evolution by natural selection. Darwin immediately wrote to his friend, the geologist Charles Lyell, to express his surprise at having been "forestalled." "I never saw a more striking co-incidence," Darwin wrote, referring to a short manuscript he composed in 1842 (but had never published). It laid out his view of natural selection (Browne 2006), a view that was identical to the one Wallace had sent him, hoping that Darwin would approve it and arrange for its publication.

What to do? Darwin's friends, Lyell and Joseph Dalton Hooker, a botanist and explorer, thought that Darwin should not let go of the claim that his 1842 manuscript was the original source (by date) of the theory of natural selection. So they put a double paper before the Linnean Society of London, with Wallace's manuscript and Darwin's findings traced back to his 1842 manuscript.

It was read on July 1, 1858, and subsequently published, thus establishing shared priority for the theory of natural selection (Browne 2006). For the next 13 months Darwin labored assiduously to complete *Origin of Species*. It was published on November 24, 1859, and sold out before the end of the day. Six editions appeared in Darwin's lifetime, the last in 1872.

Darwin died in 1882, Spencer in 1903. Each was famous as a philosopher: Darwin in natural history and biology; Spencer in philosophy (current denotation) and what we would today call social science. Both had a theory of evolution. Darwin's centered on the similarity of human agency—as the selection force in the breeding of plants and animals that causes variation within domesticated forms of life—and natural selection among forms of life where human agency does not hold sway, but chance does, and with chance in the case of natural selection, and human intervention in the case of breeding, leading to descent with modification where reproduction occurs. Darwin's theory based on those principles plus adaptation to the environment and reproductive success (survival of the fittest), became the foundation of modern biological science. Much was added (and much continues to be added) to form what, today, is known as the neo-Darwinian consensus. Accretions to the basic Darwinian theory include Mendelian inheritance and the mechanism of heredity, the discovery of the structure of DNA, cell biology and the biology of multi-cellular organisms, DNA and protein expression, the mathematics of population biology, new ways of classifying the fossil record, cooperation as an evolutionary force and so on (Blute 2010; Simpson 2011: 258–59).

On the other hand, Spencer's evolutionism slid (but not on his account) into something different. By the time he died, much of his philosophy had been transformed by others into morally compromised libertarian-type ideologies appealing to those who supported conflict (elimination of the unfit) and justified racism, selective sterilization, strict limitations on immigration, colonial supremacy, unrestricted warfare and, even, genocide, each seen as a progressive evolutionary step by promoters or as a retrograde evil by those opposed (Hofstadter 1944). One can trace a line from the latter part of the nineteenth century through the midpoint of the twentieth century and find on it the organized sources of programs, practices and policies whose common feature is human intervention (direct or indirect) in the process of human reproduction. These include various eugenics and hereditarian movements, and cults and practices believed to enhance fitness and, thus, reproductive success (Kenneally 2014: 49–65; Hau 2003; Whorton 2000).

However, Spencer, himself, was nowhere near the center of eugenics or the linking of class position to fitness. As Sica points out, he was feted in America by the plutocrats of the time who "comforted themselves with this denatured Spencerianism: since they had all the money and power, they must *ipso facto* be 'the best.'[Yet, a]s in Darwin, [fit] simply denoted creatures who, given their environment, were most likely to survive" (2112: 94).

Bonner

John Tyler Bonner, Professor Emeritus of Biology at Princeton University, is an expert on slime molds (Jabr 2012). As well he has published a number of books that reach across various fields in biology. One in particular is useful here, as it lays out a comparative analysis of the evolution of culture in the animal kingdom (Bonner 1980). While written 35 years ago, the book remains valuable for its biological reading of culture cast in language suited to a broad readership. Also, it explicitly deals with the evolution of the brain or brain-like functionality across single-celled and multi-cellular forms of life as the key to the evolution of culture.

For sociologists and social theorists, the book has special interest on account of its origin. Bonner writes:

> The stimulus for this book came in 1975 when I was invited to a Daedalus Conference organized by Talcott Parsons and Hunter Dupree on the relation of biological evolutionary theory to social science. From this small meeting of anthropologists, sociologists, psychologists, neurobiologists, and evolutionary biologists I gained a full appreciation of my own confusion on the subject and a desire to do something about it. (1980: vii)

By 1978 Bonner had a draft manuscript in hand that he circulated to a large number of readers for critical feedback. It was also presented to a group of Princeton social scientists who in the spring of 1978 had organized a weekly seminar on sociobiology. Bonner discussed his draft in three of the sessions.

Among the sociologists in attendance, Bonner mentions Susanne Keller, Marion Levy, Norman Ryder and Robert Wuthnow. He gives special thanks to "my old friend Marion Levy for [...] giving me a better understanding of how I could say something that might be useful to the sociologist" (viii). In fact, Bonner attributes an observation to Levy that in my view should be prominently displayed on the walls of every department of sociology:

> There is a tendency to oppose the words biological and cultural, but Marion Levy has pointed out to me why this is unfortunate. Culture [...] is a property achieved by living organisms. Therefore in this sense it is as biological as any other function of an organism, for instance, respiration or locomotion. Since I am stressing the way information is transmitted, we could call one *cultural evolution* and the other *genetical evolution* with the understanding that they are both biological in the sense they both involve living organisms. (Bonner 1980: 10–1)

Bonner defines culture as the transfer of information by behavioral means, especially teaching and learning. The contrast is with the transmission of genetic information passed by the inheritance of genes from one generation to the next. Both forms of information (culture and genes) require the behavior of organisms within a species for transmission to occur: teaching and learning for culture, reproductive behavior for genes.

The understanding of genetical evolution requires an understanding of natural selection. Modern biology equates natural selection with the variation of individual organisms in a reproducing population of a species (Bonner 1980: 14). Variation in turn depends upon biological reproduction that includes the whole life cycle from egg and sperm formation to fertilization, birth, co-development (parent and offspring) and, death. Development and phenotypical change during the life cycle are part of the reproductive process (Bonner 1980: 15).

Genetical evolution requires selection at the stage of meiosis and the transfer and recombination of molecules in hereditary units. That process drives genetical evolution. Cultural evolution on the other hand occurs where noticeable innovation affects the transfer of information via the learning and/or teaching processes. Genetical evolution passes information from one person at a time to another person. Although that happens in cultural evolution, too, in general the specificity of cultural evolution is much lower than for genetic evolution and much more rapid. Understanding what is transpiring in the transfer of cultural information among individuals is, obviously, dependent on having an understanding of the medium of transfer (usually spoken or written language) and the gestures that are common among a local group of a species.

What is the relation between information in the form of genes and information in the form of culture? Although some may tend to conflate and mix genetical and cultural evolution in the search for understanding, Bonner takes the strong position that understanding can only arise where there is a clear distinction between the two forms of information transmission. Simply put all forms of life—plant and animal—use genetical information and depend upon its successful transmission to reproduce the species they are part of.

Genes are always necessary to ensure the continuation of a species and its varieties. However, only in the case of plants are they necessary and sufficient. Where animals appear in evolutionary history, especially the so-called higher animals, genes are necessary but not entirely sufficient to ensure reproductive success. Culture is needed to deal with motility in the animal kingdom and the adaptive problems that arise from movement through space, especially in the search for food. According to Bonner, brains first appeared in evolutionary history to deal with that problem (1980: 72–75).

The brain, from primitive to complex forms, is the inventor and transmitter of culture. Culture by definition is the information that the brain makes possible and communicates through the senses. But without genetic transmission from generation to generation there would be no brain. Genes code for the appearance and development of the brain. So culture is dependent on genes that underwrite the formation and development of the brain that is necessary for culture to be invented, transmitted and used by those who understand it. The relation among genes, the brain and culture is circular.

Human culture has enormous adaptive value. It makes possible things that cannot be done by gene transmission alone.[7] Along the evolutionary path emerged the ability to produce complex symbolic content. Language and writing were invented. The capacity appeared for art, religion, forms of work (including gathering and storing food) and beyond. On the scale of the cosmic time line these things happened quickly and very recently. How did an ancestral primate outpace his "cousins" so to speak and become human, meaning acquiring the brain humans have?

According to Bonner, primate behavior underwent an important genetic change that enabled cultural transmission to increase in volume and complexity at a super-fast rate. Rather than make the brain larger by restructuring it—something that would have required a vast amount of time and countless gene changes—a few changes that affected the timing of development changed. Thus,

> [t]he brain was simply allowed to grow for a longer period of time than the rest of the body. By this clever ruse, a small genetic change produced a larger brain, [which] was masterly at handling memes in a variety of ways including complex teaching. (Bonner 1980: 197)[8]

The neo-Darwinian framework within which Bonner does his professional research and his wide-ranging forays into organizing and narrating facts arising from research across the biological spectrum provide guidance for both the biologist and social theorist, and also for their research communities. Whether any side has an interest in using the work of researchers and scholars such as Bonner and, for that matter, crossover theorists such as Blute (2010) in sociocultural and biological neo-Darwinism is an interesting and open question.

In the past those on one side could disregard with impunity the work of those on the other side. Divided (tribal?) academic loyalty—is she a biologist or sociologist, for example?—bore a lot of toxic freight. In part that was because of mutual ignorance of the work of the other. But there are also examples of what some would deem to be the misapplication of assumptions underlying work on one side of the divide to problems that lie on the other side of the divide. An egregious example is the insistence that the human genome codes directly for human behavior as the genomes of the species within the order of, say, Hymenoptera (ants, wasps, etc.) code for their behavior (Wilson 1975).

Perhaps the most promising development at the present time for breaking down the wall of separation between biologists and sociologists is the rapidly advancing research on the brain and various aspects of neuroscience. This has been enabled by the development of brain imaging techniques (PET, fMRI, etc.) that trace brain activity in various ways. One then can leave behind such speculative notions as vitality (see Goethe above) and replace them with "pictures" of what the brain is doing at the genetic–protein expression level, where the culture behind behavior operates.[9]

This has relevance for understanding what goes on in religious behavior. For example, the Buddhist-inspired notion of mindfulness has been explored via fMRI scans of the brains of monks (BBC News, 2011). The area of the brain that drives attentiveness lights up. Thus, there is a correlation between the neural activity in the brains of those trained in meditation behavior and their practice of meditation. But the calming effect of meditative practice may not apply to everyone. If so, one would expect that genetic variants (typically small) would exist that regulate protein expression in the area of the brain devoted to attentiveness.

There is much recent research on the link between personal religiosity and religious behavior in America and its ameliorative effects on stressors and mental health (see for example Ellison et al. 2012: 493–511). And Krause has explored the effects of giving and receiving social support on the link between stressors and mortality in church contexts. Among other things he has shown that the provision of support to those subjected to stress attenuates mortality among church-going providers (Krause 2015: 22).

Embedding properly designed brain-imaging studies within the research programs of high-level social scientists such as Ellison and Krause would go beyond the correlations observed at the phenotypic level and provide information on the neural activity of the brain—where the action lies, so to speak.[10] As genomic science advances, the study of brain soothers that are triggered by religious interaction, ritual and belief may shed light on the question of whether, for some, church contexts work simply by virtue of self-selection attributable to genetic factors. The brain soothers that are triggered for some people in a church context may not be aroused for others because of genetic variation and its interaction with culture, especially that part of culture labeled "experience."[11]

Bellah

There are those dwelling within the pages of this volume who have accorded Bellah high honor and respect as a peer, including the volume's honoree. And I have enjoyed Tiryakian's presence at many meetings of the Association for the Sociology of Religion where, over the years, he has served graciously as a commentator, critic and presenter, always providing apt words that reveal his superb intellect, knowledge of the subdiscipline (sociology of religion), voracious reading habits—especially of history and philosophy—love of things French, and good humor.

At the August 2013 meetings of the Association for the Sociology of Religion and the American Sociological Association, convened shortly after Bellah's unexpected death that July, his life and work as a scholar were recognized and discussed by panels of distinguished colleagues. Tiryakian appeared on those panels and also took advantage of an appropriate moment at a regular Association for the Sociology of Religion session to comment on Bellah. He said that in his view Bellah's *Religion in Human Evolution* would do for the twenty-first century what Pierrre Teilhard de Chardin's *The Phenomenon of Man* had done for the twentieth century. What might that have been?

Teilhard de Chardin was a Jesuit paleontologist and geologist who had a role in the discovery of Peking Man, a pre-historic skull that enhanced knowledge about human evolution. Teilhard considered evolution and faith to be compatible. Hence, *The Phenomenon of Man* (1959), published after his death. But, as Macquarrie (1983: 11) noted:

> When Teilhard announces at the beginning of *The Phenomenon of Man* that he proposes *only to see*, that is to confine himself to phenomena, he sets out on a path of immanence from which he eventually breaks out only by a *tour de force*.

Bellah's problem is the opposite of Teilhard's. By claiming the emergence of the Axial Age with its dominant theme of critical transcendence, Bellah then has to find immanence (the body and brain of genetic evolution) and do so in a way that includes reproductive phenomena. A *tour de force* from the other side, so to speak, that fully recognizes biological evolution is required. Is he successful?

Of the reviews to date of *Religion in Human Evolution*, one in particular stands out. It appeared in the American Sociological Association's *Contemporary Sociology: A Journal of Reviews*, at the time under the editorship of Alan Sica. It was the lead review in volume 41, issue 6 of 2012 and was published back-to-back with Bellah's (2012) response.

The reviewer was Karl F. Morrison, Gotthold Lessing Professor of History and Poetics Emeritus, Rutgers University, and a professor of history, at the

University of Chicago, before retirement. The title of this review is "The Holy of Holies was Empty: Robert Bellah's Quest for Wisdom." Bellah's response is entitled "Das Ewig-weibliche: A reply to Karl Morrison." The German phrase translates as "The Eternal Feminine," words that appear in a number of literary sources, but most famously in Goethe's drama, *Faust*.

Morrison's critique and Bellah's response constitute one of the richest exchanges in academic debate that I have read. A full discussion here would require a long essay with journeys into the far corners of the study of religion in the humanities and social sciences—for example, Walter Benjamin's apprehension of the difference between North German Lutheranism and the Counter-Reformation (Simpson 1999: 59–72). Early on in his review essay, Morrison writes:

> One eloquent aspect of the intricate intellectual structure in this book is the spaces he has left empty. For example, so far as I can tell, there is not one reference to a woman, or to women, in this binary account of religion in evolution, though human evolution has occurred through sexual reproduction. Bellah also marginalizes emotion, though sexual reproduction has also commonly been of a piece with visceral emotion, and religion without emotion is a pale thing. (721)

Bellah is surprised and quickened by Morrison's charge. Far from overlooking women, Bellah says that he mentions them everywhere in his book. Kalapalo initiation ceremonies are carried out for boys and girls alike, and the groups that perform their great rituals are divided not by kinship but by gender. The importance of the All-Mother ritual among the Australian Aborigines is underlined. Among the Navajo, Changing Woman is the basic figure. In the Axial cases female deities play important roles: Asherah in early Israel; Athena, Hecuba, Antigone in Greek mythology and drama. The Daoists in ancient China placed the feminine above the masculine.

To demonstrate the importance of women in his book, Bellah says that he could have entitled it "The Eternal Feminine" (2012: 734). That is so because, over eons of human existence, women (mostly) have provided the nurturing and care during the long period of development and growth of the human infant that, according to Bellah, leads into childhood and adolescent play that is the foundation stone and source (in the French sense) of religion in human evolution.

The Eternal Feminine is a protean and plastic concept with a range of what might be called "applications" in various literary sources (O'Brien 2012). Nevertheless, Bellah does not seem to realize that had he chosen it as his title he would have obscured Goethe's intent. For Goethe, the Eternal Feminine refers to Faust's yearning and desire for Gretchen and her response, which culminates in a stigmatizing unwanted pregnancy. It is not a reference to the attachment of mothers and infants, although the yearning and desire of lovers and the bonding of mothers and their babies do go hand-in-hand, one preceding the other.

Bellah misses Morrison's point. None of the examples that Bellah adduces to counter the charge that women are not mentioned in his book refer to sexual behavior between men and women, that is, sexual intercourse without which there is no human reproduction.[12] It was Darwin's genius, and Wallace's, too, to recognize fertilization as part of the process that results in descent with modification, the full description accounting for variation among and between species. That is not part of Bellah's use of the word *evolution* in his title *Religion in Human Evolution*, nor was it part of his use in the title of the 1964 paper, "Religious Evolution."

Morrison goes so far as to state that *Religion in Human Evolution* is not a treatise on evolution at all. It is a description of certain themes in the cosmopolitan culture of the West, a culture of and for elites, and that has been globalized, a culture that is steeped in the belief that its rules of thinking rest on the (imagined) superiority of a turn to the theoretic among the tutors of the civilized world. I agree.

Notes

1   See the bibliography published in Bellah and Tipton (2006: 523–42).
2   Bellah's comparators (thus meaning: 1925–29 birth cohort; Harvard University PhD. in anthropology/sociology; significant work in religion) include Clifford Geertz and Edward Tiryakian.
3   In this chapter references to Goethe's work translated and published in English are found in Goethe 2009 and cited herein by page number in that book.
4   The English translation is found in Goethe (1988).
5   This section has a biographical slant. The standard modern biography of Darwin is Browne 1995 and 2002. Paul Johnson's recent popular biography (2012) is concise and accessible. Browne 2006 provides a narrative about the writing and publication of *Origin of Species*.
6   Darwin was a well-to-do person of the English gentry. He was married into the Wedgewood (pottery) family. He supported himself and his family and funded his research on the proceeds of his investments (Johnson 2012: 49–53).
7   It also makes things possible that have no apparent adaptive value or even destructive consequences that may continue to be selected over long periods of time (Baldus 2014).
8   A meme is a unit of culture analogous to a gene. The physicality of a gene is obvious. A meme on the other hand is difficult to pin down. What is its origin? One could answer "the brain," but that begs the question. My preferred locus is within the quantum mechanics and neurochemistry of the brain. That, of course, borders on triviality because everything within the brain–body exists at the quantum level. One can observe

genes at a level above the quantum, and from their physicality deduce the quantum. So far as memes go, there is physicality in speech, gesture, sound, etc., but it is a fleeting phenomenon that may leave a trace in the brain (memory). On the concept of memes, see Dawkins (1976); Blute (2010).

9   Imaging techniques do not literally make a picture at the cellular level; fMRI highlights blood flow that maps brain activity by area. PET uses radio-labeled chemicals that are injected into the bloodstream and are designed to "find" and attach to a neurotransmitter at a receptor where the amount of the neurotransmitter that is present is detected by the level of radioactivity.

10 Such studies could go a long way toward increasing the minuscule amounts of explained variance that are typically reported in stress–social support studies.

11 McGuire and Tiger (2009: 125–40) provide a useful review of studies of the neurochemistry of the brain/body and its correlations with social interaction, ritual behavior and beliefs in Christian and Islamic contexts.

12 A character in the French cult film starring Alan Bates, *The King of Hearts*, 1966, puts it very well: "The world is so simple. It's just men and women."

References

Baldus, B. 2014. "Contingency, Novelty and Choice: Cultural Evolution as Internal Selection." *Journal for the Theory of Social Behaviour*, April 8. DOI:10.1111/jtsb.12065.

BBC News. 2011. "Brains of Buddhist Monks Scanned in Meditation Study." http://www.bbc.co.uk/news-us-canada-12661646.

Bellah, R. N. 1957. *Tokugawa Religion: The Values of Pre-Industrial Japan*. Glencoe, IL: Free Press.

——— 1964. "Religious Evolution." *American Sociological Review* 29, no. 3: 358–74.

——— 1967. "Civil Religion in America." *Daedalus* 96, no. 1: 1–21.

——— 1970. *Beyond Belief: Essays on Religion in a Post-Traditional World*. New York: Harper and Row.

——— 2011. *Religion in Human Evolution: From the Paleolithic to the Axial Age*. Cambridge, MA, and London: Belknap Press of Harvard University Press.

——— 2012. "Das Ewig-weibliche: A reply to Karl Morrison." *Contemporary Sociology: A Journal of Reviews* 41, no. 6: 733–38.

Bellah, R. N., R. Madsen, W. M. Sullivan, A. Swidler and S. M. Tipton. 1985. *Habits of the Heart: Individualism and Commitment in American Life*. Berkeley: University of California Press.

Bellah, R. N. and S. M. Tipton, eds. 2006. *The Robert Bellah Reader*. Durham, NC, and London: Duke University Press.

Blute, M. 2010. *Darwinian Sociocultural Evolution: Solutions to Dilemmas in Cultural and Social Theory*. New York and Cambridge: Cambridge University Press.

Bonner, J. T. 1980. *The Evolution of Culture in Animals*. Princeton, NJ: Princeton University Press.

Browne, J. 1980. "Darwin's Botanical Arithmetic and the 'Principle of Divergence 1854–1858.'" *Journal of the History of Biology* 13, no. 1: 53–89.

——— 1995. *Charles Darwin: Vol. 1 Voyaging*. London: Jonathan Cape.

——— 2002. *Charles Darwin Vol. 2 The Power of Place*. London: Jonathan Cape.

——— 2006. *Darwin's Origin of Species: A Biography*. Crows' Nest, AU: Allen & Unwin.

Dawkins, R. 1976. *The Selfish Gene.* Oxford: Oxford University Press.

Ellison, C. G., M. Bradshaw, N. Kuyel, and J. Marcum. 2012. "Attachment to God, Stressful Life Events, and Changes in Psychological Distress." *Review of Religious Research* 53, no. 1: 493–511.

von Goethe, J. W. 1988. "The Metamorphosis of Plants." In *Goethe's Collected Works Vol. 12 Scientific Studies,* edited and translated by Douglas Miller. New York: Suhrkamp.

———— 2009. *The Metamorphosis of Plants.* Introduction and photography by Gordon L. Miller. Cambridge, MA, and London: The MIT Press.

Hau, M. 2003. *The Cult of Health and Beauty in Germany: A Social History, 1890–1930.* Chicago and London: The University of Chicago Press.

Hofstader, R. 1944. *Social Darwinism in American Thought 1860–1915.* Philadelphia: University of Pennsylvania Press.

Jahr, F. 2012. "How Brainless Slime Molds Redefine Intelligence." http://www.Scientific American.com/article/brainless-slime-molds/

Johnson, P. 2012. *Darwin: Portrait of a Genius.* New York: Penguin Books.

Kenneally, C. 2014. *The Invisible History of the Human Race: How DNA and History Shape Our Identities and Our Futures.* New York: Viking.

Krause, N. 2015. "Making the Work We Do More Relevant: Using Religion and Health as a Template." *Sociology of Religion* 76, no. 1: 14–29.

Malthus, T. 1798. *An Essay on the Principle of Population.* London: Johnson.

Macquarrie, J. 1983. "William Temple: Philosopher, Theologian, Churchman." In *The Experiment of Life: Science and Religion,* edited by F. K. Hare, 3–16. Toronto: University of Toronto Press.

McGuire, M. T. and L. Tiger. 2009. "The Brain and Religious Adaptation." In *The Biology of Religious Behavior: The Evolutionary Origins of Faith and Religion,* edited by J. R. Feierman, 125–40. Santa Barbara: Praeger.

Morrison, K. F. 2013. "The Holy of Holies was Empty: Robert Bellah's Quest for Wisdom." *Contemporary Sociology: A Journal of Reviews* 41, no. 6: 721–32.

O'Brien, E. P. 2012. "The Meaning of the Eternal Feminine in Goethe's Drama Faust." "Electronic Theses, Treatises and Dissertations." Paper no. 5076. http://diginole.lib. fsu.edu/etd/5076.

Sica, A. 2012. "Classical Sociological Theory." In *The Wiley-Blackwell Companion to Sociology* 1st Edition, edited by G. Ritzer, 82–97. London: Blackwell Publishing.

Simpson, J. H. 1999. "A Scrapbook of Lessons for the Modern from the (New) Baroque: Discontinuity, Gazing, Glancing, Listening." In *Going for Baroque: Cultural Transformations 1550–1650,* edited by F. Guardiani, 59–72. Ottawa: Legas.

———— 2011. "Afterward: What Is History?" In *History, Time, Meaning and Memory,* edited by B. Jones Denison, 255–64. Leiden and Boston: Brill.

Teilhard de Chardin, P. 1959. *The Phenomenon of Man.* London: Collins.

Whorter, J. C. 2000. *Inner Hygiene: Constipation and the Pursuit of Health in Modern Society.* New York: Oxford University Press.

Wilson, E. O. 1975. *Sociobiology: The New Synthesis.* Cambridge, MA: Belknap Press of Harvard University Press.

Wolfe, A. 2011. "The Origins of Religion, Beginning with The Big Bang." *The New York Times Sunday Book Review,* September 30: 1. A review of Robert N. Bellah. 2011. *Religion in Human Evolution.* Cambridge, MA: The Belknap Press of Harvard University Press.

Chapter 12

THE "AXIAL AGE" VS. WEBER'S COMPARATIVE SOCIOLOGY OF THE WORLD RELIGIONS

John Torpey

This chapter explores the notion of the "Axial Age," much-discussed of late, and compares it with Weber's comparative sociology of the world religions. In contrast to the coherence and similarity of developments implied in the Axial Age thesis, this chapter argues that Weber was more inclined to emphasize the differences between the various world religions and their divergent consequences for the worldviews of those socialized into them.

Recent developments in the field of economic history raise profound problems for what has long been known as "the Weber thesis" or "the Protestant ethic thesis"—the idea that it was Protestantism, and especially Calvinism, that (however inadvertently) provided the "spirit of capitalism." Commencing with the work of Kenneth Pomeranz in his landmark 2000 book, *The Great Divergence: China, Europe, and the Making of the Modern World Economy*, the view has increasingly prevailed that, contrary to earlier accounts, Europe only surged ahead of the rest of the world economically around the beginning of the nineteenth century. This view has subsequently been endorsed, if on various grounds, by such authors as the ancient historian Ian Morris (2010) and the economist Angus Deaton (2013). For his part, Michael Mann (1986: 377) has argued that the crucial developments underlying European hegemony—in particular, the "normative pacification" provided by medieval Catholicism, lowering transaction costs among the inhabitants of the then-obscure West European peninsula—were in place centuries before the Protestant Reformation. Taken together, these analyses raise doubts about whether "the Protestant ethic thesis" can be seriously said to explain Europe's rise to dominance of the modern world, unless one is prepared to countenance the claim that it took two hundred years or more for the "Protestant ethic" to supply the necessary push toward the European economic takeoff.

Max Weber's comparative sociology of the world religions was based precisely on this notion, however. Weber's studies of the religions of China, India and ancient Palestine were oriented toward illuminating their "economic ethics"—in other words, the ways in which their doctrines were or were not conducive to giving birth to "modern rational capitalism," as Weber characterized the new economic order. Defining the explanandum in these terms was testimony to Weber's preoccupation with questions raised about the modern world by Karl Marx; it is not too much to say that most of Weber's scholarly efforts were in some sense a response to Marx's historical materialism. Weber was intent to show that, no matter how profound the impact of modern capitalism and of class struggles in the modern world, class analysis alone would never be able to make sense of the world; religions shaped worldviews and either facilitated or retarded the emergence of the capitalist ethos. But this understandable preoccupation on Weber's part may have distracted us from the more defensible core of his writings on religion, which stresses the divergent trajectories of different religious traditions.

Against this background, we may need to re-think fundamentally our "reception" of Weber's oeuvre, de-emphasizing his analysis of the causes of the rise of capitalism and focusing instead on the tools he has supplied us for the purpose of social analysis generally. A crucial step toward this goal would be an end to the practice in many sociology programs of reading only *The Protestant Ethic and the Spirit of Capitalism* among Weber's writings, which inevitably tends to leave students with the impression that Weber was concerned only with analyzing the rise of capitalism and to have Protestantism in the starring role of midwife. Here, the recent debate on the so-called Axial Age helps clarify Weber's understanding of social analysis as against that of his putative advocates who defend the Axial Age thesis, which posits a certain coherence and uniformity in the responses by several of the cultures of the ancient world to comparable problems of human development. In order to unpack this argument, let us begin with a brief explication of the Axial Age thesis.

The Idea of an Axial Age

Shortly after World War II, the German philosopher Karl Jaspers (1953: 1) proposed the idea that the middle centuries of the first millennium BCE constituted an "Axial Age," a watershed period during which "man as we know him today came into existence." Jaspers argued that the world's major civilizations—what William McNeill (1963) and others would call the Eurasian *ecumene*—faced comparable developmental challenges that led to a series of major breakthroughs in human thought. In particular, the Chinese, Indians, Greeks and the Jews of Israel are said to have developed *theoria*—"thinking about thinking," "criticism" and similar advances in reflection upon the world in which they lived. Commentators have ascribed to the period the development of the notion of "transcendence"—of this world by another world (Eisenstadt 1982)—or of the very possibility of "religious rejections of the world" on the basis of "the exaltation of another realm of reality as alone true and valuable" (Bellah 1964: 359). These developments were embodied above all in the emergence of Confucianism, Buddhism, prophetic Judaism and classical Greek philosophy. Somewhat awkwardly, and despite the prevalence of a lively pantheon of gods in the Greek world, the latter had relatively little to do with religion as we normally think of it, but rather was a case of humans taking their destiny into their own hands in an unprecedented manner.

Nonetheless, Jaspers and those who have followed his lead have tended to emphasize the coherence of this epoch as a stage in the development of human ratiocination. This view has been criticized by some historians who see it as an unwarranted intrusion of philosophers and theologians into the domain of the historian. One example of this critique comes from the pen of Jan Assmann, the German Egyptologist, who wrote: "The idea of the Axial Age is not so much about 'man as we know him' [today] and his/her first appearance in time, but about 'man as we want him' and the utopian goal of a universal civilized community" (Assmann 2012: 401). But this has not necessarily been the view among historians across the board. The Axial Age thesis had an early defender in the renowned historian of Islam, Marshall Hodgson (1963: 244), who wrote of the period that "Jaspers has with reason called this the 'Axial Age,'" an epoch that "resulted in the presence everywhere [in Eurasia] of selective intellectual standards which permitted intercultural influences to proceed on the level of abstract thought."

In his magnum opus, *Economy and Society* (1978: 447), Max Weber remarks on the importance of the "Prophetic Age" during the period singled out by Jaspers, but refers in quotation marks to the "prophets" of ancient Greece in recognition of the fact that these were not religious thinkers in the mold of the Jewish prophets, Zoroaster, the Hindu sages or the Buddha. Nor does Weber place much stress on the particular period in which these developments occurred; he indicates that the Prophetic Age took place mainly in the eighth and seventh centuries BCE, but that some of these prophetic movements "reached into the sixth and even the fifth century" (Weber 1978: 442). On the basis of these comments, Bellah (2005: 75–76) suggests that Max Weber's comparative sociology of the world religions "implies something like the Axial Age hypothesis."

Weber's Comparative Sociology of the World Religions

That may well be the case, yet one might also argue that Weber was more inclined to emphasize the *variation* in the "directions" of the "world rejection" that emerged in this Prophetic Age than their commonality. In Weber's view, the crucial dimension of these developments was not so much temporal as geographic and cultural. Immediately after this discussion of the Prophetic Age, Weber highlights a crucial distinction between two forms of prophecy: the East Asian and South Asian forms of prophecy, for which the Buddha set the standard, were "exemplary," whereas those originating in the Near East and typified by Zoroaster and Muhammad were "ethical" in character. The differences between these two basic types of prophecy, according to Weber, set these world religions on divergent paths that would lead to profoundly different religio-cultural trajectories—and, of course, divergent economic and social outcomes.

But then, beyond the ethical/exemplary distinction, there were also significant differences in emphasis and outlook among the various religions that emerged across the Eurasian landmass over the past three millennia. Let us begin with India. The so-called Aryan invaders who entered India from the northwest in roughly the middle of the second millennium BCE were nature-worshippers. That archaic form of religion would, in time, be superseded by Vedic Brahmanism—a priestly religion associated with "books of knowledge" (Vedas) that were also poems addressed to the gods, seeking their approbation and assistance. From the ancient poets, the priestly stratum inherited the responsibility for purveying, whether by writing or in speech, the sacred hymns and mantras, which were regarded as powerful magic and accessible only to the religiously qualified.

The canonical text of Brahmanism was the *Rig Veda*, which is thought to have been composed well before 1000 BCE but not written down before about 600 BCE. Like the *Qur'an*, the *Rig Veda* was thought to have been divinely revealed poetry and was followed by prose commentaries that elaborated the rules and rituals of the faith. Because they marked out a special role for the Aryan priestly class, the commentaries were referred to as the Brahmanas. Vedic religion was organized to a high degree by sacrifice and, as in Zoroastrianism—the dominant religion of ancient Persia—sacrifice was unfailingly accompanied by fire. Indeed, the god of fire, Agni, was the most frequently mentioned god in the *Rig Veda*. Aryan households were expected to offer sacrifices to the gods five times daily, either by the Brahman head of household or by his Brahman priest or cook, from whom anyone would take food because of his high, non-polluting status (Wolpert 2000: 43). As guardians of, and go-betweens with, the spiritual world, the Brahman priests had, by the middle of the first millennium BCE, come to occupy positions of earthly power as well as of religious authority.

In its explanation of the cosmos, the *Rig Veda* outlines a social hierarchy that sprang from the anatomy of the original cosmic man: the *brahmans*, or priests, came from his mouth; the *kshatriyas*, the warriors, from his arms; the *vaishyas*, the merchants, artisans, and farmers, from his legs; and the *shudras*, the servants, from his feet. The *shudras* were probably originally the indigenous people conquered by the lighter-skinned Aryans from western Asia, and the emergence of this category to supplement the three-class order familiar from European society (those who pray, those who fight and those who work) helped institute a profound color-consciousness that ever since has been "a significant factor in reinforcing the hierarchical social attitudes that are so deeply embedded in Indian civilization" (Wolpert 2000: 32). These social arrangements would, of course, characterize Indian society until very recent times.

When, in the middle of the first millennium, the Magadha dynasty came to dominate a substantial portion of the Ganges Plain, the Brahmans had come, along with the warrior class (*kshatriyas*), to be crucial pillars of rule, though they were also much less political in their self-understanding than were Confucian sages. Instead, Brahmans were becoming an educated status group, owning land and controlling village life through their dominance of ritual. Meanwhile, the quadripartite *varna* system had become a pervasive element of northern India social life. The *shudras*, who brought up the bottom of the social and religious hierarchy, were regarded as ritually unclean and, hence, consigned to the lowest occupations. (Eventually, another group, the absolutely unclean "untouchables," would be added as well; see Wolpert 2000: 42). More especially, they were forbidden to hear the Vedic mantras, possibly on pain of death or excruciating punishment, such as having molten lead poured in their ears. By this time Brahmanism had become associated with a traditionalistic defense of their own privileges and of ritual—a ritual that was strongly bound up with sacrifice and, hence, with killing. And, of course, there was a good deal of killing going on in the society at large, despite the Magadha conquest of the Gangetic Plain. The *Mahabharata*, the epic tale thought to reflect Indian life in approximately 1000 BCE but composed several centuries later, is "drenched in the blood of endless warfare" (Wolpert 2000: 38). The Brahmana era was thus one in which social hierarchy had become sharp, political authority centralized and unprecedentedly powerful, and religious life to a considerable extent a defense of this power and inequality.

In this context, there arose disquiet among thoughtful people concerning the direction of their society, provoking a variety of novel responses to their situation. Perhaps the first development to discuss is the Upanishads, the first of which were composed in approximately the eighth century BCE but whose canonization was not secured until the late centuries of the first millennium BCE. In contrast to the stress in the *Rig Veda* on mantras and sacrifices as the means to salvation, the Upanishads promoted the idea of wandering in the forest in search of understanding. Thus emerged the figure of the mendicant ascetic who renounced conventional life in favor of the pursuit of wisdom; in the process, a rationalistic side was imparted to Indian religiosity. Along with the quest for wisdom, the Upanishads instructed that yoga exercises prepared the body for the abandonment of human striving, desire and their consequent frustrations. The "quiescent, mindless, motionless inactivity of *moksha*" (Wolpert 2000: 46)—"release" from suffering—now became the chief goal of Vedantic meditation. *Moksha* could be achieved by knowledge of the self, which required control over oneself and one's desires. At the same time, the idea of *samsara*—an endless cycle of birth, death, and re-birth from which the individual can be freed only with great difficulty or good fortune—comes to the fore. The linkage between *karma* and *samsara* emerges here as "a distinguishing axiom of Indic civilization" (Wolpert 2000: 47).

Max Weber viewed the idea of *karma* as the most complete, systematic solution of the "theodicy problem"—the question of the relation of God to the world—ever invented. Weber shows that the idea of *karma* entails the creation of a world in which all acts have consequences for the person's fate in the next life; the person is enjoined to behave well in order to merit rebirth in a better station or, ideally, to be released entirely from the wheel of rebirth. As a result of this all-encompassing conception of the place of ethical action in the world, "the dualism of a sacred, omnipotent, and majestic god confronting the ethical inadequacy of all his creatures is altogether lacking" (Weber 1978: 526). Weber would seem to have been contrasting the *karma* doctrine and its consequences with the ethical implications of the Jewish god created during roughly the same period in Israel/Palestine. As we have seen, Weber distinguishes between "ethical" and "exemplary" forms of salvation religion, and Hinduism clearly lies on the latter side of the divide between these two types.

While the concepts of *karma* and *samsara* would play a crucial role in subsequent Indian religion, this did not necessarily mean that they always played the same role in different religious traditions. Let us first consider Jainism, which arose around 500 BCE and persists today as a small minority religion in India, perhaps comparable to Mormonism in the United States in its distinctness from but rootedness in the religion from which it departed. At the outset, however, Jainism was a major source of a new worldview. The religion was associated with the teachings of Mahavira, a north Indian aristocrat who renounced his privileges and adopted a peripatetic life of teaching and contemplation. The Jains argued that all things, living or nonliving, had a soul, and viewed *karma*—the principle of causation—as a substance that accumulated upon the soul to the extent that the individual acted in the world. Thus the Jains understood salvation in terms of "the escape of the soul from its adhering *karma* and its upward flight to live on forever in a realm of pure bliss" (Farmer et al. 1977: 104). Salvation could only be achieved, however, by adherence to an extremely stringent series of rules that forbade killing, stealing, lying, sexual activity, and the ownership of property. The prohibition on killing and on causing any suffering—which the West came to know, through Gandhi, as the principle of *ahimsa*—was interpreted so strictly that Jains could not kill their own food; it had to be harvested by laymen. Mahavira is thought to have slowly starved himself to death in his attempt to live up to the strictures against killing. To this day, Jains will sweep a chair before sitting down so as to insure that no living thing might die in the process. Due to the prohibition on harming living things, devout Jains have tended to avoid agricultural occupations and to be urbanites in mercantile occupations. The rewards of such a life of voluntary privation might seem paltry, but it continues to attract adherents—though understandably relatively few. At the time that it emerged, Jainism represented an extreme version of the renunciation that would characterize much subsequent Indian religiosity.

Buddhism arose in this same historical context; Mahavira and the Buddha ("the enlightened one") were roughly contemporaries, living on either side of the year 500 BCE. Siddhartha Gautama was a young noble who could look forward to a life of power and comfort, but he threw it all away in favor of wandering in search of the truth of existence. That truth, he concluded, was that this world was essentially an illusion, and that there was little to seek in this life. In contrast to Jainism, there were no souls or selves to save in Buddhism. Instead, the aim was to avoid accumulating *karma* by stanching desire. Despite the lack of a soul to which *karma* could adhere, as in Jainism, Buddhists nonetheless regarded the accumulation of *karma* as inevitable for the unenlightened. They thus sought release—*moksha*—from entanglement in the world and the attainment of *nirvana*, a state beyond desire and, hence, beyond its frustrations. This exalted state was attainable more or less only by ascetic monks who, however, relied on laypeople for alms and donations. Those laypersons were at best likely to be able, through proper performance of the duties of their station, to be reborn as beings somewhat closer to enlightenment, release and *nirvana*. In these respects, while diverging from the religious practices and ideas of Vedic religion and lacking any stake in its social arrangements, Buddhism failed to challenge to any great degree the social structures inherited from Brahmanism. The Buddhist *sangha* (brotherhood) gathered in monasteries, which gave them an organizational backbone and, in time, a thriving economic base. The monasteries symbolized the Buddhists' retreat from the world, even if they did not entirely abandon workaday life because they depended on the laity for their upkeep. Having started as an effort to purify Brahmanism and rid it of its objectionable qualities from *within* educated Brahman circles (Collins 1998: 205), Buddhism gradually came to challenge it from a separate and organizationally superior position.

Taken together, the emergence of Jainism and Buddhism might be seen as Vedic Brahmanism's Protestant Reformation. Early Buddhism resembles Lutheranism in the sense that it rebelled against the worldliness of its "mother-ship," Brahmanism (finding in the more established vehicle a distraction from piety and a misuse of faith), and offered a refurbished doctrine meant to re-secure the connection to the sacred under very different terms— especially the doctrine of nonviolence (*ahimsa*). Buddhism also was marked by a greater "reasonableness" than Jainism, a more relaxed quality comparable to Lutheranism's less extreme rejection of established ecclesiastical authority when compared with the Reformed Protestant sects. In contrast, Jainism was more similar to Reformed Protestantism, which was marked by rather greater rigor in the injunctions of the faith that they developed. Like Calvinism, Jainism took for granted that the greater the suffering of the believer, the better for his soul. Meanwhile, Buddhism was the only movement of its time to require that its monks preach to the laity, maintaining important links to them when others such as the Jains insisted on pure virtuoso religiosity. Finally, however, having conceived of the world as chiefly a realm of suffering, Buddhism's ethics were somewhat more oriented toward relieving the suffering of others than was Lutheranism's insistence on "faith alone" as the guarantor of salvation. Since Buddhism valued "good *karma*," it was also prepared to countenance good works as appropriate efforts on the path to salvation. Jainism encouraged non-harming as a path to salvation, but commanded little else in the way of helping others. In that regard, it might be said to have promoted a more individualistic orientation to the world, one not especially concerned about the fate of others. In this it differed notably from Reformed Protestantism's stress on a God-fearing community intently concerned about the fate of one another's souls.

The Protestant Reformation analogy goes only so far, however. In contrast to the Christian faiths, which remain separated despite centuries of ecumenical soul-searching, Hinduism in India later would reinterpret the Buddha as a reincarnation of Lord Vishnu and re-absorb Buddhism into itself. Like a stream that divides in one place, only to converge again further downhill, Hinduism first spawned and then ingested Buddhism, such that it disappeared from its Indian birthplace, with the final coup de grace being administered by hostile Muslims in the early second millennium CE. Carried off by wandering monks seeking a more hospitable place to worship, Buddhism subsequently came to be more associated with East and Southeast Asia than with the land of its historical origins. Buddhism and Jainism emerged at first from the Brahmanic context, but their rejection of some of its elements and elaboration of novel stresses led to the foundation of new faiths with common roots but also with very different features.

Next, we must examine a more or less contemporaneous development on Asia's western fringe, in what we now call the Middle East. This was the emergence of prophetic Judaism, which invented a radically new relationship between a people and its god(s), as intimated above in Weber's discussion of the *karma* doctrine. We should first of all clarify the meaning here of "prophecy." This activity had less to do with our sense of "divining the future" and more to do with the interpretation of the will of the gods. Thus, although they were sometimes foretelling the downfall of some tyrant for misbehavior, the prophets were chiefly articulating their understanding of the gods' commands to the people. In doing so, they reinforced the idea that the Israelites should follow one god above all others. This stress on the worship of one god to the exclusion of others, or at least above those others, arose against the background of intense pressure on the "Children of Israel," those who believed that their god had given them special claim to lands at the eastern end of the Mediterranean (Farmer et al. 1977: 96).

The Jewish prophets of the early first millennium BCE are traditionally thought to have built on the cult of Yahweh. Yet recent scholarship (Bellah 2011: 287) suggests that the original god of Israel was not Yahweh, but El, and that ancestor worship was perhaps more important in ancient Israel than later became the case. The importance of El rather than Yahweh in early Jewish history helps make sense of the very name "Israel" (*Yisra-el*), which literally means "he who strives with god."[1] Thus was created a conception of god as one with whom a people wrestles, at least metaphorically. In the words of Diarmaid MacCulloch (2009: 50), the Jews are unusual in that they "struggle against the one whom they worship. [...] The relationship of God with Israel is intense, personal, conflicted." That relationship was also novel in the sense that it was based on a covenant binding the people to their god and creating a powerful bond between them.

According to Bellah, this view of the relationship was borrowed from Assyrian precursors which, however, involved king and subjects, not god and people. In approximately 722 BCE, the Jews in Israel suffered destruction at the hands of the conquering Assyrians. The Assyrian ruler, Aššur, demanded loyalty to himself as god-king. As victims of the Assyrian onslaught, the Jews rejected those demands in favor of fealty to one god and one god only—Yahweh. The name of the ninth-century prophet Elijah, which means "Yahweh is my god" (MacCulloch 2009: 58), suggests the growing convergence of El with Yahweh and their gradual acceptance as synonyms. Insistence on the exclusive worship of Yahweh arose as an effort by the prophets, who were keenly attuned to the external threats to the Hebrews, to promote one particular god as the savior of the Jewish people.

In the process, the prophets created the notion of a remote, all-powerful creator deity to whom they owed their chief obedience, above and beyond any earthly being. "A God who is finally outside society and the world provides the point of reference from which all existing presuppositions can be questioned. [...] It is as if Israel took the most fundamental symbolism of the great archaic civilizations—God, king and people—and pushed it to the breaking point where something dramatically new came into the world" (Bellah 2011: 322). That something new was the idea of a people beholden to their obligations to their god, and vice versa. Against this background, the Hebrew prophets called the Jewish people—individually and collectively—to live up to their covenant with Yahweh/God. This emphasis frequently brought them into conflict with their earthly rulers. For example, the very idea of a monarchy could be seen as inconsistent with the obligation to give one's obedience to God, and there remain to this day orthodox Jews who object to the existence of the state of Israel as a blasphemous betrayal of Jewish ideals.

Then there were the criticisms of the specific policies of the kings. Thus the prophet Elijah inveighed against the corruption of King Ahab and his wife Jezebel and prophesied his doom. In the eighth century BCE, the Judean prophet Isaiah chastised the wealthy for their exploitation of the poor. But, ultimately, the message of the prophets was that it was the duty of every individual to honor the covenant with Yahweh. The ethical duties were outlined in the Ten Commandments, traditionally ascribed to Moses's divine inspiration. Obedience to God's commandments would, in turn, result in God's approbation and the security and prosperity of the people. The notion that worldly success was a reward for religiously correct behavior promoted what Weber called the Jews' "frank respect for wealth"; the ascetic idea that "the love of money is the root of many evils" would await the New Testament. The notion that the Jews were the chosen people of God also complicated the ethical terrain, promoting an in-group morality that regarded non-Jews as possible objects of usury while prohibiting such behavior with regard to fellow Jews. As prophetic Judaism developed, there emerged a deep and abiding tension between the particularism of the Jews' covenant with Yahweh and the implicit universalism of the ethical creed. Yahweh's commands were, in principle, valid for everyone, due to his remoteness and omnipotence. This all entailed a powerful push toward ethical concerns in Judaic religion and its successors.

As is well known, Judaism was the progenitor of Christianity, but the latter's conception was not, so to speak, immaculate; instead, Christianity was the product of a Hellenized Jewish culture that took root on the eastern fringes of the Roman Empire. Its outlook derived in many ways from Greek precursors, filtered through Roman reworkings of that inheritance. We must therefore consider some of the elements of classical Greek culture that echoed down into later developments.

The Greeks of fifth-century Athens famously created a form of social organization widely regarded as unprecedented among state-bearing societies. That organization was the *polis* or "city-state," the institution from which we derive our words for "politics" and "policy," not to mention "police." While it is often thought that the form of government in the fifth-century *polis* was "democracy," this was by no means necessarily the case; *poleis* could be ruled by illegitimate usurpers, oligarchies, or the mob. Even when the *polis* was ruled "democratically," we should understand that this democracy involved only about one-fifth of the adult male population. Among those who participated, however, it was a *direct* democracy, relying on face-to-face assemblies and debates over matters concerning the city-state. The Athenians thus invented a form of government that included many ordinary people and, more importantly for our purposes, made decisions on the basis of persuasion and without divine sanction. The link between divinity and rule, so characteristic a feature of previous states, was broken. Even if the gods were very much part of their world, the *ecclesia* ("assembly," but later the basis for the Italian *chiesa* (church) and of our term *ecclesiastical*), which made decisions for the *polis* did not need the sanction of the gods to do as they chose to do.

Greek religion was also remarkably human-centered for its time. In contrast to the phantasmagorical figures we associate with Indic religiosity, the Greek gods were represented as larger-than-life versions of human beings and conceived very much in human terms. Temples were homes for the gods, not places of worship. Meanwhile, in classical Greece of the fifth century, there was no separate priestly stratum; Greek priests were officials of the state "in exactly the same sense as generals or treasurers or market commissioners [...] with the same tenure and rotation of office, as the others" (Finley 1963: 48).

Meanwhile, the bards who passed down the stories from the heroic period that followed the collapse of Mycenaean civilization around 1200 BCE were just that, poets, not priests on the Brahmanic model who guarded sacred knowledge and dispensed it for a fee. The gods played a central role in those stories and, according to Herodotus, it was Homer who "first fixed for the Greeks the genealogy of the gods, gave the gods their titles, divided among them their honors and functions, and defined their images" (cited in Finley 1963: 26). But, unlike the Vedas, which were the property of the Brahmana priests, the stories were understood as the common possession of all Greeks and, while the gods were very human-like, the degree to which human beings in those stories were also raised up to a level close to the gods was striking.

The Greeks also exhibited a pronounced desire to make sense of the empirical world, a practice that we now know as philosophy. Two of the most remarkable of the "lovers of wisdom," Plato and Aristotle, bequeathed to posterity resources for thinking about the world that continue to generate insight and discussion. For present purposes, Plato is perhaps the more important figure, as he contributed ideas about religion that would have profound ramifications later on. First, he advanced a conception of God as perfect oneness. Like the Jews, Plato also stressed transcendence in his view of God. Yet, in contrast to the god of the Hebrews, who were busy wrestling with each other, Plato's conception of a perfect god was passionless and unchanging. This would later help provide Christianity with a conception of divinity as remote and impervious to influence, the "deus abscondidus" that, Weber argued, left the Calvinist in "an unprecedented state of inner loneliness" about the fate of his or her soul. In addition, Plato mused about the existence of an individual soul, a spark of immortality that outlived and was ultimately more real than the mortal housing in which it existed in this life. Such a view differed sharply from the Jews' attitudes on the matter at this period; until the time of the Maccabean revolt in the second century BCE, Jewish writings suggest "that human life comes to an end and, for all but a few exceptional people, that is it" (MacCulloch 2009: 70). The preoccupation with life after death would prove one of the major features that would permit later observers to regard "Christianity" as something other than the Judaism from which it originally emerged.

In some ways like the Greeks, the Chinese during the middle of the first millennium BCE also underwent a period of profound reflection on the human being's place in the world. Just as Plato has been the central figure in Western philosophy, Confucius has played a similarly decisive role in subsequent East Asian thought. Yet the teachings of Confucius revolve around questions of correct ritual and of goodness rather than of the individual's relationship with a divinity. Hence, like the developments associated with classical Athens, Confucianism has long been regarded as strongly "secular" in character. Against the background of much violence, Confucius was above all concerned with recovering the supposed harmony of earlier days by way of a return to the proper performance of ritual. Confucius insisted that, while it was important to be in tune with the desires of Heaven, human beings choose their own fate. They could thus choose to do right or to do wrong, and the cultivation of "the gentleman" involved training toward inner reserve and self-control, with the aim of producing an individual who was no one's "tool."

The "secular" qualities of Confucianism have raised questions ever since about whether or not these doctrines should be regarded as a "religion." For Weber, "Confucianism is rationalist to such a far-going extent that it stands at the extreme boundary of what one might possibly call a 'religious' ethic" (Weber 1945: 293). In *The Religion of China*, Weber (1951) describes Confucianism as a philosophy of rational adjustment to the world, but one that could also coexist peaceably with the "magic garden" of Taoism. Indeed, one of the remarkable features of Chinese religiosity is its capacity for cohabitation among a variety of belief systems. Chinese religion thus lacks the tendency toward exclusivism that characterizes all the major faiths that originated to its west—Judaism, Christianity, Islam and Hinduism.

In any case, Weber contrasted Confucianism's accommodative impulses toward the world with the otherwise similarly rationalistic impulses of Puritanism. In Weber's view, whereas Confucianism sought to inculcate adjustment to the world as it is, Puritanism instilled the sense of a tension with the world that led the Calvinist to want to transform the world. It made the Puritan into a "tool of the divine"; in contrast, the Confucian gentleman could not, as stated above, be anyone's tool. "The Confucian owed nothing to a supramundane God; therefore, he was never bound to a sacred 'cause' or an 'idea'" (Weber 1951: 236). In sum, according to Weber, Confucianism inculcated a radically "optimistic" outlook that was at odds with the dictates of an ethical god enjoining action in this world to make it more consistent with the god's strictures about how the world should be. It was thus ethically inadequate, particularly not up to the level of reformed Protestantism and its demands on the believer.

Robert Bellah (2011) has argued that this understanding of Confucianism is fundamentally wrong-headed. In Bellah's view, Confucius's insistence that the rulers properly observe the time-honored rituals supplied the foundation for the notion that China's rulers needed to serve the interests of their subjects—otherwise, their legitimacy as rulers would be squandered. This is the background to the idea that Chinese rulers have "the mandate of heaven," but also that they can lose that mandate if they fail to live up to its requirements. Beyond this, however, there is also in Confucianism "an ideal of human self-cultivation leading to an identification with an ultimate moral order, with the *Dao* and the will of Heaven, that is available to individuals, however grim the social situation and however much they may seem to have 'failed' to bring good order to society" (Bellah 2011: 476). Confucianism and other Chinese systems of thought thus instilled in both the Chinese people and their rulers moral standards that entailed a tension with the prevailing order of things; these systems of ideas were not merely modes of adjustment to the status quo. Thus, Bellah argues, "given Weber's enormously influential analysis of China as a stagnant, traditional society, it is perhaps well to point out that such was not the heritage of the Axial Age to later Chinese history" (Bellah 2011: 279). The reason for Weber's misunderstanding may again perhaps be traced to his preoccupation with the "economic ethics of the world religions," rather than with their political proclivities.

Conclusion

These reflections on the varied directions of "religious rejections of the world" suggest the important difference in outlook that characterizes Weber's sociology of the world religions and the impulses of the Axial Age thesis. I have emphasized the ways in which, for better or worse, Weber was more inclined to stress the divergent features of the various religions that emerged from the ancient world and late antiquity. Weber was more likely to stress the complex implications of these doctrines for the worldviews of those who embodied them, whereas the notion of an Axial Age stresses the shared basic unity of the intellectual–religious breakthrough that is said to have occurred in the middle centuries of the first millennium BCE. Weber's lack of commitment to any strong notion of a coherent "age" keeps him immune from the unavoidable debate generated by the Axial Age thesis over the periodization of the emergence of "man as we know him today," and hence from the necessity of jerry-built fixes that allow for the belated inclusion of later traditions the proximate origins of which lie outside the Axial Age. Christianity and Islam thus emerge from Weber's explorations as fully equal "world religions" that shaped world history just as much as any that originated in the Prophetic Age. The Axial Age thesis thus calls our attention to certain developments that laid down the tracks of later patterns, but it distracts us from a more satisfactory understanding of the religious forces that created the world as we know it now.

Note

1 Bellah (2011: 287) writes that the word Israel means "El rules," and notes that this would also buttress the notion of El as the Israelites' chief god before the rise of Yahweh to that position.

References

Bellah, R. 1964. "Religious Evolution." *American Sociological Review* 29, no. 3: 358–74.
——— 2005. "What Is Axial about the Axial Age?" *European Journal of Sociology* 46, no. 1: 69–87.
——— 2011. *Religion in Human Evolution: From the Paleolithic to the Axial Age*. Cambridge, MA: Harvard University Press.
Collins, R. 1998. *A Sociology of Philosophies: A Global Theory of Intellectual Change*. Cambridge, MA: Belknap Press of Harvard University Press.

Deaton, A. 2013. *The Great Escape: Health, Wealth, and the Origins of Inequality*. Princeton, NJ: Princeton University Press.

Eisenstadt, S. N. 1982. "The Axial Age: The Emergence of Transcendental Visions and the Rise of Clerics." *European Journal of Sociology* 23, no. 2: 294–314.

Farmer, E. L., G. R. G. Hambly, D. Kopf, B. K. Marshall, and R. Taylor. 1977. *Comparative History of Civilizations in Asia*, Vol. 1: 10,000 B.C. to 1850. Reading, MA: Addison-Wesley.

Finley, M. I. 1963. *The Ancient Greeks*. New York: Penguin.

Hodgson, M. G. S. 1963. "The Interrelations of Societies in History." *Comparative Studies in Society and History* 5, no. 2: 227–50.

MacCulloch, D. 2009. *Christianity: The First Three Thousand Years*. New York: Viking.

Mann, M. 1986. *The Sources of Social Power*, Vol. 1: *A History of Power from the Beginning to A.D. 1760*. New York: Cambridge University Press.

McNeill, W. H. 1963. *The Rise of the West: A History of the Human Community*. Chicago: University of Chicago Press.

Morris, I. 2010. *Why the West Rules—For Now: The Patterns of History and What They Reveal About the Future*. New York: FSG.

Pomeranz, K. 2000. *The Great Divergence: China, Europe, and the Making of the Modern World Economy*. Princeton, NJ: Princeton University Press.

Weber, M. 1945. "The Social Psychology of the World Religions." In *From Max Weber: Essays in Sociology*, edited by H. H. Gerth and C. Wright Mills, 267–301. New York: Oxford University Press.

———— 1951. *The Religion of China: Confucianism and Taoism*. Translated and edited by Hans H. Gerth. New York: Oxford University Press.

———— 1978. *Economy and Society: An Outline of Interpretive Sociology*, edited by G. Roth and C. Wittich. 2 vols. Berkeley: University of California Press.

Wolpert, S. 2000. *A New History of India*. 6th ed. New York: Oxford University Press.

EDWARD A. TIRYAKIAN'S PUBLICATIONS

Books and Edited Volumes

Tiryakian, E. A. 2009. *For Durkheim: Essays in Historical and Cultural Sociology.* Surrey, Burlington, and Aldershot: Ashgate.

———— 2005. *Ethnicity, Ethnic Conflicts, Peace Processes: Comparative Perspectives.* Whitby, ON: de Sitter Publications.

———— 2004. *Rethinking Civilizational Analysis.* London: Sage Publications (coedited with S. A. Arjomand).

———— 1990. *The Evaluation of Occupations in a Developing Country: The Philippines.* New York: Garland Publishing.

———— 1985. *New Nationalisms of the Developed West.* London: Allen & Unwin Crofts (coedited with R. Rogowski).

———— 1984. *The Global Crisis: Sociological Analyses and Responses.* Leiden: E. J. Brill.

———— 1974. *On the Margin of the Visible: Sociology, the Esoteric and the Occult.* New York: Wiley Interscience.

———— 1971. *The Phenomenon of Sociology: A Reader in the Sociology of Knowledge.* New York: Appleton–Century–Crofts.

———— 1970. *Theoretical Sociology: Perspectives and Developments.* New York: Appleton–Century–Crofts (coedited with J. C. McKinney).

———— 1963. *Sociological Theory, Values and Sociocultural Change: Essays in Honor of Pitirim A. Sorokin.* New York: The Free Press (Reprinted in 1967, Harper Torchbooks; Revised in 2013 with a new Introduction, New Brunswick, NJ).

———— 1962. *Sociologism and Existentialism: Two Perspectives on the Individual and Society.* Englewood Cliffs, NJ: Prentice–Hall (Reprinted in 1979, New York: Arno Press).

Articles, Chapters and Book Reviews

1955

"Apartheid and Education in the Union of South Africa." *Harvard Educational Review* 25: 242–59.

1957

"Apartheid and Religion." *Theology Today* 14: 385–400.

Review of Samuel Koenig's *Man and Society. American Scientist* 45, no. 3.

1958

"The Prestige Evaluation of Occupations in an Underdeveloped Country: The Philippines."
American Journal of Sociology 63: 390–99.

"Methodology and Research." In *Contemporary Sociology*, edited by J. S. Roucek, 151–66.
New York: The Philosophical Library (Republished in 1961. *Readings in Contemporary American Sociology*, edited by J. S. Roucek. Paterson, NJ: Littlefield, Adams and Co.).

1959

"Aftermath of a Thermonuclear Attack on the United States: Some Sociological Considerations." *Social Problems* 6: 291–303.

"Occupational Satisfaction and Aspiration in an Underdeveloped Country: The Philippines." *Economic Development and Cultural Change* 7: 431–44.

1960

"Quelques Aspects Négatifs de l'Education de Masse dans les Pays Sous–Développés." *Tiers–Monde* I: 161–73.

"Durkheim and Ethics." *American Sociological Review* 25: 405–6.

"Apartheid and Politics in South Africa." *The Journal of Politics* 22: 682–97.

1961

Review of Ambrose Reeves's *Shooting at Sharpeville. Africa Report* 6, no. 4.

Review of Peter Calvocoressi's *South Africa and World Opinion. Africa Report* 6, no. 5.

Review of W. E. Brown's *The Catholic Church in South Africa. Africa Report* 6, no. 5.

1962

Sociologism and Existentialism: Two Perspectives on the Individual and Society. Englewood Cliffs, NJ: Prentice–Hall.

"An Important Addition to Princeton's Africana." *The Princeton University Library Chronicle* 32: 178–81.

Review of Georges Gurvitch's *Dialectique et Sociologie. American Sociological Review* 27, no. 5.

1963

Editor, *Sociological Theory, Values, and Sociocultural Change: Essays in Honor of Pitirim A. Sorokin.* New York: The Free Press of Glencoe (Reprinted by Harper Torchbooks Edition, 1967).

Review of Medard Ross's *Psychoanalysis and Daseinsanalysis. American Sociological Review* 28, no. 5.

1964

"Introduction to a Bibliographical Focus on Emile Durkheim." *Journal for the Scientific Study of Religion* 3: 247–54.

"Durkheim's 'Two Laws of Penal Evolution.'" *Journal for the Scientific Study of Religion* 3: 261–66.
Review of Pitirim A. Sorokin's *A Long Journey*. *American Sociological Review* 29, no. 4.
Review of Maurice Natanson's *Philosophy of the Social Sciences: A Reader*. *American Sociological Review* 29, no. 6.

1965

"Existential Phenomenology and the Sociological Tradition." *American Sociological Review* 30: 674–88. (Reprinted in Gunter W. Remmling, ed. 1973. *Towards the Sociology of Knowledge: Origin and Development of a Sociological Thought Style*. London: Routledge & Kegan Paul).
Review of John J. Carroll's *The Filipino Manufacturing Entrepreneur*. *American Sociological Review* 30, no. 6.

1966

"Reply to Kolaja and Berger." *American Sociological Review* 31: 260–64.
"A Problem for the Sociology of Knowledge: The Mutual Unawareness of Emile Durkheim and Max Weber." *Archives Européennes de Sociologie* VII: 330–36 (German translation in Wolf Lepenies, ed. 1981. *Geschichte der Soziologie* 4, Frankfurt am Main: Suhrkamp).
Review of Pierre van den Berghe's *South Africa: A Study in Conflict*. *Social Forces* 44, no. 3.

1967

"On the Relationship of Student and University." *Duke Alumni Register* 53 (August): 19–22.
"Sociological Realism: Partition for South Africa?" *Social Forces* 46 (December): 208–21.
"Le Sacré et le Profane dans la Destruction Coloniale et Construction Nationale." *Revue de l'Institut de Sociologie* 2–3: 203–16.
"A Conceptual Scheme of Societal Change and its Lead Indicators." In Samuel Klausner, ed., *Theory and Method in the Study of Total Societies*, 69–97. New York: Frederick A. Praeger.
"Le Premier Message d'Emile Durkheim." *Cahiers Internationaux de Sociologie* 43: 21–23.
Review of Edwin S. Munger's *Afrikaner and African Nationalism: South African Parallels and Parameters*. *Africa Report* 12, no. 8.

1968

"Pitirim A. Sorokin." In *International Encyclopedia of the Social Sciences*, vol. 15, 61–64. New York: Macmillan–Free Press.
"Typological Classification." In *International Encyclopedia of the Social Sciences*, vol. 16, 177–86. New York: Macmillan–Free Press.
"The Existential Self and the Person." In *The Self in Social Interaction* vol. I, edited by Ken Gergen and Chad Gordon, 75–86. New York: John Wiley and Sons.
"Vers une Sociologie de l'Existence." In *Perspectives de la Sociologie Contemporaine*, edited by Georges Balandier, 445–65. Paris: Presses Universitaires de France.
"Sociological Reflections on Theological Education." *The Duke Divinity School Review* 33 (Spring): 69–74.

"Pitirim A. Sorokin." *Cahiers Internationaux de Sociologie* 44: 171–72.
Review of Erving Goffman's *Interaction Ritual. American Sociological Review* 33, no. 3.

1969

Sociologismo y Existencialismo (Spanish edition of *Sociologism and Existentialism*), Buenos Aires: Amorrortu Editores.
Review of Phillip Bosserman's *Dialectical Sociology. Social Forces* 47, no. 4.

1970

McKinney, J. C. and E. A. Tiryakian, eds. *Theoretical Sociology: Perspectives and Developments.* New York: Appleton–Century–Crofts.
"Structural Sociology." In *Theoretical Sociology: Perspectives and Developments*, edited by J. C. McKinney and E. A. Tiryakian, 111–35. New York: Appleton–Century–Crofts.
"Remarques sur une Sociologie du Changement Qualitatif." In *Sociologie des Mutations*, edited by G. Balandier, 83–94. Paris: Editions Anthropos.
Review of Talcott Parsons' *Politics and Social Structure. Social Forces* 49, no. 2.

1971

Editor, *The Phenomenon of Sociology: A Reader in the Sociology of Sociology.* New York: Appleton–Century–Crofts.
"Introduction to the Sociology of Sociology." In *The Phenomenon of Sociology: A Reader in the Sociology of Sociology*, edited by E. A. Tiryakian, 1–15. New York: Appleton–Century–Crofts.
Japanese edition of *Sociologism and Existentialism*. Tokyo: Misuzo Shobo.
Review of Gabriel Tarde's *On Communication and Social Influence. American Journal of Sociology* 76, no. 6.
Review of Alvin Gouldner's *The Coming Crisis of Sociology. Journal of Scientific Study of Religion* 10, no. 4.

1972

"Esotérisme et Exotérisme en Sociologie" (La Sociologie dans l'Ere Du Verseau). *Cahiers Internationaux de Sociologie* 52: 33–50.
"Toward the Sociology of Esoteric Culture." *American Journal of Sociology* 78: 491–512.
Review of Stanford M. Lyman and Marvin B. Scott's *A Sociology of the Absurd. Contemporary Sociology* 1, no. 3.

1973

"Sociology and Existential Phenomenology." In *Phenomenology and the Social Sciences* vol. I, edited by Maurice Natanson, 187–222. Evanston: Northwestern University Press.
"Sociological Perspectives on the Stranger." *Soundings* 56 (Spring): 45–58 (Republished in Sallie TeSelle, ed. 1973. *The Rediscovery of Ethnicity*. New York: Harper Colophon).

Review of G. C. Hallen and R. Prasad's *Sorokin and Sociology. Contemporary Sociology* 2, no. 4.

Review of Charles W. Lachenmeyer's *The Language of Sociology. American Journal of Sociology* 79, no. 3.

1974

Editor, *On the Margin of the Visible: Sociology, the Esoteric, and the Occult.* New York: Wiley Interscience/John Wiley and Sons.

"Reflections on the Sociology of Civilizations." *Sociological Analysis* 35 (Summer): 122–28.

"Contestation de la Rationalité: Progrès ou Régres?" In *Croissance et Développement: Analyse Multidisciplinaire*, Proceedings of the Association Internationale des Sociologues de Langue Française, 37–41.

Review of David Sudnow's *Studies in Social Interaction. Social Forces* 52, no. 4.

Review of Steven Lukes's *Emile Durkheim: His Life and Work. American Journal of Sociology* 79, no. 6.

Review of Robert N. Bellah's *Emile Durkheim on Morality and Society. American Journal of Sociology* 80, no. 3.

1975

"Neither Marx nor Durkheim ... Perhaps Weber." *American Journal of Sociology* 81 (July): 1–33.

Review of S. N. Eisenstadt's *Tradition, Change, and Morality. Social Forces* 53, no. 4.

Review of Werner J. Cahnman's *Ferdinand Tonnies: A New Evaluation. Social Forces* 54, no. 1.

Review of Ernest Wallwork's *Durkheim: Morality and Milieu. Journal of the American Academy of Religion* 43, no. 2.

Review of Andrew M. Greeley's *Ecstasy: A Way of Knowing. Contemporary Sociology* 4, no. 2.

1976

"De l'Exotérique à l'Esotérique: Vers un Nouveau Sens de la Modernité." In *Spécificité et Théorie Sociale*, edited by Anouar Abdel–Malek, 321–32. Paris: Anthropos.

"Altruism in Sociology." *Zygon* 11 (September): 211–12.

"Biosocial Man, Sic et Non" (Review essay of Edward O. Wilson, *Sociobiology: The New Synthesis*). *American Journal of Sociology* 82 (November): 701–6.

Review of Peter M. Blau's *Approaches to the Study of Social Structure. Administrative Science Quarterly* 21 (September): 516–19.

Review of Fred E. Katz's *Structuralism in Sociology: An Approach to Knowledge. Contemporary Psychology* 21, no. 11.

Review of T. O. Beidelman's *W. Robertson Smith and the Sociological Study of Religion. Contemporary Sociology* 4, no. 1.

1977

"Les Mouvements Nationaux Régionaux." *Etudes des Mouvements Nationaux Régionaux*, Proceedings of the Association Internationale des Sociologues de Langue Française, Paris.

"On Discovering Durkheim" (review essay of Durkheim's *Textes*, 3 vols.). *Contemporary Sociology* 6, no. 1.

1978

"The Time Perspectives of Modernity." *Society and Leisure/Loisir et Société* 1 (April): 125–57.

"Durkheim and Husserl: A Comparison of the Spirit of Positivism and the Spirit of Phenomenology." In *Phenomenology and the Social Sciences, A Dialogue*, edited by Joseph Bien, 20–43. The Hague: Martinus Nijhoff.

"Emile Durkheim." In *A History of Sociological Analysis*, edited by Tom Bottomore and Robert Nisbet, 187–236. New York: Basic Books.

"La Fin d'une Illusion et l'Illusion de la Fin." *Le Progrès en Question*, Proceedings of the 9th Colloquium of the Association Internationale des Sociologues de Langue Française. Paris: Editions Anthropos, 2: 381–403.

Review of Mary Douglas's *Implicit Meanings. Sociological Quarterly* 19, no. 2.

Review of Anthony Giddens' *New Rules of Sociological Method. American Journal of Sociology* 83, no. 4.

Review of Yash Nandan's *The Durkheimian School: A System and Comprehensive Bibliography. Contemporary Sociology* 7, no. 4.

1979

"The Significance of Schools in the Development of Sociology." In *Contemporary Issues in Theory and Research: A Metasociological Perspective*, edited by William E. Snizek, Ellsworth R. Fuhrman and Michael K. Miller, 211–33. Westport, CT: Greenwood Press. (Translated in 1981 as "Die Bedeutung von Schulen fur die Entwicklung der Soziologie," In *Geschichte der Soziologie*, vol. 2, edited by Wolf Lepenies, 31–68. Frankfurt: Suhrkamp.

"L'Ecole Durkheimienne à la recherche de la société perdue: La sociologie naissante et son milieu culturel." *Cahiers Internationaux de Sociologie* 66 (January–June): 97–114.

"Les Etats–Unis en tant que Phénomène Religieux." In *Histoire Vécue du Peuple Chrétien*, vol. 2, edited by Jean Delumeau, 433–58. Toulouse: Editions Privat.

Sociologism and Existentialism (integral reprint of 1962 edition). New York: Arno Press ("*Perennial Works in Sociology*" collection).

"Beyond Words—African Style" (review of Willy De Craemer's *The Jamaa and the Church: A Bantu Catholic Movement in Zaire*), *Contemporary Sociology* 8 (July): 541–43.

Review of Mark Traugott's *Emile Durkheim on Institutional Analysis. Contemporary Sociology* 8, no. 4.

1980

"Post–Parsonian Sociology." *Humboldt Journal of Social Relations* 7 (Fall/Winter): 17–32 (Reprinted in 1991, *Functionalist Sociology*, edited by Paul Colomy, 409–24. Hants, England, and Brookfield, VT: Elgar).

"Quebec, Wales and Scotland: Three Nations in Search of a State." *International Journal of Comparative Sociology* 21 (March–June): 1–13.

"Talcott Parsons (1902–79)." *Cahiers Internationaux de Sociologie* 68 (January–June): 171–72.

"The Mythologist and the Sociologist." *The Mankind Quarterly* 21 (1): 53–70.
Review of Audrey Borenstein's *Redeeming the Sin: Social Science and Literature. The South Atlantic Quarterly* 79, no. 1.

1981

Guest editor, special issue, "*Durkheim Lives!*" *Social Forces* 59 (4) (in honor of E. K. Wilson).
"Sexual Anomie, Social Structure, Societal Change." *Social Forces* 59 (4): 1025–53.
"Sociological Dimensions of Uprootedness." In *Uprooting and Development: Dilemmas of Coping with Modernization*, edited by George V. Coelho and Paul Ahmed, 131–52. New York: Plenum Publishing.
"The Sociological Import of a Metaphor: Tracking the Source of Max Weber's 'Iron Cage.'" *Sociological Inquiry* 51 (1): 27–33.
"The Politics of Devolution: Comparative Aspects of Quebec, Wales, and Scotland." *Comparative Social Research* 4: 33–64.
"The Elementary Forms as *Revelation*." In *The Future of the Sociological Classics*, edited by Buford Rhea, 114–35. London: Allen & Unwin.
"Le Mythologue et le Sociologue." In *Georges Dumézil* 83–100. Aix en Provence: Pandora Editions.
"Sexual Anomie in Prerevolutionary France." *Proceedings 1981*, Proceedings of the Consortium on Revolutionary Europe, 31–50.
"A (Sociological) Tale of Two Cities." *Contemporary Sociology* 10 (6): 768–71.

1982

"A Sop to Cerberus: Response to Besnard." *Social Forces* 61(1): 287–89.
"Puritan America in the Modern World: Mission Impossible?" *Sociological Analysis* 43(4): 351–67.
Review of William R. Beer's *The Unexpected Rebellion. Social Forces* 60, no. 4.
Review of Ruth A. Wallace and Alison Wolf's *Contemporary Sociological Theory. Contemporary Sociology* 11, no. 4.
Review of Benjamin Nelson's *On the Roads to Modernity: Conscience, Science, and Civilizations. Sociological Analysis* 43, no. 1.

1983

Tiryakian, E. A. and N. Nevitte. "A Typology of Nationalism." In *Introductory Readings in Government and Politics*, edited by Mark O. Dickerson, T. Flanagan and N. Nevitte, 116–25. Toronto: Methuen.

1984

"L'Anomie sexuelle en France avant la Révolution." *Cahiers Internationaux de Sociologie* 76 (1984): 161–84.
Editor, *The Global Crisis: Sociological Analyses and Responses*. Special double issue of the *International Journal of Comparative Sociology* 25 (1–2) (Also published as a paperback by E. J. Brill, Leiden).

"Introduction" and "The Global Crisis as an Interregnum of Modernity." In *The Global Crisis: Sociological Analyses and Responses*, edited by E. A, Tiryakian, 1–3, 123–30, Leiden: Brill.

"From Underground to Convention: Sexual Anomie as an Antecedent to the French Revolution." *Current Perspectives in Social Theory* 5 (1984): 289–307.

Review of Seymour Leventman's *Counterculture and Social Transformation. Social Forces* 63, no. 1.

Review of Bernard Barber's *The Logic and Limits of Trust. Society* 22, no. 1.

1985

Tiryakian, E. A. and R. Rogowski, eds. *New Nationalisms of the Developed West.* London: George Allen & Unwin.

"Introduction." In *New Nationalisms of the Developed West*, edited by E. A. Tiryakian and R. Rogowski, 1–13. London: George Allen & Unwin.

Tiryakian, E. A. and N. Nevitte. "Nationalism and Modernity." In *New Nationalisms of the Developed West*, edited by E. A. Tiryakian and R. Rogowski, 57–86. London: George Allen & Unwin. (Translated in 1991. In *Študije o ethnonacionlizmu*, edited by Rudi Rizman. Ljubljana, Slovenia: Zbornik).

"The Changing Centers of Modernity." In *Comparative Social Dynamics: Essays in Honor of Shmuel N. Eisenstadt*, edited by E. Cohen, M. Lissak and U. Almagor, 131–47. Boulder, CO: Westview Press.

"Journal d'un sociologue américain au Québec: 1953–1978." In *Continuité et Rupture: Les Sciences Sociales au Québéc*, edited by G–H Lévesque, 237–43. Montreal: Presses Universitaires de Montreal.

"Georges Gurvitch"; "Henri Saint–Simon"; "Jean–Paul Sartre"; and "Pitirim A. Sorokin" (biographical articles). In *The Social Science Encyclopedia*, edited by A. Kuper and J. Kuper. Leiden and London: Routledge and Kegan Paul.

"L'Actualité Méthodologique de Gurvitch et de Mannheim." *Recherches Sociologiques* (Belgium) 16 (2): 219–27.

"Le Sagittaire Inconnu." In *Une Anthropologie des Turbulences: Hommage à Georges Balandier*, edited by M. Maffesoli and C. Rivière, 44–47. Paris: Berg International Editeurs.

"On the Significance of Dedifferentiation." In *Perspectives on Macro–Sociological Theory*, edited by S. N. Eisenstadt and H. J. Helle, 118–34. London and Beverly Hills: Sage.

Review of Wayne Meeks's *The First Urban Christians. American Journal of Sociology* 90, no. 5.

Review of Joseph Katarba and Andrea Fontana's *The Existential Self in Society. American Journal of Sociology* 91, no. 3.

1986

"Modernity as an Eschatological Setting: A New Vista for the Study of Religions." *History of Religions* 25 (4): 378–86.

"Sociology's Great Leap Forward: The Challenge of Internationalization." *International Sociology* 1 (2): 155–71 (Reprinted in 1990 in *Globalization, Knowledge and Society*, edited by Martin Albrow and Elizabeth King, 63–78. London and Newbury Park, CA: Sage. Also reprinted in 1990 in *Group Portrait: Internationalizing the Disciplines*, edited by Sven Groennings and David S. Wiley, 179–95. New York: The American Forum).

"Preface." In *Structures of Knowing: Current Studies in the Sociology of Schools*, edited by Richard C. Monk, xi–xviii. Lanham, MD: University Press of America.

"Hegemonic Schools and the Development of Sociology." In *Structures of Knowing: Current Studies in the Sociology of Schools*, edited by Richard C. Monk, 417–41. Lanham, MD: University Press of America.

"1984 + 1 ... Your Turn, Monsieur Tocqueville." In *The Tocqueville Review*, vol. 7 1985/86, edited by Jesse R. Pitts and Olivier Zunz, 63–65. Charlottesville, VA: University Press of Virginia.

Review of Jacques Ellul's *The Humiliation of the Word*. *Contemporary Sociology* 15, no. 6.

Review of Robert N. Bellah et al.'s *Habits of the Heart*. *Sociological Analysis* 47, no. 2.

Review of Albert Bergesen's *The Sacred and the Subversive: Political Witch–Hunts as National Rituals*. *Review of Religious Research* 27, no. 2.

1987

"Sexuelle Anomie und Sozialer Wandel." *Vermessene Sexualität*, vol. I, edited by Alexander Schuller and Nikolaus Heim, 23–39. Berlin and Heidelberg: Springer–Verlag (translation of "Sexual Anomie, Social Structure, Societal Change" 1981).

Review of Piotr Sztompka's *Robert K. Merton: An Intellectual Profile*. *Contemporary Sociology* 16, no. 5.

Review of Arthur J. Vidich and Stanford M. Lyman's *American Sociology: Worldly Rejections and their Directions*. *American Journal of Education* 95, no. 2.

Review of Robert J. Brym's *Anglo–Canadian Sociology*. *Canadian Journal of Sociology* 12, no. 3.

1988

"From Durkheim to Managua: Revolutions as Religious Revivals." In *Durkheimian Sociology*, edited by Jeffrey Alexander, 44–65. New York: Cambridge University Press (Republished in 2005 in *Sociology: A Reader* (in Polish), edited by Piotr Sztompka and Marek Kucia. Krakow: Znak Publishers).

"Sociology's Dostoyevski: Pitirim A. Sorokin." *The World & I* 3 (9): 569–81.

"Nationalism, Modernity, and Sociology." *Sociologia Internationalis* 26 (2):1–17.

"Les contresens de la modernisation." In *La Sociologie et les Nouveaux Défis de la Modernisation*, edited by A. Custódio Gonçalves, A. Teixeira Fernandes and C. Lalive d'Epinay, 131–36. Porto (Portugal): Faculdade de Letras do Porto.

"Durkheim, Mathiez, and the French Revolution: The Political Context of a Sociological Classic." *Archives Européennes de Sociologie / European Journal of Sociology* 29: 373–96.

1989

"Nacionalismo, Modernidad y Socioloia." In *Sociología des Nacionalismo*, edited by Alfonso Perez–Agote, 143–61. Vitoria, Spain: Servicio Editorial de la Universidad del Pais Vasco.

"1968 en perspective – l'ambiguïté de la modernité." *Revue de l'Institut de Sociologie* (Belgium) 1988 (3–4): 201–9 (special issue *Les Nouveaux Enjeux de l'Anthropologie – Autour de Georges Balandier*, edited by G. Gosselin).

"'1968' en Retrospective et Prospective." In *Le Lien Social. Identités personnelles et solidarités collectives dans le monde contemporain*, vol. I bis, Université de Genève: Actes du XIIIe Colloque, Association Internationale des Sociologues de Langue Française, 584–90.
Review of Wade Clark Roof and William McKinney's *American Mainline Religion: The Changing Shape and Future. Society* 26, no. 3.

1990

"On the Shoulders of Weber and Durkheim: East Asia and Emergent Modernity." In *Asia in the 21st Century: Challenges and Prospects*, edited by Kim Kyong–Dong and Su–Hoon Lee, 3–25. Seoul: Panmun Book Co.
The Evaluation of Occupations in a Developing Country: The Philippines (with a new introduction). New York: Garland Publishing.
"Gurvitch et Parsons: Maître et Maître d'Ecole." *Sociologia Internationalis* 28 (1): 19–25.
"Exegesis or Synthesis? Comments on 50 years of *The Structure of Social Action*." *American Journal of Sociology* 96 (September): 452–55.
Review of Mitchell Aboulafia's *The Mediating Self: Mead, Sartre, and Self–Determination in Symbolic Interaction* 13, no. 1.
Review of Katherine O'Sullivan See's *First World Nationalisms: Class and Ethnic Politics in Northern Ireland and Quebec. Canadian Journal of Sociology* 14, no. 1.
Review of Nikolai Genov's *National Traditions in Sociology. Social Forces* 69, no. 1

1991

"Modernisation: Exhumetur in Pace (Rethinking Macrosociology in the 1990s)." *International Sociology* 6 (June): 165–80.
Guest editor, "Robert K. Merton in Review Symposium." *Contemporary Sociology* 20 (July): 506–30.
"Evaluating the Standard: An Introduction to Sociological Metrology." *Contemporary Sociology* 20 (July): 506–10.
"L'Exceptionnelle Vitalité Religieuse aux Etats–Unis: une Relecture de *Protestant–Catholic–Jew*." *Social Compass* 38 (September): 215–38.
Review of Michael S. Kimmel's *Revolution: A Sociological Interpretation. Contemporary Sociology* 20, no. 5.
Review of Melvin L. Kohn's *Cross–National Research in Sociology. Theory, Culture and Society* 8 (November).

1992

"Dialectics of Modernity: Reenchantment and Dedifferentiation as Counterprocesses." In *Social Change and Modernity*, edited by Hans Haferkamp and Neil J. Smelser, 78–94. Berkeley and Los Angeles: University of California Press.
"Pathways to Metatheory: Rethinking the Presuppositions of Macrosociology." In *Studies in Metatheorizing in Sociology*, edited by George Ritzer, 69–87. Newbury Park, CA: SAGE.
"From Modernization to Globalization." *Journal for the Scientific Study of Religion* 31(3): 304–10.
"L'Enseignement de la Sociologie aux Etats–Unis." In *Actes de la Rencontre internationale sur l'Enseignement de la Sociologie*, edited by Ion Aluas and Gabriel Gosselin, 7–11. Paris:

Association Internationale de Sociologues de Langue Française, and Cluj: Université "Babes–Bolyai," Cluj–Napoca.

1993

"White Women in Darkest Africa: Marginals as Observers in No–Woman's Land." In *Melanges Pierre Salmon*, vol. 2, *Histoire et ethnologie africaines*, edited by G. Thoveron and H. Legros, special issue of *Civilisations* (Brussels) 41 (1–2): 209–38.

"Die Neuen Welten und die Soziologie: Eine Übersicht." *Berliner Journal für Soziologie* 4: 521–37.

"American Religious Exceptionalism: A Reconsideration." *Annals of the American Academy of Political and Social Science*, vol. 527 (May): 40–54.

"Nationalist Movements in Advanced Societies." *Perspective on Nationalism and War*, edited by John L. Comaroff and Paul C. Stern, 131–55. New York: New School for Social Research, Center for Studies of Social Change (Published in revised form in 1995 as "Nationalism and Modernity: A Methodological Appraisal." In *Perspectives on Nationalism & War*, edited by J. L. Comaroff and P. C. Stern, 205–35. Gordon & Breach).

1994

Editor, special issue "The 100th Anniversary of Durkheim's *Division of Labor in Society*." *Sociological Forum* 9, no. 1.

"Revisiting Sociology's First Classic: *The Division of Labor in Society* and its Actuality." *Sociological Forum* 9 (March): 3–16.

"Durkheim et Weber, cousins germains?" In *Durkheim, Weber: vers la fin des Malentendus?*, edited by Monique Hirschhorn and Jacques Coenen–Huther, 19–26. Paris: L'Harmattan.

"The New Worlds and Sociology." *International Sociology* 9 (June): 131–48.

Review of Danny L. Jorgensen's *The Esoteric Scene, Cultic Milieu, and Occult Tarot. Symbolic Interaction* 17, no. 4.

1995

"Trois métacultures de la modernité: Chrétienne, gnostique, chthonienne." In *L'Univers de la Culture: Hommage à Fernand Dumont*, edited by Simon Langlois and Yves Martin, 375–90. Laval, Quebec: Presses Universitaires de Laval.

"Modernization in a Millenarian Decade: Lessons for and from Eastern Europe." In *Social Change and Modernization: Lessons from Eastern Europe*, edited by Bruno Grancelli, 249–64. Berlin and New York: Walter de Gruyter.

"Collective Effervescence, Social Change and Charisma: Durkheim, Weber and 1989." *International Sociology* 10 (September): 269–81.

"L'actualité de la Sociologie dans les Balkans." In *L'Europe face aux nouveaux défis: Actes du colloque de l'AISLF à Sofia*, edited by Sylvie Bardèche, 3–8. Paris: L.S.C.I./IRESCO.

Review of Jennifer M. Lehmann's *Durkheim and Women. American Journal of Sociology* 100, no. 5.

Review of Walker Connor's *Ethnonationalism: The Quest for Understanding, in Contemporary Sociology* 24, no. 4.

1996

"Rethinking Modernization: Legacies of Parsons and Hilbert." Working Paper FS III 96–40x. Berlin: Wissenschaftszentrum Berlin für Sozialforschung (WZB), Abteilung Sozialstruktur u. Sozialberichterstattung.

"Envisioning the History of Sociological Thought" (Review of Donald N. Levine's *Visions of the Sociological Tradition*. *Sociological Forum* 11, no. 4.

"Three Metacultures of Modernity: Christian, Gnostic, Chthonic." *Theory, Culture & Society* 13 (February): 99–118.

1997

"The Wild Cards of Modernity." *Dædalus* 126 (Spring): 147–81.

Review of Saul Newman's *Ethnoregional Conflict in Democracies: Mostly Ballots, Rarely Bullets. The Annals of the American Academy of Political and Social Science* 550 (March).

Review of Samuel P. Huntington's *The Clash of Civilizations and the Remaking of World Order*. *American Journal of Sociology* 104, no. 2 (September).

1998

"Secession, Modernity and Autonomy." *Society* 35, no. 5 (July–August): 49–58.

"Neo–Modernisierung. Lehren für die und aus der postsozialistischen Transformation." *Postsozialistische Krisen. Theoretische Ansätze und empirische Befunde*, edited by Klaus Müller, 31–52. Leverkusen, Opladen, Germany: Verlag Leske & Budrich.

"From LePlay to Today." *Comparative & Historical Sociology* (newsletter of ASA Section on Comparative and Historical Sociology) 11 (1): 1–4.

1999

"Religion." *The Encyclopedia of Political Revolutions*, edited by Jack Goldstone, 417–20. Washington, DC: Congressional Quarterly.

"War: the Covered Side of Modernity." *International Sociology* 14 (4): 473–89.

(German translation "Krieg: Die verborgene Seite der Moderne." In *Die Gegenwart des Krieges. Staatliche Gewalt in der Moderne*, edited by Wolfgang Knöbl and Gunnar Schmidt, 194–213. Frankfurt/Main: Fisher Taschenbuch Verlag). (Spanish translation 2004. "La Guerra: La Cara Oculta de la Modernidad." In *Modernidad y vioencia colectiva*, edited by Josetxo Beriain, 63–78. Madrid: Centro de Investigaciones Sociológicas).

"An Emergent French Connection: Revisiting Parsons's Durkheims." *Agenda for Sociology. Classic Sources and Current Uses of Talcott Parsons's Work*, edited by Bernard Barber and Uta Gerhardt, 53–86. Baden–Baden (Germany): Nomos Verlagsgesellschaft.

Review of N. J. Allen, W. S. F. Pickering, and W. Watts Miller's *On Durkheim's Elementary Forms of Religious Life. American Journal of Sociology* 105, no. 1.

2000

"Parsons's Emergent Durkheims." *Sociological Theory* 18, no. 1: 60–83.

Review of Niklas Luhmann's *Observations on Modernity. Contemporary Sociology* 29, no. 6.

2001

"Der Kosovo–Krieg und die Rolle der Vereiningte Staaten." *Berliner Journal für Soziologie* 11 (2): 201–16.

"Some Challenges for Sociology in the New Era." *New Horizons for Sociological Theory and Research*, edited by Luigi Tomasi, 315–36. Aldershot and Burlington: Ashgate.

Editor, special issue "Rethinking Civilizational Analysis." *International Sociology* 16, no. 3.

"Introduction: The Civilization of Modernity and the Modernity of Civilizations." *International Sociology* 16 (3): 277–92.

"Time to Change the Calendar? Sacred and Secular Problems of Crossing the Millennium." *International Review of Sociology / Revue Internationale de Sociologie* 11 (3): 419–29 (special issue *Space, Time and the Sacred I Modernity / Postmodernity*, edited by Richard H. Roberts).

"Traditions in Sociology." In *International Encyclopedia of the Social & Behavioral Sciences*, vol. 23, edited by Neil J. Smelser and Paul Baltes, 15824–29. Oxford: Pergamon/Elsevier.

2002

"Third Party Involvement in Ethnic Conflict: the Case of the Kosovo War." *The New Balkans: Disintegration and Reconstruction*, edited by George A. Kourvetaris, V. Roudometof, K. Koutsoukis, and A. G. Korvetaris, 207–28. Boulder, CO: East European Monographs.

Review of Richard Münch's *The Ethics of Modernity: Formation and Transformation in Britain, France, Germany and the United States. American Journal of Sociology* 107, no. 6.

2003

"De Sainsaulieu à Zola par Gurvitch: L'engagement intellectuel." *Construction d'identités, construction de sociétés* (Actes du Colloque Royaumont en l'honneur de Renaud Sainsaulieu), edited by Sylvie Bardèche, 185–88. Paris: CNRS/Laboratoire de Sociologie du Changement des Institutions.

"Le Travail chez Durkheim." In *Les classiques et le travail*, edited by Daniel Mercure, 229–50. Quebec City: Presses de l'Université Laval.

Elizabeth D. Ezell, Martin Seeleib–Kaiser, and Edward A. Tiryakian. "National Identity Issues in the New German Elites: A Study of German University Students." *International Journal of Comparative Sociology* 44 (3): 280–308.

"The Modernity of Civilizations and the Civilization of Modernity." In *The Transformation of the 21st Century & Life–Culture Salim*, World Life–Culture Forum 2003, Paperback, 1–20. Suwon, Korea: Kyonggi Cultural Foundation.

Review of Hans Joas's *War and Modernity. Contemporary Sociology* 32, no. 4.

"Response to Harris." *Contemporary Sociology* 32, no. 6.

2004

"Is There a Future for Sociology in the Bioglobal Age?" *The Dialogical Turn. New Roles for Sociology in the Postdisciplinary Age*, edited by Hans Joas and Charles Camic, 223–46. Lanham, MD: Rowman & Littlefield.

"Assessing Multiculturalism Theoretically: *E Pluribus Unum, Sic et Non.*" In *Governance in Multicultural Societies*, edited by John Rex and Gurharpal Singh, 1–18. Aldershot: Ashgate Publishing Ltd.

Arjomand, S. A. and Edward A. Tiryakian, eds. *Rethinking Civilizational Analysis*. London: Sage.

Arjomand, S. A. and Edward A. Tiryakian. "Introduction." In *Rethinking Civilizational Analysis*, edited by S. A. Arjomand and Edward A. Tiryakian, 1–13. London: Sage.

"Civilizational Analysis: Renovating the Sociological Tradition." In *Rethinking Civilizational Analysis*, edited by S. A. Arjomand and Edward A. Tiryakian, 30–47. London: Sage.

"'Old Europe/New Europe': Ambiguities of Identity." In *Migration in the New Europe: East–West Revisited*, edited by Agata Gorny and Paolo Ruspini, 215–31. London: Palgrave Macmillan.

Guest editor, special issue, *Ethnicity, Ethnic Conflicts, Peace Processes: Comparative Perspectives. International Journal of Comparative Sociology* 45, nos. 3–4 (July–September).

"Introduction: New Comparative Perspectives on Ethnicity and Ethnic Conflicts." In *Ethnicity, Ethnic Conflicts, Peace Processes: Comparative Perspectives*, edited by E. A. Tiryakian, *International Journal of Comparative Sociology* 45 nos. 3–4: 147–59.

2005

"From the Welfare State to the Warfare State." *Contexts* 4 (2): 23–24.

"Three Levels of Teaching Durkheim." *Teaching Durkheim on Religion*, edited by Terry F. Godlove, 29–50. Oxford and New York: Oxford University Press.

Editor, *Ethnicity, Ethnic Conflicts, Peace Processes: Comparative Perspectives*. Whitby, ON: de Sitter Publications.

"September 11 and the Actuality of Durkheim." In *Cambridge Companion of Durkheim*, edited by Jeffrey Alexander and Philip Smith, 305–2. Cambridge and New York: Cambridge University Press.

"Talcott Parsons and the Human Condition." In *After Parsons. A Theory of Social Action for the Twenty–First Century*, edited by Victor Lidz, Renée Fox, and Victor Bershady. New York: Russell Sage.

"Comparative Analysis of the Civilization of Modernity: 1203 and 2003." In *Comparing Modernities: Pluralism versus Homogeneity. Essays in Homage to Shmuel Eisenstadt*, edited by Eliezer Ben–Rafael and Yitzhak Sternberg, 287–308. Leiden and Boston: Brill.

"Modernizing German National Identity." In *Die Ordnung der Gesellschaft. Festschrift zum 60. Geburtstag von Richard M nch*, edited by Hans–J rgen Aretz and Christian Lahusen, 229–56. Frankfurt A/M, Berlin, New York, Oxford: Peter Lang.

2006

"Tocqueville in New Orleans ... Before and After Katrina." *Sociation Today* 4, no. 1 (Spring).

"Gabriel Tarde"; "Alain Touraine" and "Tradition." In *Cambridge Dictionary of Sociology*, edited by Bryan Turner. Cambridge: Cambridge University Press.

"Trois Salutations." In *Sociologie et Société Québécoise: Présences de Guy Rocher*, edited by Céline Saint–Pierre and Jean–Philippe Warren, 341–46. Montréal: Les Presses de l'Université de Montréal.

"A Sociologist for the 21st Century: Pitirim Sorokin." In *Integralism, Altruism and Reconstruction. Essays in Honor of Pitirim A. Sorokin*, edited by Elvira del Pozo Aviño, 31–41. Biblioteca Javier Coy de Estudios Norteamericanos, PUV: Valencia.

"For the Nation ... but Which One?" In *Worlds in Sociology: In Honor of Professor Georgi Fotev*, edited by Pepka Boyadjieva, L. Deyanova, S. Koleva and K. Koev, 431–42. Sofia: St. Kliment Ohridski University Press (in English and Bulgarian).

Review of Jonathan S. Fish's *Defending the Durkheimian Tradition: Religion, Emotion and Morality. Contemporary Sociology* 35, no. 5.

2007

"Emile Durkheim and Social Change." In *The Blackwell Encyclopedia of Sociology*, vol. III, edited by George Ritzer, 1261–64. Oxford and Malden, MA: Blackwell Publishing.

"Pitirim A. Sorokin." In *The Blackwell Encyclopedia of Sociology*, vol. IX, edited by George Ritzer, 4619–23. Oxford and Malden, MA: Blackwell Publishing.

"Have Sociological Passport, Will Travel." *Sociologists in a Global Age: Biographical Perspectives*, edited by Mathieu Deflem, 239–63. Aldershot and Burlington: Ashgate.

"Introduction" to reissue of Pitirim A. Sorokin's *The United States and Russia*. New Brunswick, NJ: Transaction Publishers.

"When is the Nation No Longer?" In *Nationalism in a Global Era: The Persistence of Nations*, edited by Andreas Sturm, Mitchell Young and Eric Zuelow, 55–74. Routledge Studies in Nationalism and Ethnicity, London and New York: Routledge.

"Coping with Collective Stigma: the Case of Germany." In *Identity, Morality, and Threat: Studies in Violent Conflict*, edited by Daniel Rothbart and Karina Korostelina, 359–98. Lanham, MD: Lexington/Rowman & Littlefield.

"Sociological Theory, Constructal Theory and Globalization." In *Constructal Theory of Social Dynamics*, edited by Adrian Bejan and Gilbert W. Merkx, 147–60. Norwell, MA: Springer Science & Business Media, Inc.

"The Meshing of Civilizations: Soft Power and the Renewal of the Civilization of Modernity." In *Modernity at the Beginning of the 21st Century*, edited by Volker Schmidt, 89–113. Newcastle: Cambridge Scholars Publishers.

Review of Wilson Carey McWilliams's "The Active Society Revisited." *American Journal of Sociology* 112, no. 6.

"Civilization." In *Encyclopedia of Globalization*, vol. 2, edited by Roland Robertson and Jan Aart Scholte, 147–50. New York: Routledge.

2008

"Sociology, Schools in." In *International Encyclopedia of the Social Sciences*, 2nd ed., edited by William A. Derity, 9–12. Framington Hills, MI: Macmillan Reference USA/Thomson Gale.

2009

For Durkheim. Essays in Historical and Cultural Sociology. Surrey and Burlington: Ashgate.

"Avant–Garde Art and Avant–Garde Sociology: 'Primitivism' and Durkheim ca. 1905–1913." In *For Durkheim. Essays in Historical and Cultural Sociology*, 167–87. Surrey and Burlington: Ashgate.

"No Laughing Matter: Applying Durkheim to Danish Cartoons." In *For Durkheim. Essays in Historical and Cultural Sociology*, 239–69. Surrey and Burlington: Ashgate.

"Global Altruism: Some Considerations." In *Handbook of Public Sociology*, edited by Vincent Jeffries, 409–27. Rowman & Littlefield.

"Modernity and the Second Return of Mechanical Solidarity." In *Raymond Boudon: A Life in Sociology*, edited by Mohamed Cherkaoui and Peter Hamilton, 1–22. Oxford: The Bardwell Press.

"Durkheim's Reflection on the Crisis ... But Which One?" *Durkheimian Studies/Etudes Durkheimiennes* 15: 26–38.

2010

"The (Im)morality of War: Some Sociological Considerations." In *Handbook of the Sociology of Morality*, edited by Steven Hitlin and Stephen Vaisey, 73–93. Springer.

"Civilization and Globalization." In *Handbook of Globalization*, edited by George Ritzer. New York: Routledge.

2011

Editorial introduction to a special issue, *Imagined Communities in the 21st Century*. *The American Behavioral Scientist* 55 (10): 1291–93.

"The Neglected Religious Factor in 'Imagined Communities,'" in *Imagined Communities in the 21st Century*. *American Behavioral Scientist* 55 (October): 1395–1414 (special issue edited by E. A. Tiryakian)

"A Sociological Odyssey: The Comparative Voyage of S. N. Eisenstadt." *Journal of Comparative Sociology* 11 (August): 241–50.

2012

"Civilization." In *Encyclopedia of Globalization*, edited by George Ritzer, 209–17. New York: Wiley–Blackwell.

"Early Reviews of *The Elementary Forms of Religious Life*." *Journal of Classical Sociology* 12 (3–4): 513–25.

2013

"We're Not Dopes" (comments on Etzioni). *Issues in Science and Technology* 20/21 (Winter).

2014

"Civilization in the Global Era: One, Many ... or None?" *Social Theory and Regional Studies in the Global Age*, edited by Said A. Arjomand, 91–112. Albany: SUNY Press.

Tiryakian, E. A. and Jonathan Morgan. "Solidarity, Yesterday and Today." In *The Palgrave Handbook of Altruism, Morality and Solidarity: Formulating a Field of Study*, edited by Vincent Jeffries, 249–71. New York: Palgrave Macmillan.

"Theorizing Human Rights" (Review of Hans Joas). *New Genealogy of Human Rights*. *Contemporary Sociology* 43 (2): 187–90.

2015

"Emile David Durkheim (1858–1917)." In *Key Sociological Thinkers*, 3rd ed., edited by Rob Stones. London: Palgrave Macmillan.

INDEX

Lightning Source UK Ltd.
Milton Keynes UK
UKOW02n1205290916

284106UK00003B/17/P